The PMP Cram Sheet

This Cram Sheet provides the distilled, key facts about the PMP exam. Review these important points as the last thing you do before entering the test center. Pay close attention to those you feel you need to review. A good exam strategy is to transfer all the facts you can recall from this Cram Sheet to a piece of paper once you sit to take the exam.

IMPORTANT PMI THEMES

1. The project manager is ultimately responsible and accountable for the project.

2. Projects should be aligned and prioritized with the organization's strategic direction.

3. The earlier in the project lifecycle, the more risk for the project and the more influence management has on it.

4. Historical records and lessons learned are very valuable.

5. Stakeholder management is an ongoing, continuous process throughout the project lifecycle.

6. The success or failure of a project is determined during project planning.

7. The Work Breakdown Structure (WBS) is a "must-have" for any project manager and serves as the basis for most project planning.

8. The person (people) who will do the work should estimate the work.

9. The most important task and skill of the project manager is effective project communication.

10. The project team should be involved in all project-planning activities.

11. The project plan is an all-encompassing document and must contain cost and schedule baselines in order to determine project performance during execution.

12. Project changes will occur. Changes should be expected, planned for, and well managed when they occur.

13. Earned value is the best project-controlling technique.

14. The project team should solve its own problems and resolve its own issues whenever possible.

15. Quality is planned into a project, not inspected in.

16. Risk management is an ongoing, continuous process performed by the entire project team.

17. Preventing a risk event is always preferred to mitigating a risk event.

18. Closing processes (administrative closure) should occur at the end of each project phase, not just at the end of the project.

19. "Lessons learned" describe the knowledge the team and stakeholders gained by actually performing the project and are an invaluable source of project management information.

PROJECT FRAMEWORK

1. A *project* is a temporary endeavor undertaken to create a unique product or service.

2. A *program* is a group of related projects managed in a coordinated way.

3. *Project management* is the application of knowledge, skills, tools, and techniques to project activities to meet project requirements.

4. A *deliverable* is a tangible, verifiable work product.

5. The PMBOK project management process groups are Initiating, Planning, Executing, Controlling, and Closing.

6. Project management processes can repeat within the project lifecycle, and they generally repeat with each project phase.

7. The three organization types are functional, matrix (weak, balanced, or strong), and projectized.

8. As an effective project manager, you are expected to be a good manager and a good leader.

9. The "triple constraint" paradigm is used to show the effects that competing demands can have on a project.

PROJECT INITIATION

1. Initiation is the first step in the scope management process.

2. Initiation formally authorizes a project to begin or to continue to the next phase.

3. Initiation formally links a project to the work and to the strategic objectives of the organization.

4. Someone external to the project team and higher up in the organization must issue the project charter.

5. The project charter gives the project manager authority to "get the job done."

6. The project charter establishes the targets for the project.

7. A signed contract can serve as a project charter.

8. The two types of project selection methods are benefit measurement methods and constrained optimization methods.

9. Management by Objectives (MBO) supports project initiation by linking projects to corporate objectives.

10. MBO supports project management through its use of goal-setting and periodic reviews.

11. Many project management activities during initiation are further elaborated during planning.

PROJECT PLANNING

1. The project planning process entails 21 of the 39 PMBOK processes.

2. The project plan is much more than a project schedule. It is an all-encompassing document used as the basis for project controlling and executing.

3. A project charter is not a project plan.

4. The WBS is not the project schedule.

5. The WBS serves as the foundation for most project-planning activities.

6. The WBS should include all the work of the project and should be developed with the project team.

7. The granularity of the WBS depends on what detail is needed for effective management and control.

8. Scope definition generates the WBS. Activity definition generates the activity list.

9. A project schedule must meet three key criteria to be complete: It must have buy-in, be achievable, and be realistic and formal.

10. Developing a project schedule is a four-step process: (1) define work activities; (2) identify activity/task relationships; (3) estimate effort and duration of each activity; (4) apply calendar and resources to build a schedule.

11. Network diagrams highlight relationships among project activities.

12. The three types of project network diagrams are Activity-on-Node (most popular), Activity-on-Arrow (uses dummy activities), and GERT (uses loops and conditional branches).

13. Estimating should be performed (or approved) by the person doing the work.

14. Key project success factors (cost, time, scope, resources) should be managed to baselines and only changed when an approved project change has been executed.

15. All assumptions used in estimating should be documented.

16. Historical information is vital to improving estimates.

17. The key facts about the "critical path" in a project schedule are as follows:
    - It's the longest sequence of activities.
    - There is zero slack (float).
    - It's the focus of any schedule-compression activity.

18. The three scheduling techniques are CPM (uses one estimate), PERT (uses three estimates), and GERT (can show various project outcomes).

19. The Monte Carlo technique is the most popular simulation scheduling technique and is also used for risk analysis.

20. The three methods for presenting the project schedule are milestone charts, Gantt charts, and network diagrams.

21. The two most popular methods for compressing the schedule are *crashing* (adding resources to critical path tasks) and *fast tracking* (performing critical path tasks in parallel).

22. Cost estimates for an activity are affected by activity duration, resource rates, and risk level.

23. The three levels of estimating accuracy are order of magnitude (-25% to +75%), budget (-10% to +25%), and definitive (-5% to +10%).

24. The risk management plan is not a risk response plan.

25. All project management activity should be "thought about" and planned.

26. Effective project management is proactive.

27. The "core" planning processes are those that must be done in a specific sequence.

28. The "facilitating" planning processes are always performed, are not optional, and directly impact many of the core planning processes.

29. The formality and detail of each supplemental plan will vary depending on project need.

30. Ninety percent of a project manager's time is spent communicating. Communication is the most important project management skill.

31. Remember the three C's in project communications: Be clear, concise, and courteous.

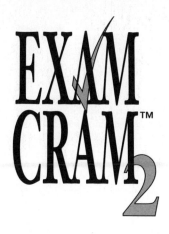

PMP
Practice
Questions

David Francis, PMP, MBA

CERTIFICATION

PMP Practice Questions Exam Cram 2

Copyright © 2005 by Que Publishing

International Standard Book Number: 0-7897-3256-4

Library of Congress Catalog Card Number: 2004108917

Printed in the United States of America

First Printing: November 2004

07 06 05   4 3 2

Trademarks

Warning and Disclaimer

Bulk Sales

Que Publishing offers excellent discounts on this book when ordered in quantity for bulk purchases or special sales. For more information, please contact

> **U.S. Corporate and Government Sales**
> **1-800-382-3419**
> **corpsales@pearsontechgroup.com**

For sales outside of the U.S., please contact

> **International Sales**
> **international@pearsoned.com**

Publisher
Paul Boger

Executive Editor
Jeff Riley

Acquisitions Editor
Steve Rowe

Development Editor
Steve Rowe

Managing Editor
Charlotte Clapp

Project Editor
Dan Knott

Copy Editor
Jessica McCarty

Proofreader
Wendy Ott

Technical Editor
Sara Strock

Publishing Coordinators
Pamalee Nelson
Sharry Gregory

Multimedia Developer
Dan Scherf

Designer
Anne Jones

Page Layout
Cheryl Lynch

CERTIFICATION

Que Certification • 800 East 96th Street • Indianapolis, Indiana 46240

A Note from Series Editor Ed Tittel

You know better than to trust your certification preparation to just any-body. That's why you, and more than 2 million others, have purchased an Exam Cram book. As Series Editor for the new and improved Exam Cram 2 Series, I have worked with the staff at Que Certification to ensure you won't be disappointed. That's why we've taken the world's best-selling certification product—a two-time finalist for "Best Study Guide" in CertCities' reader polls—and made it even better.

As a two-time finalist for the "Favorite Study Guide Author" award as selected by CertCities readers, I know the value of good books. You'll be impressed with Que Certification's stringent review process, which ensures the books are high quality, relevant, and technically accurate. Rest assured that several industry experts have reviewed this material, helping us deliver an excellent solution to your exam preparation needs.

Exam Cram 2 books also feature a preview edition of MeasureUp's powerful, full-featured test engine, which is trusted by certification students throughout the world.

As a 20-year-plus veteran of the computing industry and the original creator and editor of the Exam Cram Series, I've brought my IT experience to bear on these books. During my tenure at Novell from 1989 to 1994, I worked with and around its excellent education and certification department. At Novell, I witnessed the growth and development of the first really big, successful IT certification program—one that was to shape the industry forever afterward. This experience helped push my writing and teaching activities heavily in the cer-tification direction. Since then, I've worked on nearly 100 certification-related books, and I write about certification topics for numerous websites and for *Certification* magazine.

In 1996, while studying for various MCP exams, I became frustrated with the huge, unwieldy study guides that were the only preparation tools available. As an experienced IT professional and former instructor, I wanted "nothing but the facts" necessary to prepare for the exams. From this impetus, Exam Cram emerged: short, focused books that explain exam topics, detail exam skills and activities, and get IT professionals ready to take and pass their exams.

In 1997 when Exam Cram debuted, it quickly became the best-selling computer book series since "...*For Dummies*," and the best-selling certification book series ever. By maintaining an intense focus on subject matter, tracking errata and updates quickly, and following the certi-fication market closely, Exam Cram established the dominant position in cert prep books.

You will not be disappointed in your decision to purchase this book. If you are, please contact me at etittel@jump.net. All suggestions, ideas, input, or constructive criticism are welcome!

Ed Tittel

About the Author

David Francis, PMP, is one of the lead authors of the original *PMP Exam Cram 2* book and has been a project manager and business analyst for more than 10 years. He has worked as a consultant, instructor, and writer for the analysis, design, development, and implementation of complex projects and programs. Projects have included working with companies such as Dow Chemical, EDS, Cisco Systems, SBC, Clarian Healthcare, RCI, Capgemini, and other Fortune 500 companies.

David teaches certification, undergraduate and graduate Project Management classes as an adjunct faculty member at Indiana Institute of Technology, Keller Graduate School of Management, and Indiana University-Purdue University Indianapolis. He serves as the Director of Education for the Project Management Institute (PMI), Central Indiana Chapter and has contributed to the success of numerous educational opportunities for the chapter. David has provided curriculum development and delivery of Project Management educational programs to thousands of students and for clients including Eli Lilly and Company, Ameritech, Rolls Royce, Covance, Vifi, Conseco Insurance, Praxair, and other organizations. He has also developed and taught numerous PMP certification classes and frequently sponsors new PMP study groups and programs.

David's educational background includes an MBA from Butler University and a BA from Indiana University. Certifications include Project Management Professional Certification (PMP), IT Programming Competency Certification, Microsoft Office Suite Certification, Project Management Certification (IUPUI), and Microsoft Project Software Certification.

Professional affiliations have included the American Society for Training and Development (ASTD); Project Management Institute (PMI); Organizational Effectiveness Institute; Center for Business Partnerships; Association of Quality and Participation (AQP); Indianapolis Business and Professional Exchange; Central Indiana Quality Leadership Forum (IQLF); Indiana Quality, Productivity, and Involvement Council (IQPIC); Indianapolis Ambassadors; Toastmasters; and Indiana Labor Management Council.

David provides consulting, training, and development through his company, The Project Management Company, and can be contacted at David@ProjectManagementCompany.com.

For more information about The Project Management Company and its programs, visit www.ProjectManagementCompany.com.

About the Coauthors

Sara Strock, PMP, MBA, holds an MBA from The Ohio State University, an AAS from Ivy Tech State College in Indianapolis, and a bachelor's degree in music from Bowling Green State University.

Sara has worked in the IT field for more than 20 years, participating in and managing projects in a variety of industries including insurance, pharmaceutical, banking, travel, manufacturing, and financial. Her projects have ranged in business disciplines from customer relationship management (CRM) to security. Sara obtained her PMP certification in 2001, and is an active member of her local PMI chapter. She is currently working in a Project Management office for an insurance company.

As an author, Sara has published articles ranging from job hunting to spirituality, as well as tech editing several books for Que Publishing.

Emelee N. Mitchum, PMP, MBA, is a PMP-certified IT consulting manager with more than eight years of consulting experience. Her background includes three years in group benefits consulting and sales and five years in the IT industry. Her primary areas of professional expertise include

➤ Business requirements assessment and documentation

➤ Business process reengineering

➤ Package implementation

➤ Project Management and leadership

She is currently working as a project manager on a PeopleSoft Benefits Administration project for a hospital in Cincinnati through an Indianapolis consulting firm.

Emelee's educational background includes an MBA from Indiana University and a bachelor's degree in mathematics from DePauw University. In her spare time, she enjoys volunteering with the Junior League of Indianapolis and traveling.

Dedication

. . . .

As I enter into the development for our second book, I want to again thank my parents, Millard and Norma Francis, for their love and faith throughout my life. Many thanks to my brothers, Mitchell and Jeffrey Francis, and my grandfather, Ed Tackett, for their support and enthusiasm over the years.

—*David Francis, MBA, PMP*

Acknowledgments

Preparing this second book has been a challenge and a labor of love. I would like to thank my family, friends, relatives, colleagues, and co-workers. All of you have been an inspiration to me in some way or another. Additional thanks to Steve Rowe, Jeffrey Riley, Sara Strock, Emelee Mitchum, Jessica McCarty, Dan Knott, Que Publishing, and all of the talented people that worked on the original *PMP Exam Cram 2* book and this new study guide. Continued thanks to *PMP Exam Cram 2* coauthor, Greg Horine, for his work on the first book.

I would also like to thank Indiana University-Purdue University Indianapolis (Ron Lindle, Lorean Kegeris), Indiana Institute of Technology (Dr. Sheela Yadav, Ph.D.; Sandy Bradley; Angela Snyder), Keller Graduate School of Management (Julie Smith, Antoinette Hein), University of Indianapolis (Dr. Bruce Strom, Ph.D.), PMI, and the PMI Central Indiana Chapter and Board of Directors for its support of the Project Management profession and PMI programs.

—*David Francis, MBA, PMP*

Contents at a Glance

Table of Contents

Introduction

What Is This Book About?

Welcome to *PMP Practice Questions Exam Cram 2*! The aim of this book is solely to provide you with practice questions complete with answers and explanations that will help you learn, drill, and review for the PMP certification exam.

Who Is This Book For?

If you have studied the PMP exam's content and feel you are ready to put your knowledge to the test, but you are not sure you want to take the real exam yet, then this book is for you! Maybe you have answered other practice questions or unsuccessfully taken the real exam, reviewed, and want to do more practice questions before going to retake the real exam; if so, this book is for you, too! Please note that this book shouldn't be your only vehicle for PMP study. The PMP exam is a difficult and challenging exam, so be sure you use plenty of study materials and use this book as a drill, review, and practice vehicle. Also check with your local PMI chapter to see if it can provide support to you with a study group or other PMP educational opportunities.

What Will You Find in This Book?

As mentioned before, this book is all about practice questions! This book is separated according to the topics you will find in the PMP exam. Each chapter represents an exam topic, and in the chapter you will find three elements:

➤ **Practice Questions**—These are the numerous questions that will help you learn, drill, and review.

➤ **Quick Check Answer Key**—After you have finished answering the questions, you can quickly grade your exam from this section. Only correct answers are given here. No explanations are offered yet, though!

➤ **Answers and Explanations**—This section offers you the correct answers as well as further explanation about the content posed in that question. Use this information to learn why an answer is correct and to reinforce the content in your mind for exam day.

You will also find a CramSheet at the beginning of this book, specifically written for this exam. This is a very popular element that is also found in the corresponding *PMP Exam Cram 2* study guide (ISBN-0-7897-3037-5). This item condenses all the necessary facts found in this exam into one, easy-to-handle tear card. The CramSheet is something you can take with you to the exam location and use as a last-second study aid. Please note that you can't take it into the exam room, though!

Hints for Using This Book

Because this book is a paper practice product, you might want to complete your exams on a separate piece of paper so you can reuse the exams over and over without having previous answers in your way. Also, a general rule of thumb across all practice question products is to make sure you are scoring well into the high 80%–90% range in all topics before attempting the real exam. The higher the percentages you score on practice question products, the better your chances are for passing the real exam. Of course, we can't guarantee a passing score on the real exam, but we can offer you plenty of opportunities to practice and assess your knowledge levels before entering the real exam.

Need Further Study?

Are you having a hard time correctly answering these questions? If so, you probably need further review. Be sure to see the sister product to this book, the *PMP Exam Cram 2* by Que Publishing (ISBN-0-7897-3037-5), for further review.

We Want to Hear from You!

As the reader of this book, *you* are our most important critic and commentator. We value your opinion and want to know what we're doing right, what we could do better, what areas you'd like to see us publish in, and any other words of wisdom you're willing to pass our way.

As an executive editor for Que Publishing, I welcome your comments. You can email or write me directly to let me know what you did or didn't like about this book—as well as what we can do to make our books better.

Please note that I cannot help you with technical problems related to the topic of this book. We do have a User Services group, however, where I will forward specific technical questions related to the book.

When you write, please be sure to include this book's title and author as well as your name, email address, and phone number. I will carefully review your comments and share them with the author and editors who worked on the book.

Email: feedback@quepublishing.com

Mail: Jeff Riley
            Executive Editor
            Que Publishing
            800 East 96th Street
            Indianapolis, IN 46240 USA

For more information about this book or another Que Publishing title, visit our website at www.examcram2.com. Type the ISBN (excluding hyphens) or the title of a book in the Search field to find the page you're looking for.

Project Management Framework

Exam Prep Questions

1. George works for a medium-size IT consulting company and likes his job. He recently became involved with an upgrade of his company's IT system, and it will likely become an ongoing activity for him in addition to his other responsibilities. What describes the work that George is doing for this new assignment?

   ❑ A. It is an attractive project and he should take it.
   ❑ B. Because the project has several phases, it will use a lot of resources.
   ❑ C. His new work is an interesting program for the company.
   ❑ D. He should look for a new job.

Quick Answer: **15**
Detailed Answer: **16**

2. Projects come in all sizes and shapes. Many times, project managers must draw from their "toolbox" of processes, tools, or methodologies. How many knowledge areas are described in the Project Management Body of Knowledge (PMBOK)?

   ❑ A. 2—core processes and facilitating processes
   ❑ B. 9
   ❑ C. 5—initiation, planning, execution, control, and closing
   ❑ D. 39

Quick Answer: **15**
Detailed Answer: **16**

3. What areas does project integration management include?

   ❑ A. Plan development, execution, and scope management
   ❑ B. Execution, time management, and scope planning
   ❑ C. Change control, execution, and plan development
   ❑ D. Cost management, integrated change control, and cost estimating

Quick Answer: **15**
Detailed Answer: **16**

Quick Check

Quick Answer: **15**
Detailed Answer: **16**

4. Project human resource management includes numerous "soft" skills that are not easy to learn, and many project managers require additional training or development to effectively schedule and coordinate resources. Human resource planning includes all of the following, except
   - ❑ A. Team skills analysis
   - ❑ B. Staff acquisition
   - ❑ C. Team development
   - ❑ D. Organizational planning

Quick Answer: **15**
Detailed Answer: **16**

5. Many organizations have different definitions for Project Management because the profession encompasses so many industries. Consequently, the Project Management Institute (PMI) describes Project Management as
   - ❑ A. The processes and tools in order to complete a project
   - ❑ B. The use of knowledge, tools, and techniques to meet requirements
   - ❑ C. Industry specific because the definition changes based upon whatever industry the company is involved with
   - ❑ D. Initiation, planning, execution, control, and closeout of a project

Quick Answer: **15**
Detailed Answer: **16**

6. When an iterative type of approach is used with projects, there are several incarnations that occur throughout the entire process. Each of these iterations is called
   - ❑ A. A prototype
   - ❑ B. Deliverable
   - ❑ C. A work product
   - ❑ D. Progressive elaboration

Quick Answer: **15**
Detailed Answer: **16**

7. A *waterfall* methodology is commonly utilized with IT projects. There are several steps in the process, which includes all of the following except
   - ❑ A. Testing and implementation
   - ❑ B. Analysis and development
   - ❑ C. Requirements
   - ❑ D. Design and customer buy-in

8. The difference between core processes and facilitating processes is

Quick Answer: **15**
Detailed Answer: **16**

- ❑ A. Core processes take more time and resources.
- ❑ B. Core processes are performed in the same sequence and facilitating processes are intermittent.
- ❑ C. Facilitating processes often require micromanagement in order to be completed on time.
- ❑ D. Core processes are not performed in the same sequence and facilitating processes are.

9. The president and the vice president of marketing for a software development services organization hold a meeting to discuss a change to a key task in the design phase of a project. After the discussion, they tell the project manager to make the appropriate changes. This scenario is an example of

Quick Answer: **15**
Detailed Answer: **16**

- ❑ A. Proactive senior management
- ❑ B. A project-based organization
- ❑ C. Effective decision making
- ❑ D. A project coordinator role

10. Which of the following statements about the project expeditor or the project coordinator role is correct?

Quick Answer: **15**
Detailed Answer: **17**

- ❑ A. The project expeditor does not make decisions.
- ❑ B. The project coordinator does not make decisions.
- ❑ C. The project coordinator has no authority.
- ❑ D. The project expeditor focuses on completing the project on schedule.

11. The project selection process must be well thought out in order for the project to be successful and the stakeholders to be satisfied with the outcome. Which one of the following steps is not part of the project selection process?

Quick Answer: **15**
Detailed Answer: **17**

- ❑ A. List assumptions.
- ❑ B. Develop resource wage structures.
- ❑ C. Gather data and information for each opportunity.
- ❑ D. Develop a set of criteria against which the opportunity will be evaluated.

12. A work breakdown structure, a status report, and a responsibility assignment matrix are frequently used throughout a project. However, their usage might be iterative. These are examples of

Quick Answer: **15**
Detailed Answer: **17**

- ❑ A. Project Management tools
- ❑ B. Work products
- ❑ C. Milestones
- ❑ D. Deliverables

Quick Check

Quick Answer: **15**
Detailed Answer: **17**

13. A project manager for a not-for-profit organization is completing a new retail outlet project but is unable to get the planned amount of time from key resources to complete some of the critical path tasks. The key resources are focused on completing their day-to-day tasks, and the project manager does not control the work assignments for these people. This scenario is an example of what type of organization?
    - ❑ A. Balanced matrix
    - ❑ B. Tight matrix
    - ❑ C. Functional
    - ❑ D. Project coordinator

Quick Answer: **15**
Detailed Answer: **17**

14. Ambiguous jurisdiction is more common in a functional or weak matrix organization than a strong matrix or projectized organization. Why?
    - ❑ A. Projectized organizations tend to be large in size.
    - ❑ B. Conflict between a functional manager and a project manager is more common in a functional or weak matrix.
    - ❑ C. Legal issues are more frequent in a functional or weak matrix organization.
    - ❑ D. Projectized and strong matrix organizations are the best companies for a project manager to work for due to less ambiguity in scope development.

Quick Answer: **15**
Detailed Answer: **17**

15. The level of authority and autonomy that a project manager possesses is vital to his success and ability to influence the project, time, and personnel scheduling. In what type of organization does the project manager maintain a moderate to high level of authority?
    - ❑ A. Functional matrix
    - ❑ B. Balanced matrix
    - ❑ C. Strong matrix
    - ❑ D. Projectized matrix

16. The differences between managing people and leading people can be linked to a project manager's personality and ability to interact with individuals and groups. Why does a project manager need to have both leadership and management skills in order to be the most effective?

Quick Answer: **15**
Detailed Answer: **17**

- ❏ A. Project managers spend up to 90% of their time communicating with their team and stakeholders.
- ❏ B. Managers focus on resource scheduling and leaders focus on motivation.
- ❏ C. Leaders are more effective than managers.
- ❏ D. Managers focus on processes and leaders are more people oriented.

17. Colleen wants to make sure she eliminates any potential projects that might go before the project review board and be vetoed due to lack of research and planning. She understands that the needs identification is part of the initial phase of a project. What does it *not* start with?

Quick Answer: **15**
Detailed Answer: **18**

- ❏ A. A problem
- ❏ B. An opportunity
- ❏ C. A need
- ❏ D. An idea

18. The world is becoming more of a global economy all of the time. Project managers will need the ability to interact and manage remote resources, and outsource tasks in order to meet strict deadlines. Looking at the differences and advantages of working with various cultures and nationalities, numerous advantages for creative scheduling of resources become evident. Which of the following statements is not true?

Quick Answer: **15**
Detailed Answer: **18**

- ❏ A. Cultural differences are always a constraint on any project.
- ❏ B. Culture is a critical lever for competitive advantage.
- ❏ C. There is a common ground for people from different cultures to work from when they help resolve project conflicts together.
- ❏ D. Only those who realize that cultural differences are a resource to leverage will survive in the twenty-first century.

19. Standards and regulations are commonplace within organizations and society. Millions of dollars are spent every year for companies to be compliant with OSHA and ISO 9000 requirements. Six Sigma certifications are desired, but costly to administer and maintain. The FDA has standards and regulations, but IBM only has standards. Why doesn't IBM have regulations?

Quick Answer: **15**
Detailed Answer: **18**

   ❑ A. IBM is a for-profit corporation and the FDA is a government entity.

   ❑ B. IBM does not utilize Six Sigma methodology but it is ISO 9000 compliant.

   ❑ C. The FDA has standards for its internal use and enforces regulations upon other organizations.

   ❑ D. Because the government develops its own laws and regulations, it is the watchdog for standards.

20. The triple constraints of Project Management are frequently discussed in other contexts such as marketing classes and a variety of other subjects. The interaction between _____, _____, and _____ can be seen as a triangle, with the three sides impacting the others.

Quick Answer: **15**
Detailed Answer: **18**

   ❑ A. quality, resources, time

   ❑ B. money, resources, quality

   ❑ C. scope, quality, planning

   ❑ D. time, scope, cost

21. There are plenty of tools and techniques that project managers can utilize in order to create synergy on a project. Some of these skills cannot be developed by reading a book and must be learned on the job. Project managers need solid communication and negotiation skills primarily because

Quick Answer: **15**
Detailed Answer: **18**

   ❑ A. They must give presentations and briefings to senior management.

   ❑ B. Getting the best deals from vendors requires these skills.

   ❑ C. They might be leading a team with no direct control over the individual team members.

   ❑ D. They must be able to effectively share their technical expertise.

22. Many people confuse operational activities with projects and do not assign appropriate resources to the tasks. Frequently, they fail because a good subject matter expert (SME) does not always make a good project manager (PM). Why?

   ❑ A. They do not understand the importance and trade-offs of the triple constraints.

   ❑ B. They do not understand what the appropriate leadership style for managing the project is.

   ❑ C. They lack social and communication skills.

   ❑ D. They can't delegate authority to subordinates.

23. There are several processes, tools, and techniques that you need to learn for the PMP exam. According to the PMBOK, the five process groups are

   ❑ A. Initiation, planning, execution, resources, and quality

   ❑ B. Initiation, scheduling, reporting, closeout, and approval

   ❑ C. Analysis, design, building, development, and support

   ❑ D. Initiation, planning, execution, control, and closeout

24. Whenever people are looking for a job, they frequently see "program manager wanted" and "project manager wanted" when reading the job listings in their local newspaper. Which of the following statements best describes the relationship between projects and programs?

   ❑ A. There are no differences between the two; they are just different terms for the same thing.

   ❑ B. A project is composed of one or more related programs.

   ❑ C. A program is composed of one or more related projects.

   ❑ D. A project is a temporary endeavor, whereas a program is permanent.

25. Soliciting feedback from stakeholders is important to the success of a project. If the project manager does not include this as part of the project development process, she can encounter plenty of problems later. The process of soliciting feedback and incorporating stakeholder ideas into the project is called

   ❑ A. Feedback loop

   ❑ B. Buy-in

   ❑ C. Progressive elaboration

   ❑ D. Project approval

26. You need to take the following items when you take the PMP exam:

Quick Answer: **15**
Detailed Answer: **19**

   ❑ A. Driver's license or photo ID and "cheat sheets"
   ❑ B. Study guides and "cheat sheets"
   ❑ C. Driver's license or photo ID, calculator, and watch
   ❑ D. PMI membership card

27. Every year, auto manufacturers introduce new model cars and retire models that do not sell or have become obsolete. Frequently, project managers work with engineers and designers to develop new styles and features that will sell in the marketplace. The cycle for an automobile that extends from the concept to the introduction to the phaseout is called

Quick Answer: **15**
Detailed Answer: **19**

   ❑ A. A project life cycle
   ❑ B. A product life cycle
   ❑ C. Product development
   ❑ D. R and D (Research and Development)

28. All projects should have basic elements in order to be planned and executed efficiently and successfully. Many project managers do not plan properly and, ultimately, the projects fail and money and resources are lost. One of the following documents authorizes and initiates the project while empowering the project manager to begin working on it. This document is known as a

Quick Answer: **15**
Detailed Answer: **19**

   ❑ A. Project charter
   ❑ B. Project plan
   ❑ C. Work authorization form
   ❑ D. Project approval requisition

29. There are numerous milestones that Suzy, an aspiring PMP, wants to incorporate into her project but she does not know how to differentiate among all of the tasks. She realizes that the first meeting of stakeholders and team members is a key element to the positive start of a project. Whether an *in-person* meeting or a *virtual* meeting, this initial gathering provides an opportunity to clarify roles, ask questions, and transfer knowledge. This is called

Quick Answer: **15**
Detailed Answer: **19**

   ❑ A. A team meeting
   ❑ B. An ad hoc meeting
   ❑ C. A kickoff meeting
   ❑ D. A project overview

30. You have recently been promoted to project manager for a clinical testing facility. The team is developing a new product that will cut down on testing interval requirements for a new seizure management medication. After you become involved with the project, you decide to add more research reports, which the customer did not request. This is an example of

    - ❏ A. Good customer service
    - ❏ B. Scope creep
    - ❏ C. Due diligence
    - ❏ D. Gold plating

31. There are distinct differences between project life cycles and project phases. Which of the following statements describes the relationship between project phases and project life cycles?

    - ❏ A. A project phase can contain one or more iterations of the project life cycle.
    - ❏ B. Collectively, the project phases are known as the project life cycle.
    - ❏ C. The project life cycle is known as the sequence of project activities, whereas phases are defined to control the overlapping activities.
    - ❏ D. The project life cycle contains the iterative, incremental elements inside a project phase.

32. The PMIS is a valuable tool for the project manager to utilize as a communication mechanism throughout the duration of the project. The communication plan is frequently a subproject of the PMIS development milestone that is used to gather, integrate, and disseminate the _____ of the Project Management processes.

    - ❏ A. outputs
    - ❏ B. tools
    - ❏ C. deliverables
    - ❏ D. scope changes

33. Susan wants to be a project manager and has done Project Management at PMC Construction Company for more than 10 years. Until she discovered the PMI, she was unaware there was a global authority on Project Management certification or benchmarking in the planning and delivery of projects. When describing the purpose of the PMBOK, it is important to note that the guide is used to provide practices and knowledge that are *generally accepted* because

Quick Answer: **15**
Detailed Answer: **20**

❑ A. They are global in perspective.

❑ B. They are applicable to most projects, most of the time.

❑ C. They provide a foundation of knowledge from which to learn for future project managers.

❑ D. Project Management is a relatively new profession that continues to build credibility.

34. Projects come in all sizes and shapes. They occur in almost every industry, including aerospace, manufacturing, information services, engineering, and life sciences. Because Project Management encompasses so many different areas and disciplines, many people have a difficult time explaining what Project Management is. Regardless of the industry, Project Management includes all of the following except

Quick Answer: **15**
Detailed Answer: **20**

❑ A. Impermanence

❑ B. Creating a unique item for consumption

❑ C. Creating a unique service

❑ D. Increasing efficiency of projects

35. A company that you previously worked for is seeking new employees and you are trying to explain the culture to a potential candidate. The company has strict policies, supervisory control, and rules. Team members are not encouraged to be individualistic nor offer feedback to upper management. Many times, the team feels its input is not valuable or implemented. This explanation describes a company that utilizes what employee management theory?

Quick Answer: **15**
Detailed Answer: **20**

❑ A. Meredith and Mann's Autocratic Management Theory

❑ B. Deming's Zero Defects Theory

❑ C. Kerzner's Earned Value Theory

❑ D. McGregor's X Theory

36. NASA developed the space shuttle over an extended period of time. When the project first began, many of the engineers had to develop their blueprints based upon a vision of what they saw as the final product. This focus on the end result is one of the keys to successful Project Management. Each time that a blueprint was revised, before the final design was approved, the team became challenged with additional work; however, it understood that

   ❑ A. Scope creep was common in a large scope project.
   ❑ B. Progressive elaborations of the blueprints accurately defined the final deliverable.
   ❑ C. New subject matter experts would be needed.
   ❑ D. The project sponsor would develop a change control document.

Quick Answer: **15**
Detailed Answer: **20**

37. *Management by projects* views aspects of ongoing operations as projects in order to apply Project Management techniques to them. This can be used to describe an organizational approach to the management of ongoing operations. Why would a company want to utilize this methodology on nonprojects?

   ❑ A. To keep project managers employed
   ❑ B. To provide better estimates about durations
   ❑ C. To allow the utilization of PM tools, such as earned value, to calculate ROI
   ❑ D. To specify the different phases within the operations

Quick Answer: **15**
Detailed Answer: **20**

38. General management includes all of the following except

   ❑ A. Staffing and planning
   ❑ B. Controlling operations of an ongoing enterprise
   ❑ C. Organizing and procurement
   ❑ D. Executing and logistics

Quick Answer: **15**
Detailed Answer: **21**

39. According to PMI, application areas are categories of projects that have common elements that exist in general management projects, but are not needed or present in all projects. Consequently, application areas are usually defined in terms of

   ❑ A. Industry groups
   ❑ B. Financial impact upon the organization
   ❑ C. Deliverables and time frames
   ❑ D. Visibility within the company

Quick Answer: **15**
Detailed Answer: **21**

40. Your new nursing resource company is doing well after its 10th year of business but, frequently, projects go over time, over budget, or both. Therefore, the new PMO director, Tom Thinwallet, has implemented new change control procedures for your projects in order to keep them in line financially. In order for Tom's change control management plan to be effective, it must

Quick Answer: **15**
Detailed Answer: **21**

   ❏ A. Be conservative.
   ❏ B. Utilize milestones as frequently as possible.
   ❏ C. Define how project deliverables can be changed.
   ❏ D. Tie stakeholder rewards to definite timetables.

41. Open-heart surgery can be viewed as a project and a program. Why?

Quick Answer: **15**
Detailed Answer: **21**

   ❏ A. Because heart usage does not have a definite ending, the project is also a program.
   ❏ B. Because the surgery requires a tremendous amount of resources, it is considered a project.
   ❏ C. The surgery is a project; the ongoing support is a program.
   ❏ D. Getting the skills and resources is a program. Scheduling and coordinating the skills and resources is a project.

42. Your team has developed a thorough project plan and risk analysis for your project. You have a tight time frame to develop a team, determine your milestones, and get everyone up to speed. The best way to communicate this information as quickly as possible is

Quick Answer: **15**
Detailed Answer: **21**

   ❏ A. Via email
   ❏ B. However it is described in the communication management plan
   ❏ C. At the kickoff meeting
   ❏ D. Through the project team

43. Amy has become involved with Six Sigma at work and she sees some parallels between Project Management and Six Sigma. She is also a firm believer that each project phase should be reviewed to determine whether the project should continue to the next phase. The review and decision to proceed with the project is

Quick Answer: **15**
Detailed Answer: **22**

   ❏ A. A kill point
   ❏ B. A milestone
   ❏ C. Based upon stakeholder expectations
   ❏ D. Time consuming and unnecessary for small projects

44. The project life cycle can be broken into five phases that tend to overlap with each other from one phase to another; however, the control phase does not overlap with a specific phase. Why?

- ❑ A. Change control management is separate from the other phases.
- ❑ B. Change control management has a plan that can be used throughout the initiation, planning, execution, and closeout of the project.
- ❑ C. Because the project sponsor is responsible for change control management, the project manager is not involved with that phase of the project.
- ❑ D. Change control extends throughout the entire project from initiation to closeout.

45. You have been assigned to manage a new supply chain solicitation and procurement process project. This enterprisewide initiative will be rolled out to 30 locations within 8 months in 3 geographical regions including Asia, Ireland, and Spain. Because of the abbreviated time frame, you must look for ways to reduce your timelines for the various tasks. By utilizing resource scheduling software, you determine several opportunities for overlapping phases in order to speed up the process. This is an example of

- ❑ A. Crashing the schedule
- ❑ B. Peak shaving
- ❑ C. Resource reallocation
- ❑ D. Fast tracking

46. Mark Smallbrain, the internationally known author and consultant, predicts that bowling will be the next fad to have a revitalization this decade. Therefore, he plans to endorse a chain of bowling franchises and invest in their vision of bowling splendor. The probability of his failure is the highest at the beginning of a project. The bowling aficionados (stakeholders) will also have the biggest impact upon the project scope at the beginning of the project. Why are the probabilities higher at the beginning of the project?

- ❑ A. Stakeholders are more fickle at the beginning of a project.
- ❑ B. Risk decreases over time and stakeholders lose vision of their original scope over time.
- ❑ C. Risk decreases as deliverables are provided and timelines and milestones are met. Stakeholder influence decreases as the scope is documented and expectations are set.
- ❑ D. A risk analysis has not been prepared and not all of the stakeholders have been identified.

47. Sam is running a one-year project that is expected to be in initiation and planning for three months, execution for six months, and rollout for three months. When will his project spend the most money?

   ❑ A. Initiation
   ❑ B. Planning
   ❑ C. Execution
   ❑ D. Control

Quick Answer: **15**
Detailed Answer: **22**

48. The software development life cycle begins with a proof of concept and progresses into the build, test, and acceptance phases as the project develops. Sometimes, differences between stakeholders can develop into conflict, which impacts the customer. As a trained, professional project manager, how do you handle this situation and resolve the customer's concerns?

   ❑ A. Let the customer vent and take notes.
   ❑ B. Schedule a meeting.
   ❑ C. Develop a change request for the customer.
   ❑ D. Resolve the matter in favor of the customer.

Quick Answer: **15**
Detailed Answer: **23**

49. A project coordinator or project leader title or position is more common in a functional or weak matrix organization because a project manager's role is only utilized on a part-time basis. In a projectized or strong matrix organization, a project manager's level of authority changes in what way?

   ❑ A. The level of authority increases because you have more control over resources.
   ❑ B. The level of authority stays the same however the autonomy increases.
   ❑ C. Coercion power is more effective in a projectized organization.
   ❑ D. The administrative staff becomes full time, so there is more emphasis on results and accountability.

Quick Answer: **15**
Detailed Answer: **23**

50. Which of the following statements best describes the relationship between project life cycle phases and Project Management processes?

   ❑ A. Project Management processes correspond one to one with project life cycle phases.
   ❑ B. Project life cycle phases can repeat within a Project Management process.
   ❑ C. Project Management processes can repeat within a project life cycle.
   ❑ D. Project Management processes are completely independent of project life cycle phases.

Quick Answer: **15**
Detailed Answer: **23**

Quick Check Answer Key

1. C	28. A
2. B	29. C
3. C	30. D
4. A	31. B
5. B	32. A
6. D	33. B
7. D	34. D
8. B	35. D
9. D	36. B
10. A	37. C
11. B	38. C
12. D	39. A
13. C	40. C
14. B	41. C
15. C	42. B
16. D	43. A
17. D	44. D
18. A	45. D
19. C	46. C
20. D	47. C
21. C	48. D
22. A	49. A
23. D	50. C
24. C	
25. B	
26. C	
27. B	

Answers and Explanations

1. **Answer C** is correct. Answer A is incorrect because his new work is not a project, it is a program. The PMI definition of a project is a "temporary endeavor undertaken to create a unique product or service." Because there is no end to the work, it would not qualify as a project. Answer B is incorrect for the same reason. Answer D should be incorrect unless George is in the wrong type of work.

2. **Answer B** is correct. Answer A is incorrect because it pertains to the processes. Answer C is incorrect because these are the five phases of a project. Answer D is incorrect because there are 39 processes, not knowledge areas, in the PMBOK.

3. **Answer C** is correct. Answer A is incorrect because it includes a knowledge area. Answer B is incorrect because it includes a knowledge area. Answer D is incorrect because it includes a knowledge area, which includes cost estimating.

4. **Answer A** is correct because Project Management human resource planning does *not* include skills analysis. Answers B, C, and D are incorrect because these are areas that are included in Project Management human resource planning.

5. **Answer B** is correct because the PMI definition of Project Management is "the application of knowledge, skills, tools, and techniques to project activities to meet project requirements." Consequently, Answers A, C, and D are incorrect.

6. **Answer D** is the best answer. Answer A is incorrect because the prototype is an output of the process. Answers B and C are incorrect because iterations are not deliverables, nor are they work products.

7. **Answer D** is correct. All of these choices are correct, except customer buy-in is not part of the process. "Waterfall" methodology includes six steps: requirements, analysis, design, development, testing, and implementation.

8. **Answer B** is correct. Answer A is incorrect because the core processes do not necessarily take more time and resources than facilitating processes. Answer C is incorrect because core processes are not usually tied with micromanagement of tasks. Answer D is incorrect because core processes are performed in the same sequence on most projects.

9. **Answer D** is correct. In this scenario, it is the *best* response. A project coordinator's authority and decision-making ability are generally limited to minor items. Senior management will generally make the significant decisions impacting the scope and success of the project. There is not enough information given to determine whether Answers A or C are correct, and in a project-based organization, the project manager would be empowered to make these decisions. Therefore, Answer B is incorrect.

10. **Answer A** is correct. A project coordinator *does* make decisions on nonmajor items impacting the project and *does* have some authority to influence the project. Therefore, Answers B and C are incorrect. The project expeditor is focused on coordinating communications and is not able to make decisions. Therefore, Answer D is incorrect.

11. **Answer B** is correct. The other step in the four-step project selection process is to evaluate each opportunity against the criteria. Wage structures are not associated with the project selection process. Answers A, C, and D are steps that are involved in the project selection process, and are therefore incorrect for this question.

12. **Answer D** is the best answer. Answer A is incorrect because this list includes outputs of Project Management processes, which could later be used as tools. Answer B is incorrect because it is not a PMBOK term. Answer C is incorrect because not all of these deliverables are significant enough to be considered milestones.

13. **Answer C** is correct. In a functional organization, the project manager has the least support and the least ability to control project resources. In a balanced matrix organization or a project coordinator situation, the project manager would be empowered with more control over resources or would be able to leverage his senior management to influence resource assignments. Therefore, Answers A and D are incorrect. Tight matrix deals with the co-location of project team members within a matrix organization and is not relevant to this question. Therefore, Answer B is incorrect.

14. **Answer B** is correct. Answer A is incorrect because it is not a correct statement and has nothing to do with ambiguous jurisdiction. Answer C is incorrect because ambiguous jurisdiction is not related to legal issues at a company. Answer D is incorrect because the statement is incorrect and is not related to ambiguous jurisdiction.

15. **Answer C** is correct. Answer A is incorrect because it is not a correct PMBOK term. Answer B is incorrect because a project manager has a low to moderate level of authority in these types of organizations. Answer D is incorrect because it is not a correct PMBOK term.

16. **Answer D** is the best answer. Answer A is incorrect because it does not answer the question. Answer B is incorrect because it is not the best answer. Answer C is incorrect because the statement is incorrect and is not related to ambiguous jurisdiction.

17. **Answer D** is the best answer. The *idea* is not the catalyst that precedes the needs identification. The *concept* or *idea* is generally the output of the needs identification process. Therefore, it is not the correct answer. Answers A, B, and C (need, problem, opportunity) are triggers that signal the needs identification process and are therefore incorrect answers for this question.

18. **Answer A** is the best answer. The statement in Answer A is not true because cultural differences are not "always" a constraint on a project. Answers B, C, and D are all true statements and therefore incorrect responses to this question.

19. **Answer C** is the correct answer. Answer A is incorrect because it does not answer the question. Answer B is incorrect, although it provides plenty of information to confuse the reader. Answer D is incorrect because a standard is "a document approved by a recognized body that provides for common and repeated use, rules, guidelines, or characteristics for products, processes, or services with which compliance is not mandatory." The government does not enforce guidelines.

20. **Answer D** is correct. Scope, quality, and cost are the triple constraints. Quality is a function of these three areas and can impact them; however, it is not considered one of the components of the triple constraint. Therefore, Answers A, B, and C are incorrect.

21. **Answer C** is correct. This is an example of looking for the *best* response. Effective negotiation and communication skills are important to the other three situations, too, but the project team leadership aspect is where these skills are essential and where they will have the greatest impact on project success. Therefore, Answers A, B, and D are incorrect.

22. **Answer A** is the best answer. Many subject matter experts are very proficient in their area of expertise; however, they do not have the other necessary Project Management attributes associated with time management, scope control, and budgeting skills. Answer B could be correct because subject matter experts frequently understand the appropriate leadership style for managing the project, but it is not the best answer. The triple constraints are the areas in which many subject matter experts encounter problems and the trade-offs they must encounter as they go forward with their project. Answer C is incorrect because subject matter experts do not routinely lack social and communication skills. Answer D is incorrect because project managers don't delegate authority to subordinates. Project managers have all the responsibility and none of the functional authority.

23. **Answer D** is the correct answer. Answer A is incorrect because quality and resources are not process groups. Answer B is incorrect because scheduling, reporting, and approval are not process groups. Answer C is incorrect because none of these are PMBOK process groups.

24. **Answer C** is correct. Answer A is incorrect because there is a definite difference between the two terms. Answer B is incorrect because just the opposite is true. Answer D is incorrect because a program is a group of projects, which are temporary endeavors.

25. **Answer B** is the best answer. Answer A is incorrect because it is not a PMBOK term for the process described in this question. Answer C is incorrect because progressive elaboration is a totally different aspect of Project Management, although buy-in might be involved in the process. Answer D is incorrect because this is not related to the buy-in process.

26. **Answer C** is the correct answer. Answers A and B are incorrect because you are not allowed to take "cheat sheets" to the test, although you need to take a driver's license or photo ID. Answer D is incorrect because you do not need to present your PMI card at the testing center.

27. **Answer B** is the correct answer. Answer A is incorrect because the project life cycle includes initiation, planning, execution, control, and closeout. Answers C and D are incorrect because product development and R and D do not extend throughout the life cycle of a product.

28. **Answer A** is the correct answer. Answer B is incorrect because a project plan is the output of the planning process. Answer C is incorrect because it is not the correct term for this question. A work authorization is a control mechanism that is used to keep the project on track by getting the correct work on time. Answer D is incorrect because this is a fake term for this question.

29. **Answer C** is the best answer. Although Answers A, B, and D may also be correct to a certain degree, Answer C is the best answer because the question describes the planning, knowledge transfer, and scheduling that is commonly done during the kickoff meeting with the stakeholders and team members.

30. **Answer D** is correct. Answer A is incorrect because you are providing a service that the customer did not request; therefore, it might not be important to her and unnecessary. Answer B is incorrect because scope creep is generally an expansion of the scope of the project at the customer's request and the customer did not request these reports. Answer C is incorrect because an additional report does not always mean increased diligence with a project.

31. **Answer B** is correct. A project life cycle is composed of one or more phases. Answers A, C, and D do not fully or accurately describe the relationship between project phases and project life cycle and are therefore incorrect.

32. **Answer A** is correct. The PMIS is used to distribute the outputs of Project Management processes. Answer B is incorrect because tools are not disseminated during a project. Answer C is incorrect because deliverables are not used to gather, integrate, or disseminate the outputs of the processes. Answer D is incorrect because scope changes are just an example of an output.

33. **Answer B** is the best answer. According to PMI, *generally accepted* indicates that the practices and knowledge are applicable most of the time. Answer A is incorrect because it does not answer the question. Although the PMBOK might not be accepted in every country around the world, it continues to expand every year. Answer C is incorrect because *generally accepted* is the focus of the question and this answer is not a full response to the question. Answer D, although true, also does not address the definition of *generally accepted*.

34. **Answer D** is correct. The PMI definition of a project is "a temporary endeavor undertaken to create a unique product or service." Therefore, Answers A, B, and C are incorrect because they encompass parts of the definition in the answer. *Temporary* indicates that the project has a definite beginning and ending. The uniqueness is what distinguishes the product or services from different types of projects.

35. **Answer D** is correct. Answer A is incorrect because Meredith and Mann did not develop an autocratic management theory. Answer B is incorrect because Deming's theories did not involve any of the X and Y theories that were developed by McGregor. Answer C is incorrect because Earned Value is not related to X or Y management theories.

36. **Answer B** is correct. The progressive elaborations of a project integrate the temporary and unique characteristics of a project. Because a project proceeds in steps over time, the progress continues forward incrementally. This process is developed thoroughly with input from the team and plenty of details. Although the characteristics are defined broadly in the beginning of the project, they begin to become more defined with each elaboration as the project progresses. Answer A is incorrect because scope creep is only common if there was poor planning for the project or an effective change control management plan was not utilized correctly. Answer C is incorrect because it is not related to the evolution of the blueprints for the shuttle. Answer D is incorrect because a change control document is generally not needed for progressive elaborations of the blueprints unless it has a major impact upon the project development.

37. **Answer C** is correct. Answer A is incorrect because project managers are not effectively utilized if they are always scheduling and coordinating resources for daily operations. Answer B is incorrect because project managers are not the best resource for providing estimates on daily operations and time allocations; people doing the actual work are the best sources. Answer D is incorrect because you do not specify different phases of ongoing operations.

38. **Answer C** is correct because procurement is not considered part of general management, although organizing is part of general management. General management also includes other supporting disciplines such as law, human resource management, and strategic planning. This frequently overlaps into areas such as financial forecasting, planning techniques, and organizational behavior. Therefore, Answers A, B, and D are incorrect because they are part of general management.

39. **Answer A** is correct. Industry groups, management specializations, technical elements, and functional departments are generally how application areas are defined. Therefore, Answers B, C, and D are incorrect because application areas are not defined in these types of terms.

40. **Answer C** is correct. The change control management plan should be described at the beginning of the project and provide details about how deliverables or other project-related artifacts can be changed during the project. If no procedures or guidelines are provided, chaos will develop because the stakeholders will not understand how they are to implement change within the project. Answer A is incorrect because a conservative approach is not always the best method to view projects if you are required to develop creative solutions to problems. Answer B is incorrect because frequent milestones are not the solution to effective change control management. Answer D is incorrect because rewards are not generally tied to the change control management process; however, rewards are frequently tied with timelines and the ability to provide projects ahead of schedule.

41. **Answer C** is correct. Open-heart surgery has a beginning and ending and therefore constitutes a project. The post-surgery maintenance and ongoing support is a program because it does not have a definite ending to the treatment. Answer A is incorrect because the heart usage timeline does not determine whether it is a project or a program. Answer B is incorrect because resource allocation does not determine whether the surgery is a project or a program. Answer D is incorrect because getting the skills and resources is not a program.

42. **Answer B** is correct. The communication management plan describes who and how the communication will be distributed. Answer A might be a fast method of distribution, but it should be explained thoroughly in the communication plan. Answer C is incorrect because the project manager does not need to wait until the kickoff meeting in order to communicate the information. If the kickoff is described in the communication management plan as the correct method to communicate this information, the kickoff is appropriate. However, the communication plan is the first source to draw from to determine if the kickoff meeting is the forum to utilize. Answer D is incorrect because it might not be the most efficient method to distribute the information.

43. **Answer A** is the best answer. The phase-end reviews are called phase exits, stage gates, and kill points because they provide a point to pause and determine whether the project should go forward or be stopped. Answer B is incorrect because the review and decision are not always milestones. Answer C is incorrect because the decision should not necessarily be based upon stakeholder expectations. Answer D is incorrect because the review and decision-making process can be swift if enough information is provided in a timely manner.

44. **Answer D** is correct. Change control management is utilized from the beginning to the end of the project in order to keep it focused with an emphasis on the time and budget. Answer A is incorrect because change control management is not separate from the other phases. Answer B is incorrect because the control plan *must* be throughout the other phases of a project. Its usage is not optional, and consistent utilization is imperative to managing scope creep and other scope expansions. Answer C is incorrect because the project sponsor is generally not responsible for the change control documentation, although it should be involved in the buy-in and approval process.

45. **Answer D** is correct. Answer A is incorrect because crashing the schedule involves scheduling extraneous amounts of resources in an attempt to decrease your timeline with the additional people. Answers B and C are incorrect because peak shaving and resource reallocation are used whenever you want to move extra resources from one time period to another. Fast tracking pushes the project along regardless of whether an approval has been completed. This can be the catalyst for the project to proceed into the next phase without loss of inertia.

46. **Answer C** is correct. The completion of milestones and deliverables provides validity to the direction of the project with an emphasis on results. The stakeholders are more involved in the beginning because the scope might be more open ended. However, this impact and involvement decreases as the scope is formalized and buy-in is achieved with the stakeholders. Answer A is incorrect because it does not correctly answer the question. Answer B is incorrect because time alone does not reduce risk, and stakeholders should not lose vision over time if the information is correctly documented and communicated. Answer D is incorrect because a risk analysis should have already begun regardless of whether the stakeholders have been identified.

47. **Answer C** is correct. The execution phase of a project has the highest level of activity and expense. The planning phase has the second-highest level of activity and expense. For most project life cycles, the intermediate phases consume the highest level of staffing and time. During the initial phase, the project begins to gain momentum as the level of activity rises. Therefore, Answers A, B, and D are incorrect.

48. **Answer D** is correct. According to PMI, differences between or among stake-holders should be resolved in favor of the customer. Coming to a win/win reso-lution is a key element to effective Project Management while aligning business priorities with customer expectations. Answer A is incorrect because taking notes is not enough to resolve the problem. Answer B is a good first step, but it is not the best response. Answer C is incorrect because this might not resolve the problem.

49. **Answer A** is correct. As you go along the continuum from a functional to a projectized organization, the level of authority for a project manager increases. Answer B is incorrect because the level of authority increases as you progress from functional to projectized organizations. Answer C is incorrect because coercion power is not as effective in Project Management as other professions, such as the military. Answer D is incorrect because it does not answer the question completely.

50. **Answer C** is correct. The Project Management processes should be executed for each project life cycle phase and/or iteration. Answer A is incorrect because the Project Management processes are used to manage the progress of the project life cycle, and project life cycle phases are not normally associated with controlling and executing processes, for example. Answer B is incorrect because it is the opposite of the correct choice. Answer D is incorrect because a rela-tionship can exist between the initiating, planning, and closing processes and traditional project life cycle phases (such as concept, analysis, and closure).

Project Initiation

Exam Prep Questions

1. Susan is a well-paid global operations executive who also enjoys consulting and teaching. She is so popular that recently she received two offers in the same day to speak at conferences as a paid presenter. At one conference, she was offered $3,000 for her presentation on a topic that she is not fond of. She was offered $2,000 at another conference to speak on resource allocation, a topic that she enjoys. Because money is no object to Susan, she decides to speak about resource allocation for $2,000 and pass on the other conference. Susan must also use a day of vacation time with a value of $2,000 to take time off work to attend the conference. What is Susan's opportunity cost to speak at the conference?

   ❑ A. $1,000
   ❑ B. $2,000
   ❑ C. $3,000
   ❑ D. $4,000

2. The purpose of a project charter is all of the following except

   ❑ A. To describe the business need(s) that the project will meet
   ❑ B. To authorize the beginning of the project
   ❑ C. To give the project manager the authority to go forward with the project
   ❑ D. To give functional power to the project manager

3. Whenever a team becomes involved with a new project, it does analysis in order to determine what the best alternatives to begin the project are. Because projects should be aligned with the organization's strategic direction, the initiation phase is the

   ❑ A. First step in the solicitation process
   ❑ B. Second step in the project life cycle
   ❑ C. Stakeholder's responsibility
   ❑ D. First step in the scope management process

4. You have started your own company based upon PMI methodologies and have been contracted by the government to develop a new interface for one of its computer applications. You develop a solution and win the bid for the contract but encounter problems at the end of the project when the customer says that you did not fulfill their needs. You are thoroughly shocked. What is your conclusion of the situation?

- ❑ A. There are always more customers available.
- ❑ B. If the customer is not satisfied, the project is not successful.
- ❑ C. Change control management was not effective.
- ❑ D. The customer did not communicate very well.

Quick Answer: **39**
Detailed Answer: **40**

5. Budiono is in the process of developing his project notebook and accumulating archive materials related to the project's work breakdown structure (WBS). The lowest level of a work breakdown structure branch is known as a _____.

- ❑ A. Work package
- ❑ B. Task
- ❑ C. Deliverable
- ❑ D. Work product

Quick Answer: **39**
Detailed Answer: **40**

6. Which of the following work products must be included in the project charter?

- ❑ A. Risk analysis
- ❑ B. Budget estimates
- ❑ C. Product description
- ❑ D. Scope statement

Quick Answer: **39**
Detailed Answer: **40**

7. During the project selection process for the new power plant infrastructure development, Roger learns about a project selection method that utilizes scoring models and a cost analysis to determine what projects he should work on and develop over time. This type of project selection method is an example of

- ❑ A. Constrained optimization
- ❑ B. Earned value
- ❑ C. Standard deviation
- ❑ D. Benefit measurement

Quick Answer: **39**
Detailed Answer: **41**

8. Ralph's Cyber Café is starting an electronic PMO office and needs fresh ideas to help the business grow. For the initial phase, the PMO director has decided to roll out the use of project charters. As a project manager, why would you be encouraged by this plan?

Quick Answer: **39**
Detailed Answer: **41**

   ❑ A. The project charter enables you to establish the business need for the project.
   ❑ B. The project charter ensures that a preliminary budget and schedule are developed.
   ❑ C. The project charter authorizes you to use organizational resources to accomplish the objectives of the project.
   ❑ D. The project charter enables you to get senior management buy-in for your Project Management approach.

9. One of the goals of management by objectives (MBO) is to ensure that objectives of one level within an organization are supportive of and aligned with the objectives of another level of the organization. This methodology has been popular within some organizations as they define their culture. Which of the following is not true about MBO?

Quick Answer: **39**
Detailed Answer: **41**

   ❑ A. It has a top-down orientation.
   ❑ B. Corrective actions are not part of the process.
   ❑ C. You need to establish clear and achievable objectives.
   ❑ D. MBO is a natural fit for Project Management.

10. As a new program manager, Mary is still trying to determine her best sources of information for the not-for-profit organization that you work for. One resource is experts. Expert judgment is mentioned in the beginning of the PMBOK because project initiation is the first process that lists expert judgment as a primary tool or technique. Which of the following would likely not be a source of expert judgment for Mary?

Quick Answer: **39**
Detailed Answer: **41**

   ❑ A. Stakeholders
   ❑ B. Industry groups
   ❑ C. Government regulatory agencies
   ❑ D. Utilities

11. Rebecca has created the project charter but cannot get it approved by senior management. Her manager and boss have asked her to begin the project anyway. Which of the following actions is the *best* thing to do?

Quick Answer: **39**
Detailed Answer: **41**

   ❑ A. Focus on other projects that have a signed charter.
   ❑ B. Start work on critical path tasks.
   ❑ C. Update the Project Risk Log.
   ❑ D. Show the manager the impact of proceeding without approval.

Quick Check

12. Cost benefit analysis and constrained optimization are two general types of project selection methods that project managers utilize when they are evaluating projects. Although various industries have different priorities and agendas, the stakeholders need to be in agreement about the selection process for the project. What is the most important criterion when an organization chooses a project selection model?

Quick Answer: **39**
Detailed Answer: **41**

    ❏ A. Organizational fit
    ❏ B. Flexibility
    ❏ C. Cost
    ❏ D. Capability

13. The payback period can become an important issue when a large scope project is developed over several years. Maureen has been assigned the responsibility of calculating the payback period for her project that is to be completed in 3 years. The internal rate of return (IRR) is 7% and the annual savings will be $800,000 per year. The total cost is $4,000,000 and the rate of return during this time period is 3%. What is the payback period of Maureen's project?

Quick Answer: **39**
Detailed Answer: **42**

    ❏ A. 3 years
    ❏ B. 4 years
    ❏ C. 5 years
    ❏ D. 13.3 years

14. Another project selection method evaluates the present value of cash inflows minus the present value of cash outflows. When evaluating the net present value (NPV)

Quick Answer: **39**
Detailed Answer: **42**

    ❏ A. A positive NPV is unfavorable.
    ❏ B. A negative NPV is unfavorable.
    ❏ C. The lower the NPV, the better.
    ❏ D. You subtract the IRR to get the future value.

15. The Acme Company is always trying to get the best return on its investment because its government funding was cut last year. If the current interest rate is 6% and the return on investment (ROI) is 1.73, the return that a company would earn if it invests in the project is the

Quick Answer: **39**
Detailed Answer: **42**

    ❏ A. IRR
    ❏ B. Benefit cost ratio
    ❏ C. Present value (PV)
    ❏ D. Earned value

16. There are numerous reasons why initiation and planning activities get confused. While determining business needs and collecting historical data during the initiation phase, the project manager also

Quick Answer: **39**
Detailed Answer: **42**

   ❑ A. Selects team members

   ❑ B. Determines deliverables and constraints

   ❑ C. Develops a risk analysis

   ❑ D. Prepares a communication plan

17. Management By Walking Around (MBWA) is a common term to refer to the interaction that a manager performs while working with his team. Daniel works for a toothpaste company and has found his company, Bright Teeth, is an ideal environment in which to apply the technique of MBWA because

Quick Answer: **39**
Detailed Answer: **42**

   ❑ A. Top management policy and goals should flow down through the management hierarchy.

   ❑ B. Project Management involves setting organizational objectives.

   ❑ C. All projects should be strongly oriented toward goals and objectives.

   ❑ D. Projects are generally handled in a matrix management environment.

18. Sometimes project managers forget all of the expenses that they can incur on a project, such as capital resources and assets. This can have an impact upon their budgets and the economic return on the project. A cost that has been incurred and cannot be reversed is known as a

Quick Answer: **39**
Detailed Answer: **42**

   ❑ A. Fixed cost

   ❑ B. Direct cost

   ❑ C. Variable cost

   ❑ D. Sunk cost

19. Ian works for a manufacturing company that has a global presence and utilizes outsourcing for many of its services. Because of the increasing cost of local resources, he must identify all of the potential options when analyzing his resource pool and determining which projects he wants to complete in the United States and which projects should be done in India. All of the following are examples of benefit-measurement methods of project selection except which one?

Quick Answer: **39**
Detailed Answer: **42**

   ❑ A. Scoring models

   ❑ B. Multiobjective programming

   ❑ C. Economic models

   ❑ D. IS steering committee review

20. Straight-line depreciation is the simplest method of depreciating an asset and is frequently utilized on a project to determine its economic feasibility. Straight-line depreciation is

Quick Answer: **39**
Detailed Answer: **43**

- ❏ A. Only applicable for direct costs
- ❏ B. Only applicable for costs that are indirectly traced to a specific product or service
- ❏ C. A cost that can increase with the interest rate
- ❏ D. A method that divides an asset's cost and its expected salvage value by its expected utilization period

21. Michelle is not an accountant and is frequently frustrated about why she needs to know financial information for her projects. Therefore, she has returned to college in order to enhance her accounting knowledge. Her company, Quikstart, is paying for her tuition if she maintains satisfactory grades. In her studies, she has found that current assets less current liabilities are equal to

Quick Answer: **39**
Detailed Answer: **43**

- ❏ A. Working capital
- ❏ B. Standard deviation
- ❏ C. Actual cost of work performed (ACWP)
- ❏ D. Estimate at completion (EAC)

22. A project charter is one of the key deliverables to come from the initiation process. The project charter should by issued by

Quick Answer: **39**
Detailed Answer: **43**

- ❏ A. One or more functional managers
- ❏ B. The head of the performing organization
- ❏ C. A manager external to the project
- ❏ D. The CFO

23. The direct cost to manufacture a replacement auto part for a 2001 vehicle is $24.97 and indirect costs (including utilities) is $4.50 per part, labor at $2,119 per month, and variable costs of $14.32. What is the wholesale cost to produce this auto part?

Quick Answer: **39**
Detailed Answer: **43**

- ❏ A. $24.97
- ❏ B. Not enough information is provided
- ❏ C. $43.79
- ❏ D. $39.29

24. During the initiation of a project, numerous ideas will surface whenever you are discussing goals and objectives for the project. SMART objectives are much easier to assign to team members when they are involved in the initiation phase rather than when assignments are distributed in an autocratic manner. SMART objectives are

Quick Answer: **39**
Detailed Answer: **43**

   ❑   A. Aligned with the organization's strategic goals
   ❑   B. Easily achievable
   ❑   C. Specific, measurable, assignable, realistic, and time based
   ❑   D. Used with the MBO management approach

25. Project Management is a relatively new profession. Frequently, the early project managers were looked upon as operations managers or some other title that did not adequately describe the work they were actually doing. Typically, the early project managers were selected by which organizational level?

Quick Answer: **39**
Detailed Answer: **43**

   ❑   A. Human resources
   ❑   B. Computer sciences
   ❑   C. Executive
   ❑   D. Engineering

26. As an experienced project manager, you know there is an inherent amount of risk with any project. During what phase of the project life cycle is the highest level of risk and uncertainty?

Quick Answer: **39**
Detailed Answer: **43**

   ❑   A. Controlling
   ❑   B. Executing
   ❑   C. Planning
   ❑   D. Initiating

27. A business analyst helps provide a beginning blueprint for the project to develop structure and encourages discussions about the needs of the project. Which document describes the business need, the quantifiable criteria that must be met by the project, and the key deliverables, as well as authorizes the project and the final product of the project?

Quick Answer: **39**
Detailed Answer: **44**

   ❑   A. Business requirements document
   ❑   B. Executive summary
   ❑   C. Project charter
   ❑   D. Gantt chart

Quick Check

28. Norma is a new product development project manager who frequently has to deal with scope creep at her company due to the various silos within her company and competing demands at each of the profit centers. She frequently becomes frustrated because her projects seem to become "never ending." Which of the following is not a scope management process that Norma can utilize?

Quick Answer: **39**
Detailed Answer: **44**

- ❑ A. Scope planning
- ❑ B. Scope reporting
- ❑ C. Initiation
- ❑ D. Scope verification

29. Jeffrey has been given the assignment to summarize his project and provide a status update for next week's steering committee meeting. As part of his presentation, he will present the scope document and associated deliverables. This scope statement provides a foundation of information to begin the project and gives the team an idea of what it is trying to accomplish. Which of the following statements is not true about a scope statement?

Quick Answer: **39**
Detailed Answer: **44**

- ❑ A. The scope statement does not include a description of project objectives, such as cost, schedule, and quality measures.
- ❑ B. The scope statement provides a documented basis for preparing the work breakdown structure (WBS).
- ❑ C. The scope statement is not developed by functional managers during the concept phase of a project.
- ❑ D. The scope statement is not the basis for the contract between the buyer and seller.

30. Project authorization is one of the processes that is associated with the initiation phase of a project. Authorizations can come in many different forms, and projects are generally authorized by all of the following except

Quick Answer: **39**
Detailed Answer: **44**

- ❑ A. Technological advances
- ❑ B. Customer request or market demand
- ❑ C. Executive year-end bonuses
- ❑ D. Business or social needs

31. There are some major differences between the project life cycle and the product life cycle. These differences can have a significant impact upon the Project Management requirements and approach utilized during the initiation process. Inputs into the initiation process include all of the following except

    ❏ A. The product charter
    ❏ B. The strategic plan
    ❏ C. The project selection criteria
    ❏ D. Historical information

32. *Tools and techniques* is a term that is frequently used in the PMBOK to describe the various options and actions that a project manager can take when faced with various situations or opportunities. The tools and techniques for the initiation processes include

    ❏ A. The communication plan
    ❏ B. Expert judgment
    ❏ C. The project budget
    ❏ D. The WBS

33. Subject matter experts (SMEs) are resources that are imperative to the success of a project. Many times, project managers are not experts in the areas they are managing and frequently must rely upon others' expertise. In which scope-management process are SMEs first used?

    ❏ A. Scope planning
    ❏ B. Scope definition
    ❏ C. Initiation
    ❏ D. Scope verification

34. Assumptions, constraints, and the project charter are three of the outputs from the initiation phase of a project. From the point of initiation, why should assumptions be documented for the team?

    ❏ A. Assumptions limit the project team's options for decision making.
    ❏ B. Assumptions might prove to be incorrect. The ability to identify these assumptions allows for baseline adjustments in case of project crisis.
    ❏ C. Assumption analysis is a key technique of risk identification.
    ❏ D. In case of schedule or budget overruns, the documentation of assumptions provides an accountability trail.

35. The assignment of a project manager to a project is one of the key outputs from the initiation process. In general, when should a project manager be assigned to a project?

   ❑ A. Before the project plan execution phase
   ❑ B. When the stakeholders choose him
   ❑ C. After the project planning is done
   ❑ D. This is decided in the WBS

Quick Answer: **39**
Detailed Answer: **45**

36. One of the deliverables that comes from the initiation phase can come in the form of a signed contract or a formalized document. This deliverable should be prepared by someone who is external to the project and utilizes this as a catalyst for the project to move forward. This deliverable is known as the

   ❑ A. Scope statement
   ❑ B. Project charter
   ❑ C. Change request
   ❑ D. Status report

Quick Answer: **39**
Detailed Answer: **45**

37. As a project manager, you are required to look at the attributes of a new hotel project in Las Vegas that will have a positive financial impact upon your organization. The cost benefit ratio is a project selection method and one way to determine whether the project is appropriate for your company. This ratio identifies the relationship between the financial cost and the benefits of a proposed project. If the cost benefit ratio for the new Las Vegas hotel project is .78,

   ❑ A. The project should go forward.
   ❑ B. The project manager will determine a plan to reduce the CR to zero.
   ❑ C. The project will be successful.
   ❑ D. It is unfavorable.

Quick Answer: **39**
Detailed Answer: **45**

38. ABC Company project manager, Doug, is not an accountant but he must make several financial decisions for his new project for the company. In his research, he has found there are several accounting-related attributes he needs to consider before he talks with the steering committee about the new project. In his presentation, he needs to describe the interest rate that makes the net present value of all cash flows equal zero. This is known as

   ❑ A. Prioritization of financial outcomes
   ❑ B. Future value (FV)
   ❑ C. IRR
   ❑ D. Present value (PV)

Quick Answer: **39**
Detailed Answer: **45**

39. Problems, opportunities, and business requirements are stimuli that management responds to by creating projects. Susan is working as a project manager for Big Chip Information Technologies and has developed several programming code changes that have revolutionized Big Chip and how it interacts with its customers. A technological advancement such as the development of the personal computer is

Quick Answer: **39**
Detailed Answer: **45**

❑ A. An advancement that the project manager should incorporate into her current projects

❑ B. Scope creep

❑ C. An advancement that the project manager should incorporate into her future projects

❑ D. A reason to authorize a project

40. You are a project manager for the redevelopment of the Hoover Dam. Your team has been provided with the scope statement, but it lacks many description details. Your team is concerned because the project is in the initiation phase and it wants to postpone it until it has more information. As the project manager, you recommend that

Quick Answer: **39**
Detailed Answer: **46**

❑ A. The team should go forward, but be cautious about the lack of details and the impact upon the timeline for the project.

❑ B. The project should not go forward until the stakeholders agree about the scope and purpose of the project.

❑ C. The team should verify the scope and realize that more details will be available as project characteristics are progressively elaborated.

❑ D. The team should review the project selection criteria for the Hoover Dam project.

41. According to the PMBOK, the _____ documents the characteristics of the product or service that the project was undertaken to create.

Quick Answer: **39**
Detailed Answer: **46**

❑ A. project definition

❑ B. product description

❑ C. scope statement

❑ D. strategic plan

42. Chuck is the project manager for a new point of sale (POS) implementation for a national grocery chain. At the beginning of the project, Chuck must rely upon input from numerous SMEs in order to make correct decisions. This tool is an example of

Quick Answer: **39**
Detailed Answer: **46**

- ❑ A. Stakeholder input
- ❑ B. Team member expertise
- ❑ C. Expert judgment
- ❑ D. Consultant intuition

43. Scott is a government employee who is new to the Project Management world. He was just promoted to this role and wants to learn more about how he can advance within his organization. During the initiation phase of his first project, why should Scott document assumptions for the project?

Quick Answer: **39**
Detailed Answer: **46**

- ❑ A. Because the assumptions might be incorrect, the ability to identify these assumptions allows for baseline assumptions in case of a project problem.
- ❑ B. Assumptions can limit the team's options for decision making.
- ❑ C. In case of schedule or budget overruns, the documentation of assumptions provides a paper trail of responsibilities.
- ❑ D. Assumption analysis is a technique for risk identification.

44. A good CFO will tell you that it is important to look at your bottom line and determine how to increase profits for the organization. Veronica, the new CFO at a local university, is taking that approach and applying it to new projects. Therefore, she wants to include costs from each phase of the project on a total expenditure line item in the annual budget. This total expenditure is known as

Quick Answer: **39**
Detailed Answer: **46**

- ❑ A. An opportunity cost
- ❑ B. A sunk cost
- ❑ C. NPV
- ❑ D. A life cycle

45. Margaret works for an American textile manufacturer that outsources several parts of its operations to an organization in Ireland. At the beginning of the outsourcing project, a charter was developed. The appropriate person to develop this charter would be

Quick Answer: **39**
Detailed Answer: **47**

- ❑ A. A manager external to the project
- ❑ B. The project manager
- ❑ C. The functional managers in America and Ireland
- ❑ D. The Irish Consulate

46. Thomas Company has purchased a new server for its IT department and expects to use it until it becomes obsolete. The server cost $4,500 and can be used for 10 years. It has a resale value of $2,000 after 5 years and a resale value of $1,000 after 7 years. It is obsolete in the 10th year. Using straight-line depreciation, calculate the expense per year for this piece of hardware:

❑ A. $4,500
❑ B. $3,500
❑ C. $2,500
❑ D. $450

Quick Answer: **39**
Detailed Answer: **47**

47. Relocating 200 employees from one building to another is your new responsibility in a recent company reorganization. Because there is a large volume of people involved with this project, a multiphase approach will be used in order to mini-mize the impact upon the workflow of the company. Consequently, payments will need to be made on leases for both locations until all employees have been moved. A lease payment on the second building is an example of a

❑ A. Project assumption
❑ B. Direct cost
❑ C. Variable cost
❑ D. Fixed cost

Quick Answer: **39**
Detailed Answer: **47**

48. Project budgets, resources, sustainability, and schedules are difficult issues to juggle. As a project manager, you are always trying to maintain a balance between all of these project aspects. These topics are known as

❑ A. Milestones
❑ B. Assumptions
❑ C. Inputs
❑ D. Constraints

Quick Answer: **39**
Detailed Answer: **47**

49. Due to market demand of the new low-carb potato chips, Louie is working a lot of hours at the local factory. Because Louie recognizes that the product introduction and life cycle are the same as with a previous product he worked on that was very successful, he anticipates this product will be successful as well, based upon

❑ A. Expert judgment
❑ B. Historical information
❑ C. Demographic studies
❑ D. The strategic plan

Quick Answer: **39**
Detailed Answer: **47**

Quick Check

Quick Answer: **39**
Detailed Answer: **48**

50. The scope management process is challenging and many times can involve a project review board to make the final determination in order to minimize scope creep. During what scope management process are SMEs first utilized?

❏ A. Scope verification

❏ B. Scope planning

❏ C. Scope definition

❏ D. Initiation

Quick Check Answer Key

1. C	28. B
2. D	29. C
3. D	30. C
4. B	31. A
5. A	32. B
6. C	33. C
7. D	34. C
8. C	35. A
9. B	36. B
10. D	37. D
11. D	38. C
12. A	39. D
13. C	40. C
14. B	41. B
15. A	42. C
16. B	43. D
17. C	44. D
18. D	45. A
19. B	46. D
20. D	47. D
21. A	48. D
22. C	49. B
23. B	50. D
24. C	
25. D	
26. D	
27. C	

Answers and Explanations

1. **Answer C** is correct because the opportunity cost is the lost money that she could have been paid for the other event if she was the speaker. Therefore, Answers A, B, and D are incorrect.

2. **Answer D** is correct because a project manager is *not* given functional authority in the charter. Answer A is incorrect because the charter should include a description of the business need(s) that the project will meet. Answer B is incorrect because the project charter does authorize the beginning of the project. Answer C is incorrect because the project charter does give the project manager the authority to go forward with the project.

3. **Answer D** is correct because the initiation phase is the first step in the scope management process and the Project Management process. The process of performing this initial analysis for a project should be considered a separate project and not part of the initiation phase of the project. Answer B is incorrect because the initiation phase is the first step in the project life cycle. Answer C is incorrect because it is not necessarily the stakeholders' responsibility to be a resource for the initiation of the project, unless they are team members.

4. **Answer B** is correct. Answer A is incorrect because without satisfied customers, we do not have potential for new projects. Answer C is incorrect because the change control management process would have likely resolved this problem. Answer D is incorrect because it is the project manager's responsibility to seek communication with the customer to set realistic expectations.

5. **Answer A** is correct. Not all branches of the WBS have to be decomposed to the same level, although each succeeding level generally has more detail. Answer B is incorrect because a task is not a definitive enough answer to describe the lowest level of the WBS. Answer C is incorrect because deliverables are the outputs of the project processes and not involved with the different levels of the WBS. Answer D is incorrect because a work product is described as a process output and not a term that would be used to describe the lowest level of a WBS.

6. **Answer C** is correct. The product description is one of the three minimal requirements of the project charter, as described by the PMBOK. The charter should also include a description of the business need(s) that the project will meet. The other choices in this question might appear in some organization's charters; however, they are not the correct answers for the test question. Therefore, Answers A, B, and D are incorrect.

7. **Answer D** is correct and illustrates the utilization of a cost benefit analysis. Answer A is incorrect because constrained optimization is a mathematical approach that uses math models and complex criteria in the selection process and is not the appropriate response to this question. Answer B is incorrect because earned value is the value of the work actually performed and not a project selection method. Answer C is incorrect because standard deviation evaluation is not a project selection method, although some of the standard deviation reports may be inputs to the project selection process.

8. **Answer C** is correct. Answer A is incorrect because the project manager cannot establish the business need alone. Remember that the charter is issued by someone external to the team. Answer B is incorrect because the project charter does not require a preliminary schedule and budget. Answer D is incorrect because the Project Management approach would be defined in the project plan.

9. **Answer B** is correct. Corrective actions are part of the process after establishing objectives and checking on the objectives. The next step is to take corrective actions. Answers A, C, and D are true statements and therefore are incorrect for this question.

10. **Answer D** is the best answer because utilities would be the least likely to provide expert advice to a not-for-profit organization concerning how to run the organization. Answer A is incorrect because stakeholders can be a valuable resource for expert judgment. Answer B is incorrect because industry groups frequently support not-for-profit organizations and can be a good information source. Answer C is incorrect because the government regulatory agencies frequently support and monitor not-for-profit organizations.

11. **Answer D** is correct. Remember the importance that PMI places on effective communications and on "doing the right thing." Answers A and C are incorrect because these would not be the best actions to take next in this situation. It is the project manager's responsibility to present all the necessary information to the sponsors and stakeholders so that they can make decisions that are in the best interest of the project, quality, and the timeline. Answer B is incorrect because the "lack of senior management approval" issue has not been dealt with yet and resolution should be pursued so the project can go forward.

12. **Answer A** is correct. The most important factor is that the project selection method be "realistic" for the organization. It needs to be consistent with its goals and objectives, and it needs to account for the capabilities of the organization. Answers B, C, and D are all incorrect because although they are key criteria when choosing a project selection model, they are irrelevant if the model is not first an effective organizational fit.

13. **Answer C** is correct. The payback period is how long it takes to recoup your investment. In this example, the cost was $4,000,000 and the savings was $800,000 per year. $4,000,000/$800,000 = 5. Therefore, Answers A, B, and D are incorrect.

14. **Answer B** is correct. A negative NPV is unfavorable because this means that cash outflows are higher than the value of cash inflows. Answer A is incorrect because a positive NPV is favorable. Answer C is incorrect because the higher the NPV, the better. Answer D is incorrect because IRR is not associated with NPV.

15. **Answer A** is correct. The internal rate of return (IRR) is the interest rate that makes the net present value of all cash flows equal zero. Answer B is incorrect because the benefit cost ratio identifies the relationship between the cost and benefits of a proposed project. Answer C is incorrect because present value (PV) is the value today of future cash flows. Answer D is incorrect because earned value is the work accomplished plus the authorized budget for the work. It is the sum of the approved cost estimates for activities completed during a given time period. This was previously called the budgeted cost of work performed (BCWP).

16. **Answer B** is correct. The deliverables and constraints are identified during the initiation phase as the inputs into the planning phase. Answer A is incorrect because team member selection is done during the planning phase of the project. Answer C is incorrect because a risk analysis is generally prepared during the planning phase of a project. Answer D is incorrect because the communication plan is also generally developed during the planning phase.

17. **Answer C** is correct. The approach of goal/objective setting and periodic evaluations is common to both MBWA and Project Management. Answer A is incorrect because projects use more than functional management hierarchy structures. Answer B is incorrect because Project Management is focused on executing organizational objectives and not on setting them. Answer D is incorrect in much the same way that Answer A is incorrect. You cannot rely on a top-down organizational flow in project environments.

18. **Answer D** is correct because a sunk cost is a project expense that will eventually need to be paid. Answer A is incorrect because a fixed cost remains constant, regardless of any change in a company's activity. Answer B is incorrect because a direct cost can be directly linked to producing specific goods or services. Answer C is incorrect because a variable cost changes in proportion to a change in the company's activity or business.

19. **Answer B** is correct. Multiobjective programming is the only constraint optimization method that is listed. Answers A, C, and D are all incorrect because they are not constraint optimization methods.

20. **Answer D** is correct. Answer A is incorrect because straight-line depreciation is not tied with direct costs. Answer B is incorrect because indirect costs are not associated with straight-line depreciation. Answer C is incorrect because the interest rate does not impact straight-line depreciation.

21. **Answer A** is correct. Answer B is incorrect because the standard deviation is not associated with current assets or liabilities. Answer C is incorrect because actual cost of work performed is not linked to current assets or liabilities. Answer D is incorrect because the estimate at completion (EAC) is utilized for this example.

22. **Answer C** is correct. The other answers could be accurate in specific situations, but their role alone does not meet the key criterion of being "external" to the project team. Answers A, B, and D are incorrect because these individuals are not external to the project.

23. **Answer B** is correct. In order to calculate the cost of the auto part, you need to know all of the costs associated with this part, which are not provided in this problem. Although there is a lot of information provided in this example, it does not provide enough information to determine a per-item cost. In order to determine the cost to manufacture each item, you need to know all costs that are directly related to the production of that specific item. Therefore, Answers A, C, and D are incorrect.

24. **Answer C** is correct. This acronym is frequently used in textbooks inside and outside of Project Management circles to explain why it is vital that you quantify objectives, set due date time frames, and assign responsibility for tasks. This common-sense approach to defining objectives can be a positive tool for a project manager. Answers A, B, and D are all incorrect because they are not the definition or the concept of SMART goals.

25. **Answer D** is correct. Early Project Management was tied with aerospace and government defense departments. The emphasis upon engineers and engineering tools was closely tied to the Project Management profession for a long time until Information Technology began to place a heavy emphasis on its utilization for the development and implementation of IT projects. In today's Project Management world, there is a heavy emphasis on Information Technology projects because many of them involve new development and a certain amount of ambiguity.

26. **Answer D** is correct. Every project has the highest level of risk and uncertainty at the initiation of the project. This is due to the fact that few, if any, of the deliverables have been provided and the milestones have not been met at the beginning of a project. As milestones are met and deliverables are provided, the risk and uncertainty decreases as you develop successes for the project. Your risk generally decreases as you proceed from the initiation phase to the planning phase to the executing phase and closeout. Therefore, Answers A, B, and C are incorrect.

27. **Answer C** is correct. Answer A is incorrect because the business requirements document does not provide project execution details that are contained in the charter. Answer B is incorrect because an executive summary generally is a brief overview of the project and does not provide granular details about the actual implementation and deliverables. Answer D is incorrect because a Gantt chart is used to show timelines for the various tasks associated with the project.

28. **Answer B** is correct. Answers A, C, and D are incorrect because they are defined by the PMBOK as scope management processes, including initiation, which is the first step in the scope management process.

29. **Answer C** is correct. The scope statement can be developed by the functional manager, or any other manager besides the project manager, during the initiation phase of the project. Answer A is incorrect because a scope statement does include these items. Answer B is incorrect because the scope statement is not directly affiliated with the work breakdown structure (WBS). Answer D is a true statement and therefore incorrect for this question. The scope statement is not the basis for a contract between the buyer and seller and is therefore not the correct response in this situation.

30. **Answer C** is correct. Project authorizations should not be exclusively based upon the impact of an executive's bonus (many people would agree that it should not ever be based upon an executive's bonus). Answers A, B, and D are common events that predicate the need for project authorization and can evolve into large scope projects.

31. **Answer A** is correct. The charter is *not* an input into the project initiation process. Inputs to the project initiation process are a product description, a strategic plan, a project selection criteria, and historical information. Answers B, C, and D are inputs into the initiation process and therefore incorrect for this question.

32. **Answer B** is correct. Answers A, C, and D are not tools and techniques used during the initiation process.

33. **Answer C** is correct. Initiation is the first step in the scope management process, and expert judgment is one of the techniques routinely utilized. Answers A, B, and D are incorrect because they would come after the initiation process.

34. **Answer C** is correct. Answer A is incorrect because constraints limit your options. Answer B is incorrect because it's not the correct process for adjusting project baselines. Answer D is incorrect because, although it's a tempting answer based on real-world experience, it's not the answer PMI is looking for, and it would be more applicable to project controlling.

35. **Answer A** is correct. The project manager should be assigned to a project as early as possible in order to allow him the opportunity to participate in the planning aspects of the project. Answer B is incorrect because the stakeholders are generally not the people that choose the project manager. Answer C is incorrect because just the opposite is correct, and the project manager should definitely be assigned to the project before the project planning is complete. Answer D is incorrect because the work breakdown structure does not mandate when the project manager will be assigned.

36. **Answer B** is correct. The project charter is one of the most important outputs of the initiation phase. Answer A is incorrect because the scope statement is not one of the outputs of the initiation phase. Answer C is incorrect because a change request is generally developed after the initiation phase of the project, not during it. Answer D is incorrect because the status report is the output of the execution phase of a project.

37. **Answer D** is the best answer. A benefit cost ratio (BCR) that is lower than 1.0 is unfavorable because you are spending more money than you are receiving benefits. Answer A is incorrect because the project manager should review the project to determine whether it should go forward and develop ways to increase the BCR to 1.0 or more. Answer B is incorrect because the BCR should not be reduced to zero. A BCR of zero indicates that the project does not have any benefits associated with the expenses of a project. Answer C is incorrect because the project will not likely be successful, unless there are benefits that outweigh the expenses and effort associated with the completion of the project.

38. **Answer C** is correct. The internal rate of return (IRR) is the return that the company would earn if it invests in the project. Answer A is incorrect because prioritization of financial outcomes is not a PMI term and not an appropriate response for this question. Answer B is incorrect because the future value (FV) is not associated with the internal rate of return. Answer D is incorrect because the present value is the value today for future cash flows.

39. **Answer D** is the best answer. Technological advances, market demand, customer requests, and legal requirements are some of the triggers that signify the need to authorize a project. Answer A is correct but not the best answer for this question. Answer B is incorrect because scope creep is not associated with the project authorization process. Answer C is incorrect because any advancement that can have a positive impact upon a project should be incorporated into projects as soon as they are available.

40. **Answer C** is correct. The project details and description will usually have less detail at the beginning of the project and will increase as the characteristics are progressively elaborated. Answer A is incorrect because the team should confirm that they understand the essence of the scope of the project, even if the details might be ambiguous at the beginning of the project. Answer B is incorrect because the project should go forward; however, the team should request further clarification of what the project scope entails. Answer D is incorrect because the project selection criteria should be established before the project begins.

41. **Answer B** is correct. The product description provides the characteristics of the service or product that the project was utilized to develop. Answer A is incorrect because project definition is not an official PMI or PMBOK term. Answer C is incorrect because a scope statement is a document that provides the description of what the project entails. Answer D is incorrect because the strategic plan is the input into the initiation process along with the strategic plan, project selection criteria, and historical information.

42. **Answer C** is the best answer. An SME (subject matter expert) provides expertise and advice to the team for the project. Expert judgment and project selection methods are tools and techniques that are utilized during the initiation of a project. Answers A, B, and D are incorrect because they are not tools and techniques that are utilized during the initiation process.

43. **Answer D** is correct. Assumptions have an inherent amount of risk and should be evaluated during the initiation phase to determine the potential impact upon the project. Answer A is incorrect because assumptions are not baselined in a project. Answer B is incorrect because assumptions do not generally limit the team's options; however, constraints can limit the team's options. Answer C is incorrect because assumptions are not correlated with the project responsibilities and do not impact the overruns on a project.

44. **Answer D** is correct. Life cycle costing includes the costs from each phase of the project life cycle when the total investment costs are calculated. Answer A is incorrect because an opportunity cost is the difference between a chosen investment and the one that is passed up. Answer B is incorrect because sunk costs are costs that have been incurred and cannot be reversed. Answer C is incorrect because net present value (NPV) is the present value of cash inflows (benefits) minus the present value of cash outflows (costs).

45. **Answer A** is correct. The project charter should be developed by someone who is external to the project. Sometimes this external person actually becomes the project sponsor and provides support to the project because she either originated the idea for the project or worked with the originator. Answers B and C are incorrect because these individuals are not external to the project. Answer D is incorrect because a government official associated with a vendor would not be involved with the development of a charter.

46. **Answer D** is correct. Straight-line depreciation is a method of depreciation that divides the difference between an asset's cost and its expected salvage value by the number of years it is expected to be used. Therefore, the calculation is

    ($4,500 [cost]) – ($0 [salvage value at obsolescence])/10 years = $450 per year.

47. **Answer D** is correct. A fixed cost is a constant expense, regardless of the level of activity within the company and does not vary based upon the level of output. Answer B could be correct because a lease payment is a direct cost, but it is not associated with a product in this case, so it is not the best answer. Answer C is incorrect because variable costs are generally associated with the manufacture of a product, and vary with the volume of product produced.

48. **Answer D** is correct. Constraints are factors that can limit the options of the team and need to be identified so they can be evaluated for their impact upon the outcomes of the project. Answer A is incorrect because milestones are goal-related achievements and not applicable to this question. Answer B is incorrect because assumptions are factors that are considered to be true, real, or certain. Answer C is incorrect because inputs are the project-related efforts and contributions that are related to outputs, tools, and techniques.

49. **Answer B** is the best answer. The experience that Louie had with the previous product life cycle is the knowledge that he can draw upon to anticipate similar results in the future. Answer A is not correct because Louie would not necessarily be considered an expert, especially if he had limited experience in that area. Answer C is incorrect because demographic studies involve the analysis of various groups of individuals to evaluate what categories they can be broken into and is not applicable to this situation. Answer D is incorrect because a strategic plan is involved as an input into the initiation process and is more related to the support of the performing organization's goals than the prediction of future sales of potato chips.

50. **Answer D** is correct. Because the change control process occurs during the entire project, from initiation to closeout, the initiation phase is the first step in the scope management process, and SMEs provide input as a tool during this phase. Answer A is incorrect because the scope verification process occurs after the initiation phase, when the SME's input is needed. Answer B is incorrect because scope planning occurs after the initiation phase of the project. Answer C is incorrect because the SME's input is needed before the scope definition process of the project.

3

Project Planning—Core Processes

Exam Prep Questions

1. The new CIO for Mega Hard Drive Corporation, Roger Bigbucks, brings John into his office to discuss a new project that has been approved to improve the security access to their corporate systems worldwide. Roger explains the key objectives of the project, general time frame, and business value. The CIO assigns John to be the project manager and ends the meeting. What is the first thing John needs to do?

   ❑ A. Determine who the key stakeholders are and have a kickoff meeting.
   ❑ B. Find out how much money he has to use for the project.
   ❑ C. Order new business cards that show he is the project manager.
   ❑ D. Begin developing the scope definition.

2. Ed is asked to audit a relatively new project that creates a web interface for warranty claims processing at a manufacturing company. The project is already in trouble with a lot of new changes, and business partners are becoming frustrated. During interviews with the project team, Ed realizes that each individual has a different view of what the project is supposed to accomplish. After reviewing the project charter, he notices that individual assignments are listed, but no objectives or high-level deliverables. What should Ed recommend the project manager do to help save this project?

   ❑ A. Have the project manager publish a description or explanation of the business need the project is going to address.
   ❑ B. Change the project charter to include objectives and high-level deliverables with individuals assigned and time frames.
   ❑ C. Develop a scope statement with the project stakeholders. .
   ❑ D. Hold a kickoff meeting to get everyone on the same page.

Quick Check

Quick Answer: **71**
Detailed Answer: **72**

3. Paul is given a project charter and is assigned to be the project manager. He is ready to begin progressive elaboration of the project scope and tasks. Which of the following tools and techniques is not appropriate for him to use at this time?

- ❏ A. Alternatives identification
- ❏ B. Analogous estimating
- ❏ C. Work breakdown structure templates
- ❏ D. Benefit cost analysis

Quick Answer: **71**
Detailed Answer: **72**

4. You are working on a new project to develop a new wireless product with ease-of-use features recommended by customers. It is as yet undetermined which features and the extent to which each feature will be incorporated into the product. You have a focus group that will continue to evaluate the features as the project goes forward. The focus group is authorized to suggest changes, as are your engineers and the quality department. As a project manager, what will help you most to minimize the effect of these changes?

- ❏ A. A change management plan.
- ❏ B. A scope management plan.
- ❏ C. Do not continue with the project until all of the features are clearly defined in the scope statement and scope definition.
- ❏ D. This is an expected part of every project. A good project manager will have a communications plan in place to be sure everyone knows what is happening on the project.

Quick Answer: **71**
Detailed Answer: **73**

5. In January, Connie, a marketing manager for a toy manufacturer, is preparing a new red-haired doll for release during the Christmas season. This means it needs to be ready to market by the February Toy Fair, where toy retailers make their choices about what toys to buy for the next year. The project manager for the toy development is in the process of ensuring the toy meets federal safety standards, which it does, but the product is running into a problem with additional non-federal safety issues that are only now being uncovered. Identify the assumption, constraint, and product description the project manager should have documented in the scope-supporting details.

- ❏ A. Assumption: The product must be ready for the market in February.

    Constraint: Safety standards.

    Product Description: Includes the fact that it is a Christmas toy.

- ❏ B. Assumption: Federal safety regulations are sufficient for a safe toy.

    Constraint: The product must be market ready by February.

    Product Description: The toy is a red-haired doll.

- ❏ C. Assumption: The project manager is responsible for the product's safety results.

    Constraint: The toy must meet federal safety standards.

    Product Description: The product is a toy.

- ❏ D. Assumption: Non-federal safety issues might come up.

    Constraint: The toy must be sold at Christmas.

    Product Description: The toy must appeal to toy retailers.

6. The AAA Cleaning Service Company is in the process of developing and marketing a new yearly bundled package of cleaning services to be available in its Eastern division and has assigned Bob Brown to be the project manager for the new product rollout. There are just a few major deliverables: Develop new contracts, create an advertising campaign, provide service training, and update the ordering system to handle the new product. Management has agreed to Bob's summary of tasks and expectations, but wants Bob to tell them how much he thinks the project will cost and how long it will take to do the rollout because marketing is anxious to begin pre-selling the service. What should Bob do first?

Quick Answer: **71**

Detailed Answer: **73**

- ❏ A. Quit. There is not enough information for Bob to be successful in this rollout.
- ❏ B. Develop a scope statement so that he is certain he has the project well defined.
- ❏ C. Create a work breakdown structure of the tasks to be done.
- ❏ D. Give an estimate of six months and $250,000 based on his prior work on other projects in different fields.

. . . .

7. Doug Johnson, the manager of operations at a small liquor distribution company, has contracted an outside firm to develop a new warehouse picking system. He is generally satisfied with their performance so far, but in some meetings, he feels they are going beyond the scope of the project as originally defined. Because the contract is time and materials, Doug wants to be sure only the work that is defined in the project scope is what gets done. What project documentation should Doug ask the project manager for?

Quick Answer: **71**
Detailed Answer: **73**

- ❑ A. The scope statement, work breakdown structure (WBS), and any approved changes.
- ❑ B. Meeting minutes from the kickoff meeting, where the project scope was discussed.
- ❑ C. The project charter.
- ❑ D. No documents are needed for review. Doug simply needs to clarify scope with the project manager.

8. The WBS is the foundation for all but which of the following?

Quick Answer: **71**
Detailed Answer: **73**

- ❑ A. Coordinated and integrated planning
- ❑ B. Performance reporting
- ❑ C. Scope management
- ❑ D. Project communication

9. Jenny is developing a WBS for her project. She knows that PMI believes these are important, but she is struggling with the structure and content of the WBS. Which of the following are not items that will help her?

Quick Answer: **71**
Detailed Answer: **73**

- ❑ A. Each WBS element should represent a single tangible deliverable.
- ❑ B. The WBS elements should be structured by organizational unit.
- ❑ C. Think through how each component contributes to the finished deliverable.
- ❑ D. All significant reporting items should be included in the WBS.

10. Ralph is a quality control reviewer for all projects at a large clothing manufacturer. He has reviewed Sally's project and feels that the cost accuracy and duration estimates need to be improved and that the project's projected end date is too far into the year. What should Sally do first?

- ❏ A. Reinterview the subject matter experts (SMEs) and ask for better estimates.
- ❏ B. Reexamine the WBS to see if it can be further decomposed, to allow for better estimating on cost and duration.
- ❏ C. Tell Ralph the estimates are sufficient. He is just a quality control guy and has no real understanding of her project.
- ❏ D. Reduce all the cost and time estimates by 10% based on Ralph's feedback.

11. Rod is new to Project Management and is trying to be sure he is following the entire set of core planning processes properly. He is in the process of developing a WBS, and realizes activity definition is next, but is confused about the difference between the two. As a seasoned project manager, and one ready to take the PMP exam, how would you describe the difference between the two to Rod?

- ❏ A. The WBS is focused on deliverables, whereas activity definition is focused on the tasks to create those deliverables.
- ❏ B. The WBS is focused on scope, and activity definition is focused on planning.
- ❏ C. No one really uses the WBS, and it is essentially the same as the activity definition. Most managers use a project planning software tool instead.
- ❏ D. WBS is focused on the project, whereas activity definition is related to the Project Management activities that must take place to ensure the project is well executed.

12. During the activity definition process on his project, Jeff realizes there are some deliverables that are missing from the scope definition process. What should he do?

- ❏ A. Simply define the additional activities.
- ❏ B. Invoke the scope change management process.
- ❏ C. Update the WBS to include the missing deliverables, and define the appropriate activities that support creating those deliverables.
- ❏ D. Check with his manager to determine if the deliverables in question need to be included in the project, and then convene the change control board.

13. *Necessary and sufficient* conditions are used in law, logic, and a number of other disciplines. In what way can a project manager benefit from the use of the necessary and sufficient concept?

Quick Answer: **71**
Detailed Answer: **74**

   ❑ A. A project manager should check to make sure he has the necessary resources and sufficient time to complete the project.

   ❑ B. It is a concept that can be used to verify the correct level of decomposition for WBS and activity definition.

   ❑ C. Project managers only use this concept with projects that involve contracts with outside vendors.

   ❑ D. There is no such concept.

Quick Answer: **71**
Detailed Answer: **74**

14. Alyea is ready to begin activity definition for her project. She has the project scope statement, a WBS, the corporate policy of defining activities to a 20-hour period, information from a meeting with her SMEs, and a team room identified, although it is not yet available. What more does she need before she starts?

   ❑ A. To identify her assumptions

   ❑ B. To identify her constraints

   ❑ C. To obtain input from experts on the project

   ❑ D. Historical information on projects similar to her own

Quick Answer: **71**
Detailed Answer: **74**

15. RF Sportswear is undertaking the construction of a new manufacturing plant. You are working with John, the project manager who is working on the project plan. He has asked for the physical plant layout plans, which you don't have yet because the project has just started. You participated in helping to develop the WBS and the activities list with John. As a former project manager, you realize what John needs, and you send him a copy of the mock-up drawing done for the steering committee and approval of the project. Why does John need the plans at this point?

   ❑ A. John is working on activity sequencing and the plans are needed for helping to determine dependencies.

   ❑ B. John needs to archive all the documents for the project in one project folder for future use.

   ❑ C. You know John is not an engineer and that he was not at the steering committee meeting.

   ❑ D. John does not need the plans, but from a management standpoint, you want to respect his authority as the project manager.

16. Your company has a policy of having every software project reviewed and approved by the Architecture Review Board prior to the construction phase of a project. You are currently in the process of activity sequencing. This is an example of what?

    ❑ A. Gatekeeping
    ❑ B. Milestone
    ❑ C. New scope for the project
    ❑ D. Project integration

Quick Answer: **71**
Detailed Answer: **75**

17. Elwood is developing his project plan for a construction project, and is currently involved in determining the dependencies between activities on his project. He is also working with a just-in-time (JIT) inventory from his suppliers. In creating his project plan, he knows that his prefabricated trusses need to arrive and be installed before he can begin to lay down the roofing. However, because he has purchased the roofing materials from the same supplier as the trusses, the roofing material will arrive at the same time as the trusses.

    In the preceding example, what is not true about the relationship between the truss installation and roof installation?

    ❑ A. It is hard logic.
    ❑ B. It is a start-to-finish relationship.
    ❑ C. It is an example of an external dependency.
    ❑ D. It is a finish-to-finish relationship.

Quick Answer: **71**
Detailed Answer: **75**

18. In the hair care industry, it is considered a "best practice" to sweep the hair from a previous client's haircut prior to seating the new client. You are a project manager, and have gone in for a haircut with your hairdresser, Jan. She has had a bad day, and has seated you before cleaning her area. This is an example of what?

    ❑ A. Bad customer service
    ❑ B. A discretionary dependency
    ❑ C. Hard logic
    ❑ D. Precedence diagramming method (PDM)

Quick Answer: **71**
Detailed Answer: **75**

19. Joe wants to choose a tool for activity sequencing. He can use all of the following except

    ❑ A. Scoring models
    ❑ B. Activity on node (AON)
    ❑ C. Arrow diagramming method (ADM)
    ❑ D. Graphical evaluation and review technique (GERT)

Quick Answer: **71**
Detailed Answer: **75**

20. Richard has a project that uses the rational unified process, and iterative tasks that loop. What would be the best sequencing method for him to use?

    Quick Answer: **71**
    Detailed Answer: **75**

    ❑ A. PDM
    ❑ B. ADM
    ❑ C. Critical path
    ❑ D. GERT

21. The White Paper Company is embarking on developing a new warehouse. Gregg, the project manager, knows the warehouse will require new systems, equipment, and construction. He has his work breakdown structure completed, and knows he will need staff in addition to equipment purchases. He has the company's purchasing policy and its temporary staffing policy at his desk for review, but doesn't really know what staff might be available for work on his project. He is about to call the Human Resources Department to ask for help. What should he ask for?

    Quick Answer: **71**
    Detailed Answer: **75**

    ❑ A. Company human resource policies
    ❑ B. A resource pool description
    ❑ C. New hire information
    ❑ D. Approved vendor information

22. After gathering the needed information from human resources, Gregg is reviewing the WBS for his new warehouse project, and is trying to separate staff needs from material needs. He needs four programmers, two construction workers who are experts in metal framing, one drywall hanger, and an electrician. He will also need the actual building materials, but he is not as familiar with construction as he is with systems development. He has looked at a couple of other similar projects, and has an idea of the manpower. What should he do to determine the material requirements?

    Quick Answer: **71**
    Detailed Answer: **76**

    ❑ A. Consult other project managers who have experience in construction.
    ❑ B. Hire a consultant for that part of the project.
    ❑ C. Check with the construction management unit of the White Paper Company.
    ❑ D. All of the above.

23. On a systems development project, John needs two program-
    mers. He knows Jeff and Rob were able to create a program in
    40 days similar to the one he wants to create on his project.
    He decides to use 40 days as his estimate. This is an example
    of what type of estimating?

    ❏ A. Parametric modeling
    ❏ B. Analogous
    ❏ C. Rule of thumb
    ❏ D. Fixed rate

Quick Answer: **71**
Detailed Answer: **76**

24. Rich is an expert Java programmer. Eric is just out of school
    and is 50% as effective as Rich. Rich thinks a certain program
    can be completed in three weeks. Where can Ray, the project
    manager, find this information so that he can put both Rich
    and Eric on the project and have it done in two weeks?

    ❏ A. The resource pool description
    ❏ B. Historical information
    ❏ C. His activity duration estimates
    ❏ D. The scope statement, which states the project must be done
           in two weeks

Quick Answer: **71**
Detailed Answer: **76**

25. Nick has a 400-square-foot room to floor. He knows it takes
    an average of 5 man minutes per square foot based on past
    jobs to lay down the flooring, including the prep work, gluing,
    and cleanup. He figures this job will take approximately 34
    man hours. At $12 per hour, this will cost him $400 to have
    the work done. This is what type of estimating?

    ❏ A. Bottom up
    ❏ B. Quantitatively based durations
    ❏ C. Analogous
    ❏ D. Cost based

Quick Answer: **71**
Detailed Answer: **76**

26. Raymond wants to give himself a few extra hours in his
    budgeted time for a construction project to account for prob-
    lems with weather or delays in delivery. This is called

    ❏ A. Padding
    ❏ B. Risk acceptance
    ❏ C. Reserve time or contingency
    ❏ D. Mitigation

Quick Answer: **71**
Detailed Answer: **76**

27. Ryan wants to keep all his documentation in order, and is currently doing duration estimating for his project. In addition to his duration estimates, what else does Ryan need to do to complete his activity duration process?

   ❑ A. Document assumptions made in estimating and update the activity list.
   ❑ B. Provide cost estimates.
   ❑ C. Provide resource requirement updates.
   ❑ D. A cost baseline.

28. Al is a project manager and is making activity duration estimates for his project based on his experience six years ago doing some similar tasks. He doesn't want to bother his project staff, who will be actually doing the work. Why is Al headed for a scheduling problem?

   ❑ A. He is not headed for a problem. Al has the expert knowledge and can therefore do the estimates.
   ❑ B. Al should be asking the staff to make or approve the estimates for the best outcome.
   ❑ C. Al is heading for project team problems by not involving his staff in the planning process.
   ❑ D. Al is not considering elapsed time.

29. Sally knows one of her key construction workers, Gordon, has a high probability of participating in a new reality building show. This would take him out of work for eight weeks, which is one fourth of the construction time. He is a long-term employee and well liked by all, and management supports his efforts regarding the show. Gordon has a 75% chance of making the show. Sally is working on her project plan and, specifically, task durations. How should she address the resource issue?

   ❑ A. Engage the project team to identify the effect of Gordon's absence on the baseline durations, and incorporate that into the duration estimates.
   ❑ B. Estimate the project as-is. There is always another worker to fill in for Gordon.
   ❑ C. Buy "key-man" insurance to mitigate the cost of Gordon being gone.
   ❑ D. Increase all activity durations assigned to Gordon by 75% because that is the expected probability of Gordon being on the reality show.

Quick Check

30. You are a seasoned project manager who has taken a new job in the engineering field, about which you know very little. You are attempting to create activity durations for your project. What resources can you use to help?

Quick Answer: **71**
Detailed Answer: **77**

 ❏ A. Prior project files from similar projects
 ❏ B. Commercial databases with information on projects like yours
 ❏ C. Consult your project team
 ❏ D. All of the above

31. Activity durations should always have which of the following?

Quick Answer: **71**
Detailed Answer: **77**

 ❏ A. Each work package identified
 ❏ B. A range of possible quantitative results
 ❏ C. Approval by management
 ❏ D. An order of magnitude associated with the duration

32. Steve is asked to provide a cost estimate for a redecorating project. How should he proceed?

Quick Answer: **71**
Detailed Answer: **77**

 ❏ A. Take the cost of raw materials and labor for each activity in the WBS. Check previous project files and consider any risks to delivery; then add 10% to account for the company profit.
 ❏ B. Add raw materials and labor costs for each activity in the WBS.
 ❏ C. Check competitor pricing, add the raw materials and labor from the WBS, and then decrease by 10% to be competitive.
 ❏ D. Use the cost of raw materials from a similar project on a house with the same floor plan.

33. I am looking to estimate the cost on a project, but I don't want to spend a lot of time on a detailed analysis. I really want a ballpark figure. What options do I have?

Quick Answer: **71**
Detailed Answer: **77**

 ❏ A. None—cost estimating requires details to be accurate.
 ❏ B. Use the cost of similar projects.
 ❏ C. Use a rule-of-thumb or per-square-foot estimate.
 ❏ D. Add up the costs on the WBS.

34. The Back-Step Furniture and Kitchen Company has been asked to provide a cost estimate for a kitchen bid. To do the project, the firm will have to borrow money to finance the cost of raw materials. What item will be most important for the cost estimator to have?

Quick Answer: **71**
Detailed Answer: **78**

 ❏ A. A low cost of materials
 ❏ B. Good credit
 ❏ C. Cheap labor
 ❏ D. Accurate activity duration estimates

. . . .

35. Edward, a former U.S. Army lieutenant, is estimating a project the way he used to in the Army. He is taking each activity, assigning its cost, and then aggregating it to a final cost estimate. This is an example of what type of cost estimating?

❏ A. Top down

❏ B. Bottom up

❏ C. Army method

❏ D. Parametric

Quick Answer: **71**
Detailed Answer: **78**

36. The sponsor of one of your projects wants to know how cost variances will be managed. He is very concerned because other projects have had serious cost overruns. What can you provide him that will give him a highly detailed and formal method for dealing with cost variances?

❏ A. A paragraph in the project plan that describes general approaches to cost management

❏ B. A weekly one-on-one with the sponsor to discuss costs

❏ C. Weekly vendor meetings

❏ D. A formal cost management plan

Quick Answer: **71**
Detailed Answer: **78**

37. Activity list updates happen during which project planning processes?

❏ A. All planning processes can result in activity list updates

❏ B. Activity sequencing and activity duration estimating

❏ C. Activity definition

❏ D. Risk planning

Quick Answer: **71**
Detailed Answer: **78**

38. One of the key outputs of the scope planning process is what?

❏ A. Project charter

❏ B. Scope statement

❏ C. Scope definition

❏ D. WBS

Quick Answer: **71**
Detailed Answer: **78**

39. As a project manager, you know the WBS is important. What are the key planning processes in which the WBS is an input?

❏ A. Cost estimating, resource planning, cost budgeting, and risk management planning

❏ B. Scope definition

❏ C. Activity duration estimating and activity sequencing

❏ D. All planning processes

Quick Answer: **71**
Detailed Answer: **78**

40. You are a project manager involved in developing a project plan for the downtown redevelopment of Kokomo, Indiana. You are now beginning to do some risk planning. What are the tools and techniques you use to develop your risk management plan?

    ❏ A. Gather high-quality data on project risks.
    ❏ B. Apply a general contingency.
    ❏ C. Use a risk template.
    ❏ D. Conduct a planning meeting.

Quick Answer: **71**
Detailed Answer: **78**

41. John provides a list of key risks and how to mitigate those risks to his manager as his risk management plan. Why is his manager, Jeff, a PMP, asking him to redo his plan?

    ❏ A. A list of project risks is an output of risk identification.
    ❏ B. The risk management plan should address approaches, tools, and data sources as well as roles and responsibilities, budgeting, timing, interpretation rules, risk thresholds, reporting formats, and tracking.
    ❏ C. The risk list should also include triggers.
    ❏ D. John has not involved the project team.

Quick Answer: **71**
Detailed Answer: **79**

42. Beth is setting up a planning meeting for developing a risk management plan for her project. Who should she invite?

    ❏ A. Just the project sponsor because his perception of how the risks will be handled is the most important
    ❏ B. The corporate risk manager
    ❏ C. The project team leaders, key stakeholders, and anyone engaged in risk management activities for the corporation, if applicable
    ❏ D. The entire project team, all stakeholders, and all of the corporate risk management department, if one exists

Quick Answer: **71**
Detailed Answer: **79**

43. Joey is new to risk management within his projects. He has typically handled risks as they come up, and adjusted time frames accordingly after discussing them with his sponsor. He is now being asked to develop a risk management plan and is complaining about having to develop a scoring and interpretation method. What advice would you give him as a seasoned PMP who is knowledgeable in risk management?

Quick Answer: **71**
Detailed Answer: **79**

- ❏ A. Developing interpretation and scoring criteria helps to ensure consistency in handling risks as they arise. It also helps to weight multiple risks at one time.
- ❏ B. A scoring mechanism is rarely used in real life. Just put a paragraph or two into the management plan with High, Medium, and Low.
- ❏ C. Scoring feeds into the risk thresholds, which determine who needs to be involved in mitigating a risk.
- ❏ D. A risk management plan is a communication tool so that all members of the project team know how risks will be handled as they are identified.

44. Why are risk tolerances and thresholds important to identify in the risk management plan?

Quick Answer: **71**
Detailed Answer: **79**

- ❏ A. Tolerances and thresholds, when documented, can help to define the target by which the project team can measure the effectiveness of the risk response plan execution.
- ❏ B. Tolerances and thresholds help to define how often the risk management process will be performed.
- ❏ C. Tolerances and thresholds determine what tools and data sources will be used in risk management.
- ❏ D. Tolerances and thresholds provide the basis for costing the risk management process as well as defining how risk activities will be recorded.

45. A risk management plan should be tailored to a given project in what ways?

Quick Answer: **71**
Detailed Answer: **79**

- ❏ A. Some companies use predefined templates for risk management plans.
- ❏ B. Certain companies have predefined roles and responsibilities as they relate to risk management.
- ❏ C. Some organizations have predefined risk management policies that must be tailored to an individual project.
- ❏ D. The risk management plan should ensure that the level and type of risk management efforts are appropriate to the level of risk and importance of the project to the company.

Quick Check

Quick Answer: **71**
Detailed Answer: **79**

Quick Answer: **71**
Detailed Answer: **79**

Quick Answer: **71**
Detailed Answer: **79**

46. Timing, as described in a risk management plan, affects how often a risk management process should be performed during the life cycle of a project. What key factor affects timing?

- ❏ A. Timing should be defined to allow for results to be developed early enough to affect decisions.
- ❏ B. Timing is scaled to project size.
- ❏ C. Timing is affected by organizational policies regarding risk management.
- ❏ D. Timing is directly related to the sponsor's risk aversion threshold.

47. You have recently been assigned to provide an accurate project schedule for a troubled data conversion project. You have reviewed the project schedule created by the previous project manager, and notice that certain task dependencies do not seem to be correctly identified. Prior to reworking the schedule, what will you need to do first?

- ❏ A. Create a network diagram to ensure task dependencies are correct.
- ❏ B. Review the resource pool description.
- ❏ C. Review the scope statement.
- ❏ D. Review the project charter.

48. The Big Bank has hired you on as a new project manager for the development and rollout of new ATM software. You are now ready to develop your project schedule. Your project has the potential to be very active during the summer months, and you know that some of your key team members are planning exciting vacations during that time. What do you need to help plan the schedule accordingly?

- ❏ A. Company holiday schedule, regular work hours for each individual, and vacation times for each project team member
- ❏ B. Where the work activity will be taking place
- ❏ C. Develop leads and lags in the tasks assigned to individuals on vacation
- ❏ D. Resource pool description

49. As a seasoned project manager, you know your sponsors and executive management are keenly interested in the project delivery date. Why are you nervous when your project sponsor wants the delivery date as soon as you've developed the schedule?

    ❑ A. Schedule development is often iterated, as are the inputs to schedule development, to provide more detailed and accurate information. Therefore, the end date is likely to change until the process has been iterated sufficiently.

    ❑ B. Your project sponsor provided you with a "drop dead" date, and your schedule does not have that date.

    ❑ C. You have not yet incorporated contingency into the schedule.

    ❑ D. The schedule has not been leveled.

Quick Answer: **71**
Detailed Answer: **80**

50. Project schedule development is the discipline of determining what?

    ❑ A. The start and finish dates for each project activity

    ❑ B. Providing a critical path by which to manage the project

    ❑ C. Providing early and late start and finish dates for the project

    ❑ D. Determining which resources should perform which tasks

Quick Answer: **71**
Detailed Answer: **80**

51. In developing a project schedule, you as a project manager need to be aware of major constraints. What are the two major time constraints that must be considered during project schedule development?

    ❑ A. Project staff vacations and corporate holiday calendars

    ❑ B. Resource capabilities and availability

    ❑ C. Imposed dates and major milestones

    ❑ D. Responsibility and geography for activities

Quick Answer: **71**
Detailed Answer: **80**

52. Why are CPM, GERT, and PERT not considered sufficient to create a project schedule?

    ❑ A. All three are tools and techniques of schedule development, not the actual schedule.

    ❑ B. As mathematical analysis tools, they simply provide the dates that are possible, and do not consider resource pool limitations.

    ❑ C. They are sufficient. Each calculates early and late start and finish dates for each activity.

    ❑ D. They are Monte Carlo techniques used to provide what-if analysis for adverse external factors on a project.

Quick Answer: **71**
Detailed Answer: **80**

53. Roger is a project manager working on a schedule for the road installation for a new housing development. He knows there will be issues related to weather, as well as a big convention in town that is directly on the delivery path for his project. He is developing his schedule and realizes his first pass shows a date that is one month later than the date expected by his managers. He is fairly sure his critical path is correct, and that his key estimates are accurate. He also knows the budget amount he is estimating is close to what his managers wanted to spend. What options does Roger have?

  ❑ A. Meet with his managers and explain his assumptions and the project schedule. Get them to buy in to the new date.

  ❑ B. Determine where he can add additional resources, thereby increasing the cost of the project, but providing the date the managers want.

  ❑ C. See where certain dependencies might be moved to take place in parallel, increasing the risk and possibly rework in the project, but meeting the date.

  ❑ D. All of the above.

54. Which project scheduling technique focuses on float to determine tasks with the least scheduling flexibility?

  ❑ A. CPM

  ❑ B. PERT

  ❑ C. Crashing

  ❑ D. Monte Carlo

55. Jennifer wants to measure and monitor the cost performance in her project. She has prepared a cost estimate, a WBS, a project schedule, and a risk management plan. What should she do at this point to ensure she is able to monitor costs effectively?

  ❑ A. Develop a schedule baseline.

  ❑ B. Develop a cost baseline.

  ❑ C. Carefully manage her expenditures according to her cost estimates.

  ❑ D. Influence the factors that cause her costs to change.

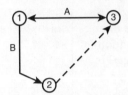

56. The preceding diagram is an example of what type of activity sequencing technique?

Quick Answer: **71**
Detailed Answer: **81**

   ❑ A. ADM
   ❑ B. PDM
   ❑ C. CPM
   ❑ D. AARP

57. You are a project manager and have created a project plan with activities, duration, resources allocated, and costs associated. Your manager is now asking you for your project plan. You are confused, because you've already sent him the plan. What is your manager really looking for?

Quick Answer: **71**
Detailed Answer: **81**

   ❑ A. A document that guides project execution and includes assumptions, planning decisions, and alternatives chosen as well as the timing of key management reviews
   ❑ B. The project charter
   ❑ C. A list of stakeholder skills and knowledge for guiding the project
   ❑ D. Organizational policies that affect project execution

58. In developing your project schedule for your home remodel, you realize room painting will take three hours and is followed immediately by the trim replacement, which has a predecessor task of restaining the trim. Although this is the correct sequence, you know the paint takes four hours to dry. To correctly sequence these activities, you need to do which of the following?

Quick Answer: **71**
Detailed Answer: **81**

   ❑ A. Add a lag time of four hours to the painting activity.
   ❑ B. Add a lead time of four hours to the trim-replacement activity.
   ❑ C. Remove the dependency between the two tasks, and manually supervise them.
   ❑ D. Change the project to have the painting done after the trim is replaced.

59. You are developing a project schedule, and your manager has asked you for the coding structure. How does the coding structure benefit your project schedule?

  ❑ A. The coding structure enables you to sort activities and pro-vide clear reporting to the individuals on the project.

  ❑ B. The coding structure is aligned with the chart of accounts to appropriately allocate the costs to the corporate accounting system.

  ❑ C. The coding structure is related only to system development projects.

  ❑ D. A and B.

60. John is studying for his PMP exam and is ready to take the test. Because he is confident about his test preparation, he asks his friend, Portia, to quiz him on several topics. Portia asks, "What part of the planning process is staff acquisition?" John's response should be

  ❑ A. Staff acquisition is not the responsibility of the project manager.

  ❑ B. Staff acquisition is a human resources knowledge area.

  ❑ C. Staff acquisition is a core planning process.

  ❑ D. Staff acquisition is a facilitating planning process.

61. A WBS is a deliverables-oriented grouping of project elements that organizes and defines the total scope of the project. How is the WBS developed?

  ❑ A. As a pictorial representation of the project team's organization

  ❑ B. As a scope artifact that is archived after completion

  ❑ C. By outside parties

  ❑ D. By defining project work in terms of deliverables and compo-nents

62. Experienced project managers understand the importance of detailed planning and how a WBS can be a good tool to provide direction and support to the project. How does a WBS help a project stakeholder?

❑ A. Stakeholders do not use a WBS—only the project team references the WBS.

❑ B. Stakeholders use a WBS to enforce contractual agreements.

❑ C. The elements assist stakeholders in developing a clear vision of the product and the overall steps to produce it.

❑ D. The WBS functions as the organizational breakdown structure (OBS) for stakeholders.

63. Getting the definition of success for the project combined with feedback and buy-in from the team members of the WBS can assist you in determining what tasks need to be done throughout the project. The WBS supports effective Project Management in all but which of the following ways?

❑ A. Separating deliverables into component parts to ensure project plan matches scope

❑ B. Assisting in determining resource needs

❑ C. Supporting resource assignments and planning

❑ D. Providing the basis for the communications plan

64. Identification of inputs and outputs to the various phases and the WBS can assist with identifying deliverables and other project-related work products. A WBS is an input to all but which of the following processes?

❑ A. Resource planning

❑ B. Risk management planning

❑ C. Activity definition

❑ D. Organizational planning

65. Decomposing tasks into smaller activities can be helpful in reducing the amount of stress associated with overwhelmingly large milestones. What is a feature of the hierarchical nature of the WBS?

❑ A. A WBS hierarchy prevents duplication.

❑ B. A WBS can be rolled up or collapsed to provide information at the appropriate level for a particular audience.

❑ C. The decomposition of tasks provides a detailed planning tool.

❑ D. The depth of a WBS is restricted to three levels, which avoids overplanning.

66. Integrated analysis of cost, schedule, and performance can only be accomplished when

Quick Answer: **71**
Detailed Answer: **82**

   ❑ A. Proper linking between the WBS and associated cost and schedule is made
   ❑ B. A performance budget baseline is created
   ❑ C. Goal achievement is measured
   ❑ D. Integration and assembly elements are included

67. Every project has its share of problems and challenges. All of the following are challenges in creating a WBS except

Quick Answer: **71**
Detailed Answer: **82**

   ❑ A. Defining excessive levels in a WBS
   ❑ B. Ensuring WBS elements are deliverable focused
   ❑ C. Identifying all key project deliverables
   ❑ D. Cost of effort to create a WBS

68. At his Indonesia-based software manufacturing company, Daniel realizes that risk management has become more important as the company continues to evolve. He needs to begin the process of incorporating risk management into all of his new projects. What is the first step in using a WBS as an effective tool for risk management?

Quick Answer: **71**
Detailed Answer: **82**

   ❑ A. Determine the probability of occurrence of risks.
   ❑ B. Review WBS elements and segment into risk events.
   ❑ C. Further define high-risk areas in the WBS.
   ❑ D. Include contingency activities in the WBS.

69. Scheduling the right resources at the right place at the right time is a project manager's responsibility and is a critical success factor for the project's successful completion. What is a key element to consider in developing a WBS when factoring in resource planning?

Quick Answer: **71**
Detailed Answer: **82**

   ❑ A. Can the quality of work be evaluated by testing?
   ❑ B. Are WBS elements compatible with accounting and payroll structures?
   ❑ C. How will element completion be determined?
   ❑ D. Can individual work assignments be managed from the reporting structure indicated by the WBS?

Quick Answer: **71**
Detailed Answer: **82**

Quick Check

70. Because he is the president of a minority-owned business, Albert has first rights to many government contracts for the new city infrastructure projects. Albert also realizes that dealing with political bureaucracy can be one of the constraints of working on government-related projects. Which of the following is a key assumption of a government design-bid-build project?

❑ A. The WBS must be more detailed.

❑ B. Alternatives must be included in the WBS.

❑ C. Of qualified bidders, the lowest bidder performs the construction.

❑ D. Real property must always be included in the WBS.

Quick Check Answer Key

1. A	28. B	55. B
2. C	29. A	56. A
3. B	30. D	57. A
4. B	31. B	58. A
5. B	32. B	59. A
6. C	33. B	60. D
7. A	34. D	61. D
8. D	35. B	62. C
9. B	36. D	63. D
10. B	37. B	64. D
11. A	38. B	65. B
12. C	39. A	66. A
13. B	40. D	67. D
14. D	41. B	68. B
15. A	42. C	69. D
16. B	43. A	70. C
17. D	44. A	
18. B	45. D	
19. A	46. A	
20. D	47. C	
21. B	48. A	
22. D	49. A	
23. B	50. A	
24. A	51. C	
25. B	52. B	
26. C	53. D	
27. A	54. A	

Answers and Explanations

1. **Answer A** is the best answer. A kickoff meeting is indeed one of the first things a project manager should schedule and is in fact the initial task in scope planning. Answer B is tempting, because the amount of money for use on the project could indeed be a constraint; ideally, however, a project manager will determine the scope, activities, and resources needed, and then develop the budget needed. Answer C is also tempting in terms of showing authority to do a project; however, John's CIO just authorized him to do the project, and a business card does not necessarily give him the authority. Answer D is incorrect because scope definition is after scope planning, and requires as input the scope statement, which is defined in scope planning.

2. **Answer C** is correct because a scope statement addresses the description of the business need, high-level objectives and deliverables, and a brief description of the project. This will help to get everyone on the same page. Answer A does not address everything that a scope statement addresses, so it is not the best answer. Answer B is incorrect because the project charter does not include resource assignments and time frames. Answer D is tempting because holding a kickoff meeting does indeed serve that purpose, but the scope statement is what will help to get the project focused correctly.

3. **Answer B** is the best answer because it is a technique associated with cost estimating. Answers A, C, and D are incorrect; because Paul is ready to begin progressive elaboration of scope and tasks, he is ready for scope planning and scope definition, and these are tools and techniques used for those tasks.

4. **Answer B** is correct. Answer A is tempting because the problem focuses on changes. However, because we are talking about the elaboration of the product's characteristics, we are talking about scope changes, and therefore Answer B is the best answer. Answer C is also tempting because it is difficult to move forward on a project until the scope is clearly defined (especially in systems development projects), but with products and certain types of web development, scope changes can be frequent, and a formal scope management plan is needed. Answer D is true from a project perspective, but does not address the scope issues.

5. **Answer B** is correct. This is an example of a PMI question that tells you what the work product or output is, but expects you to know how to use business knowledge to apply to the question. Arguments can be made for many assumptions, but in this case, the best answer is Answer B. The biggest assumption, and an incorrect one (which might have been avoided had it been stated), was that federal safety standards were sufficient to make a toy safe. The constraint is the time frame in which the toy must be ready, and part of the product description should include that the toy is a red-haired doll. Answer A is incorrect because the statement "the product must be ready for the market in February" is a constraint and not an assumption. Answer C is incorrect because the statement "the product is a toy" does not provide enough information to be considered a product description. Answer D is incorrect because the statement "the toy must appeal to toy retailers" is not a product description.

6. **Answer C** is correct. Bob has a pretty clear scope and defined deliverables. In order to be able to estimate project cost and time, the next step would be to create a work breakdown structure of the deliverables decomposed into component tasks. Answer A is incorrect because even though Bob doesn't have a lot of information at this point, as a project manager, it is his job to progressively elaborate the project. Answer B is incorrect because Bob's summary of tasks and expectations is essentially his scope statement. Answer D is incorrect because Bob cannot rely solely on his personal experience to deliver an accurate cost and time estimate.

7. **Answer A** is the best answer. Because the scope statement and WBS define the work to be done and the WBS is intended to also ensure no unnecessary work is done, Doug can look at these with the project manager to understand any differences he perceives. Answer B is incorrect because meeting minutes, although helpful historical documents, do not define the "contracted" scope. Answer C is also a helpful document, but will not tell Doug the details of what he needs to know. Answer D is tempting, but not the best answer. Reviewing the actual WBS provides a documented and clear definition vision of the end product of the project. A conversation does not.

8. **Answer D** is correct. This is tricky, because the WBS helps to facilitate communication, but is not the foundation of communication. Answers A, B, and C are all supported directly by the WBS.

9. **Answer B** is correct. A WBS should be structured with a deliverable focus. PMI feels project failure can result from nondeliverable focused WBS elements. Answers A, C, and D are incorrect because they are items that can help in the development of a WBS.

10. **Answer B** is the best answer. Although it might be true that Ralph does not have the insight into her project, Sally's first step should be to review the WBS and be sure it is at a sufficient level of detail to provide the accuracy of estimates. Answer A is incorrect because reinterviewing SMEs does not address the root of the problem. Sally can do so after she has examined the WBS. Answer C is incorrect because a good project manager will always want to produce the best quality project, and the quality control function—if it is auditing a project—probably has some knowledge of the corporate projects and general expectations. Answer D is incorrect, although it does happen often in real life.

11. **Answer A** is correct. Answer B is incorrect because, although the WBS is part of scope definition, both scope definition and activity definition are part of project planning. Answer C might be the attitude that is encountered sometimes in the real world, and Answer D describes project control processes, not activity definition.

12. **Answer C** is correct. Often in the planning process, and particularly during progressive elaboration and decomposition, missing deliverables can be identified. This does not mean they are out of scope. The WBS needs to be updated and the activities to support creating that deliverable need to be planned. Answer A is incorrect because it fails to update the WBS. Answers B and D are incorrect because failing to identify a deliverable in the scope definition process does not mean a scope change has occurred.

13. **Answer B** is correct. Using the necessary and sufficient test is a technique of decomposition. Are the lowest levels identified both necessary and sufficient to accomplish the deliverable? If not, there might be activities that need to be removed or added. Answer A is tempting because it is true, but it is not an example of the necessary and sufficient concept. Answer C can be true in that contracts often use the necessary and sufficient test as criteria for completeness, but it is not the best answer. Answer D is incorrect because *necessary and sufficient* conditions is used in law, logic, and a number of other disciplines.

14. **Answer D** is correct. Alyea has five of the six inputs to activity definition. Her constraints are the corporate 20-hour work package policy; her expert judgment comes from her SMEs, or subject matter experts; and she is assuming her team room will be ready in time for the project to start. Answers A, B, and C are incorrect because identifying assumptions, identifying constraints, and obtaining input from experts on the project are not inputs to the activity definition process.

15. **Answer A** is correct. The plans are part of the product description, which needs to be reviewed as input into the activity sequencing process. Answers B and C may be true, but they are not the best answer. Answer D is false, and therefore incorrect.

16. **Answer B** is correct. The approval by the Architecture Review Board is a milestone you want to include in activity sequencing so that you can ensure the requirements for meeting the review board's approval are met. Answer A is tempting because the question references phase-end activities; however, it is not an example of gatekeeping because the project is not being authorized to continue based only on the architecture review. Gatekeeping often involves the review of other factors as well. Answer C is incorrect because the requirement of a review board approval does not affect scope. Answer D is incorrect because project integration planning involves project plan development, execution, and integrated change control, which are not related to a review board.

17. **Answer D** is correct. The trusses must be completed before the roofing can start; therefore, the roofing has a dependency on the installation of the trusses and is a start-to-finish relationship. Answer A is incorrect because it is hard logic. Answer B is incorrect because it is not a start-to-start relationship. Answer C is incorrect because this problem is an example of an external dependency because the project depends on the supplier for the trusses and the roofing. Because they are correct statements, they are incorrect answers for this question.

18. **Answer B** is the best answer because it is related to Project Management. Although Answer A may be true, it is not the best answer. Answer C is another term for a mandatory dependency. Answer D is the acronym for precedence diagramming method, which is a technique used in activity sequencing in which activities are represented in boxes (also known as *nodes*) and are linked by precedence relationships to show the coordination of the activities that are to be performed.

19. **Answer A** is correct. Scoring models are not used with activity sequencing. Answers B, C, and D are activity sequencing tools and therefore incorrect answers to this question. Activity on node (AON) is also known as the precedence diagramming method in which activities are represented by the node. The arrow diagramming method or activity on arrow (AOA) shows the activities on the arrow. GERT is a conditional diagramming method.

20. **Answer D** is correct. Answers A, B, and C are incorrect because none of those methods allow for nonsequential activities.

21. **Answer B** is the best answer. Although company human resource policies might be useful, he already has the policies on his desk for review. New hire information provides no value added for his resourcing decisions and approved vendors are in the policies on his desk, therefore Answers A, C, and D are incorrect.

22. **Answer D** is the best answer. Gregg should get some expert advice or expert judgment in finalizing the materials requirements. Answers A, B, and C are correct statements and represent opportunities to find expert judgment and are therefore incorrect answers to this question.

23. **Answer B** is the best answer. John is using an estimate based on a project very similar to his own with staff he will be using. Answer A is incorrect because parametric modeling involves using a mathematical model to predict costs, such as dollars per line of code. Answer C is incorrect, although close; if the development project is a common item, such as putting down new flooring, a rule-of-thumb measurement can be used, although it is less accurate. Answer D is incorrect because it is not a form of estimating, but a type of pricing.

24. **Answer A** is correct. The characteristics of the resource pool, of which Rich is an expert and Eric is new, are available in the resource pool description. Answers B and C are incorrect but helpful in the resource planning tasks because they both give information on how to plan for resources. Answer D is incorrect because a scope statement, although part of inputs to resource planning, will not help Ray decide which resources to put on the project. Further, a scope statement should not indicate time frames.

25. **Answer B** is correct. Nick is using quantity of time for each work category (that is, minutes per foot). Answer A is incorrect because bottom-up estimating takes each work package and estimates it, and then rolls up to a total. Answer C is incorrect because Nick is using quantifiable data rather than a project just like the one he is doing. Answer D is incorrect because there is no such thing.

26. **Answer C** is correct. Providing additional hours as a contingency is a risk mitigation strategy; therefore, Answer C is the best answer because we are talking about time. Answer A is incorrect because padding has no basis and is not quantified as a risk or other type of estimate. Padding is highly discouraged by PMI. Answer B is incorrect because adding contingency is not acceptance of a risk, it is simply mitigation. Answer D is not the best answer, although what Raymond is doing is a form of mitigation.

27. **Answer A** is correct. In addition to duration estimates, Ryan needs to provide and document the assumptions made in doing the estimates as well as any updates to the activity list that were uncovered. Answer B is incorrect because cost estimates are an output of cost estimating. Answer C is incorrect because updates to resource requirements are an output of schedule development. Answer D is incorrect because a cost baseline is the output of cost estimating.

28. **Answer B** is correct. Al's experience is dated. He should be engaging the people doing the work to help with the estimating; therefore, Answer A is incorrect. Answer C is incorrect because it is not the best answer for this question, although it may be true. Answer D may be true, but we have not mentioned anything in the question that involves elapsed time versus actual work.

29. **Answer A** is correct. Engaging the project team and adjusting the estimates based on a possible change is the best answer. Answer B is tempting, and many companies choose to go this route, but if Gordon is a key team member, the loss and learning curves will need to be addressed. Answer C is incorrect because buying the insurance does not solve the schedule problem. Answer D is mathematically incorrect. The probability that Gordon would be gone does not translate into changing duration by the same amount.

30. **Answer D** is the best answer because Answers A, B, and C are all correct. PMI highly recommends historical data on similar projects. Commercial databases are also another source of information, as is your project team, which is assumed to have the knowledge of working on similar projects. Although Answers A, B, and C are individually correct, the combination of all three statements is the best answer.

31. **Answer B** is correct. A range of possible results +/- is the best answer. Answer A is good to have for appropriate estimating, but the estimate of a given work package does not require that all work packages be identified. Further, work packages that are identified in the activity duration process are added to the activities list as an output of activity duration estimating. Answer C is incorrect; in general, activity durations need to be done by or approved by the people actually doing the work. Answer D is tempting because order of magnitude is an estimating term; however, it is associated with cost estimates.

32. **Answer B** is correct. Answer A is tempting, but adds the profit margin, which has to do with pricing, not cost. Answer C is similar, but is dealing with competitive pricing. Answer D is tempting, but in a decorating project, the raw materials can be significantly different, even if it is the same size and type of house. Also, Answer D does not factor in labor.

33. **Answer B** is correct. Although it is less accurate than adding up individual costs from the WBS, it is less time consuming. The trade-off is accuracy. Answer A is incorrect (but tempting) because to do a more accurate cost estimate, you need to delve into the details. Answer C is tempting also, and possible, except we don't really know if the project in question can use parametric modeling. Answer D is incorrect because it takes the most time, but it is most accurate.

34. **Answer D** is correct. Accurate duration estimates are key because the Back-Step Furniture and Kitchen Company is borrowing money. The longer it borrows, the greater the cost of the job. The sooner it can collect for service rendered, the better. Answers A, B, and C are all true, but not the best answer for this question.

35. **Answer B** is correct. Estimating at the activity level and aggregating is an example of bottom-up estimating. Answer A is incorrect because top-down estimating is a more general technique. Answer C is incorrect because the Army issue in this problem is a red herring. Answer D is incorrect because parametric estimating involves quantitative measures that can be applied to any scale project.

36. **Answer D** is correct. Although a cost management plan can be informal, this is an appropriate scenario for a formal cost management plan, in which a sponsor is very concerned about costs. Answer A is incorrect because it does not adequately address the sponsor's concerns. Answers B and C may actually be part of your cost management plan, but they are not the best answers because both could be in the cost management plan.

37. **Answer B** is the best answer. Updates to the activity list are done during activity sequencing and activity duration estimating. Answer A is tempting but not correct because some of the planning processes do not focus on activity list updates. Answer C is incorrect because the output of activity definition is the creation of the activity list, not updating the activity list. Answer D is incorrect because risk planning focuses on how to approach and plan risk management activities.

38. **Answer B** is correct. The scope statement is the key output of the scope planning process. Supporting detail (assumptions) and a scope management plan are also outputs from the scope planning process, but not listed. Answer A is incorrect because that is the key output of the initiating process. Answer C is incorrect because scope definition is a planning process. Answer D is incorrect because the WBS is the key output of scope definition.

39. **Answer A** is the best answer. Answer B is incorrect because the WBS is the key output of the scope definition process. Answer C is also tempting because people often associate the WBS and activity lists. Activity duration estimating and activity sequencing rely on the activity lists that are generated from the WBS, but they are not the same thing. Although Answer D is tempting, the WBS is a key input only to the processes listed in Answer A.

40. **Answer D** is correct. A planning meeting is the technique by which you develop your risk management plan. Answer A shows a commitment to risk management, but is not a technique for planning. Answer B is used for unknown risks as a mitigation strategy. Answer C is one of the inputs to risk planning.

41. **Answer B** is correct. A risk management plan is the process by which risks will be handled during the project. Answer A is tempting, and true, but not the best answer. Answer C is also tempting because triggers are an output of risk identification. Answer D may or may not be true—we do not have sufficient information.

42. **Answer C** is the best answer. Using the key stakeholders and team leaders as well as a representative of risk management is sufficient for developing a project risk plan. Answers A and B are incorrect because they provides too narrow a viewpoint. Answer D is tempting, but an unnecessary use of time for the risk planning session. A broader group is appropriate for risk identification.

43. **Answer A** is the best answer. Although Answer B may be true, high, medium, and low is a method of scoring. Answers C and D are also true, but not the best answers.

44. **Answer A** is correct. Answer B defines the timing that should be addressed in the risk management plan. Answer C defines the methodology that should be identified in a risk management plan. Answer D touches on the budgeting and tracking that should be defined in the risk management plan.

45. **Answer D** is the best answer. The risk management plan should be appropriate to the level of risk, size of project, and importance to the company. A high risk project that is a strategic imperative for a company should have a more detailed risk management plan. Answers A, B, and C are tempting because they represent inputs to the risk management plan development.

46. **Answer A** is the best answer. Although Answers B, C, and D are true, the key factor is ensuring the risk management processes take place so that results are developed early enough to make decisions. Decisions should then be revisited periodically throughout the project.

47. **Answer C** is the best answer. The first place to start with a troubled project is to ensure the activities leading up to schedule development are accurate. Therefore, reviewing the scope statement is the first step. Answer A is tempting because dependencies are incorrect in the schedule. As a good turnaround project manager, you should also do Answers B and D and become familiar with the project.

48. **Answer A** is the best answer. Although you will need the activity attributes described in Answer B, and the resource pool from Answer D, your resource calendars are the best way to include vacation time into a schedule and develop it appropriately. Answer C is incorrect because leads and lags are used to identify real delays from order time to arrival, or curing time for cement.

49. **Answer A** is the best answer. Schedules often need to be iterated to provide accurate information. Answer B is all too often the real-world experience. However, good communication and negotiation with the project sponsor can help mitigate those types of issues. Answers C and D may be true, but we do not have enough information.

50. **Answer A** is correct. Answer B is tempting because a critical path does help to manage a project, but it is not the best answer. Answer C focuses on the project, not the activities, and therefore is incorrect. Answer D is part of scheduling, but not the primary focus.

51. **Answer C** is correct. Answer A is tempting because calendar activities relate to time and can be constraints. Answer B is incorrect because resource capabilities are not related to time. Answer D is incorrect because responsibility and geography are not related to time.

52. **Answer B** is correct. Answer A is tempting because it is true by definition, but Answer B is correct because it properly answers the question, in that these techniques do not take into account resource pool constraints. Answer C is incorrect because it provides possible early and late start and finish dates, but not the actual schedule. Answer D is incorrect because none of the three are simulation techniques.

53. **Answer D** is correct. Answer A represents good negotiating techniques for a project manager, in which given the scope, cost, and resources, a particular date is determined. Answer B represents the technique of crashing, in which additional costs are incurred to get the same work done more quickly. Answer C represents fast tracking, in which normally sequential tasks are done in parallel, increasing risk and rework.

54. **Answer A** is correct. Critical path method is a project-scheduling technique that focuses on float to determine tasks with the least scheduling flexibility. Answer B is incorrect because PERT focuses on weighted average duration estimates. Answer C is incorrect because crashing is a duration compression technique. Answer D is incorrect because Monte Carlo is a simulation technique that is used in duration estimations.

55. **Answer B** is correct. A cost baseline is used to measure and monitor project progress. Answer A is tempting because schedule baselines are often done at the same time. Answers C and D are incorrect because those activities are a part of cost control.

56. **Answer A** is correct. Answer B is incorrect because PDM (precedence dia-gramming method) puts the activities on the node. Answer C is incorrect because the critical path method generally involves durations as well as activi-ties on node. Answer D is incorrect because it is the acronym for American Association of Retired Persons.

57. **Answer A** is correct. Answer B is tempting, but a project charter initiates a project and does not provide the execution guidelines (although in real life the charter often includes these items). Answers C and D are incorrect because they are inputs to the project plan development.

58. **Answer A** is correct because the time for drying has a dependency with the painting. Answer B is incorrect because you might have some unusual conse-quences to adding lead time to the task that the drying is not associated with. Answer C is incorrect and will lead to a bad schedule. Answer D is possible, but not the best answer.

59. **Answer A** is correct. A schedule coding structure enables the users of the schedule to sort and use it better. Answer B is tempting, but the chart of accounts is related to the WBS, not the schedule. Answer C is incorrect because the coding structure is not only related to system development proj-ects. Answer D is incorrect because it ties incorrect Answer B with correct Answer A and is therefore also incorrect.

60. **Answer D** is correct. Answers A and B are true statements, but not the best answers. Answer C is incorrect because staff acquisition is not a core planning process.

61. **Answer D** is correct. Answer A is incorrect because it is a description for an organizational chart. Answer B is true in that a WBS is a scope definition arti-fact, but it is not archived. The WBS is a living document throughout a proj-ect. Answer C is incorrect because the project team likely develops the WBS.

62. **Answer C** is correct. The WBS helps to focus communication and accountabil-ity at a level of detail required to manage a project. Answer A is incorrect because stakeholders do use a WBS. Answer B is incorrect but tempting because a WBS does define scope. However, it is not used to enforce a contractual agreement. Only courts can do that. Answer D is incorrect because an OBS is an organizational breakdown structure, and is not related to project elements.

63. **Answer D** is correct. A WBS does not provide the basis for a communications plan; however, it does facilitate communication and provide a framework on which to base reporting. Answers A, B, and C are all pieces of project manage-ment that a WBS supports and are correct statements; therefore, they are incorrect answers to this question.

64. **Answer D** is correct. Answers A, B, and C are all correct statements because they use the WBS as an input to the process and are therefore incorrect answers to this question.

65. **Answer B** is correct. Answer A is incorrect because the WBS hierarchy does not prevent duplication by itself. Answer C is incorrect because a WBS is focused on deliverables and components or work packages and not on tasks. Answer D is incorrect because a WBS can be sized appropriately to the project size with as many levels as necessary.

66. **Answer A** is correct. Answer B is what is created when the proper linking takes place. Answer C is not recommended— measuring work accomplishment is preferred by PMI. Answer D is incorrect because integration tasks only need to be included in a WBS when several components are being brought together to create a higher-level deliverable.

67. **Answer D** is correct. The cost of the WBS effort creation is not a factor considered by PMI as a challenge to create a WBS and is assumed as part of a project. Answers A, B, and C are correct statements and are challenges to creating a well-defined WBS. Therefore, they are incorrect answers to this question.

68. **Answer B** is correct. Answers A, C, and D are incorrect because they are done after risk events are identified.

69. **Answer D** is correct because it is a general factor to consider in periodic reviews of the WBS. Answer A is incorrect because it is a consideration for risk and the WBS. Answer B is incorrect because it is a general consideration with regard to accounting and payroll structures are not considered in a WBS. Answer C is incorrect because determination of element completion is not a key element when developing a WBS.

70. **Answer C** is correct because this assumption will have a major impact upon how you approach the bidding on a government project. Limits on power and the use of eminent domain to obtain real property are the other two key assumptions in this example. Answer A may or may not be true, depending on the project. Answer B is incorrect because alternatives are not included in the WBS, regardless if it is a government project. Answer D is incorrect because real property is not included in the WBS.

Project Planning—Facilitating Processes

Exam Prep Questions

1. To prepare for the PMP exam, it is important to understand how all of the Project Management processes interact with each other during the entire project life cycle. During this preparation, George realizes the fundamental differences between *core processes* and *facilitating processes* is

   ❑ A. Core processes need to be done in the same order on most projects, whereas facilitating processes, although not optional, are performed intermittently and as needed.

   ❑ B. Core processes are mandatory and facilitating processes are optional.

   ❑ C. Core processes focus on developing the schedule, whereas facilitating processes focus on developing the project plan.

   ❑ D. Core processes are measured and facilitating processes are not.

   Quick Answer: **107**
   Detailed Answer: **108**

2. Rod is a friend of yours and is struggling with the definitions of quality. He believes quality is about testing. You are working with him on developing the quality management plan for a project on which you both are working. How would you describe the definition of quality planning?

   ❑ A. Quality planning is evaluating the overall project performance on a regular basis to provide confidence that the project will satisfy the relevant quality standards.

   ❑ B. Quality planning is the totality of characteristics of an entity that bear on its capability to satisfy stated or implied needs.

   ❑ C. Quality planning is the monitoring of specific project results to determine whether they comply with relevant quality standards and identifying ways to eliminate the causes of unsatisfactory performance.

   ❑ D. Quality planning is the identification of quality standards that are relevant to the project and determining how to satisfy them.

   Quick Answer: **107**
   Detailed Answer: **108**

3. At the Jumping Gymboree for children, Ellen, the owner, is planning a new location. Very much an advocate of quality, she has learned a lot from the opening of her first site and doesn't want to make the same mistakes again. She has had a lessons-learned session facilitated by a professional to ensure the organization documents the process. She is ready to start the project and wants to make sure everything at the new site and any other additional sites is of high quality. She believes she should begin her quality management plan, but does not have much information about the new site, size, or location, or really whether the project will move forward. What should she be doing instead?

Quick Answer: **107**
Detailed Answer: **108**

- ❑ A. Focus on project initiation for the new site.
- ❑ B. Establish a quality policy for Jumping Gymboree.
- ❑ C. Obtain the local building requirements and regulations.
- ❑ D. Formalize the lessons learned into a procedure for the development of new sites.

4. Jeff is a pharmacist who provides delivery orders to nursing homes. He is keenly interested in providing a high-quality service: Orders received by noon will be delivered by noon the next day. He always meets his target, and often exceeds it. However, his competitor, Ralph, is providing more services, such as 1-hour delivery, 24-hour delivery, and transportation to and from doctors' offices. His competitor is not as consistent, but is getting more and more business. How would you characterize the two businesses?

Quick Answer: **107**
Detailed Answer: **108**

- ❑ A. Jeff provides a high-grade, high-quality service, whereas Ralph provides a high-grade, low-quality service.
- ❑ B. Jeff provides a low-grade, low-quality service, whereas Ralph provides a high-grade, high-quality service.
- ❑ C. Jeff provides a low-grade, high-quality service, whereas Ralph provides a high-grade, low-quality service.
- ❑ D. Jeff provides a high-grade, low-quality service, whereas Ralph provides a low-grade, high-quality service.

5. John is trying to make a case for improving quality efforts and planning in his company. He is aware that in the quality discipline, it is axiomatic that benefits outweigh costs, but he is trying to show how the costs of quality break down for his given project within his quality management plan. What three types of costs will he highlight?

❑ A. Quality control, rework, and external

❑ B. Prevention, appraisal, and failure

❑ C. Internal, external, and stakeholder satisfaction

❑ D. Experimental, benchmarking, and flow charting

6. Carmen is developing her quality management plan for an advertising campaign project. What items must it include for it to properly address quality management for her project?

❑ A. It must be formal.

❑ B. It must be related to the advertising industry standards for quality.

❑ C. It must include information on quality control, quality assurance, and quality improvement for the project.

❑ D. It must include the advertising checklist of required steps for federal approval as well as the resources for the project.

7. You are working on a yearlong global project involving 60 different countries. The project has a large number of stakeholders because it is rolling out a new process for managing global procurement. You are in the project-planning phase of this project and working on the communication plan. What do you need to consider before you do your stakeholder analysis?

❑ A. Understand the project organization, the number of departments and disciplines involved, the number of locations and individuals involved, and whether the procurement process will need to be communicated to vendors.

❑ B. Meet with the project team to determine who would be the most likely project communication recipients.

❑ C. Obtain global email address lists from corporate communications that have been used on similar projects.

❑ D. Plan to communicate only with the project sponsor and corporate location because the project is a yearlong effort; communicating to other sites will not be necessary until the process is delivered.

Quick Answer: **107**
Detailed Answer: **109**

8. Allen Prieto, a product manager for a manufacturer of vending mechanisms for Laundromats and soda machines, is working on a communications plan for his new debit card vending mechanism. He is interested in communicating with the dealerships that sell his equipment, but knows many of them have not made the technology leap to email because the business has traditionally been handled by paper and phone. He also knows there will be a move by corporate to require dealers to be Internet capable within three months. What factors should he consider in determining his communications method?

- ❑ A. What other traditional mechanisms have been used for dealerships
- ❑ B. Immediacy of need for information because the new product will be hot and dealers will want to know about it quickly
- ❑ C. The technical details that will need to be communicated
- ❑ D. Other stakeholders on the project; dealerships are not the only interested party

Quick Answer: **107**
Detailed Answer: **109**

9. Reggie is developing a communications plan for his project. It is an informal and broadly framed statement indicating communications will be "as frequent as necessary as determined by the project control board" within his overall project plan and a communications matrix that provides the information on who will get what information when and how. What is he missing?

- ❑ A. A statement of how data will be collected and stored and corrections distributed
- ❑ B. A method for assessing information between scheduled communications
- ❑ C. A method of updating and refining the communications management plan as the project progresses
- ❑ D. A production schedule showing when each communication will be produced

10. Beth likes new technology, and is in the process of developing a communications plan for her project team. She is preparing to issue hand-held computers (PDAs) to all her project team, even though some of her team members are technology averse. Only parts of the team will be on call, and only during certain parts of the project. During her stakeholder analysis, what is Beth forgetting?

Quick Answer: **107**
Detailed Answer: **109**

❑   A.   Beth needs a communications matrix to determine when the PDA communications should be dispatched.

❑   B.   Most managers already have PDAs and she will not have to issue them.   ✗

❑   C.   Care must be taken to avoid using inappropriate technology and delivering unnecessary information to the project team members who will not need "instant" information.

❑   D.   She will need a training plan for the team members who are technology averse.

11. Human resources management as it relates to Project Management includes which of the following?

Quick Answer: **107**
Detailed Answer: **109**

❑   A.   Stakeholders, sponsors, customers, project team, and interested parties

❑   B.   Project team members and project managers

❑   C.   Project team members

❑   D.   Identifying, documenting, and assigning project roles and responsibilities, and reporting relationships

12. Denise is a rather autocratic line manager and has recently taken a position managing IT projects for a consulting firm. Her project team members will generally be changing with each new project. How would you, as an experienced project manager, advise her with regard to her management style?

Quick Answer: **107**
Detailed Answer: **109**

❑   A.   Denise has been successful as a manager in the past; she should continue the techniques that have been successful for her.

❑   B.   Remind her that she might want to alter her style because project teams are generally composed of individuals temporarily assigned to the project and new to working together.

❑   C.   Remind her that she will now rarely have direct authority over her project team members.

❑   D.   Suggest she use the X theory of human resources management.

13. Gina is a detail-oriented programmer in charge of a small software development project. She is having difficulty eliciting cooperation from her project team during the initiation phase. She has sent a detailed list of what she feels the project should be doing, but is not getting response from her team. How would you counsel her?

Quick Answer: **107**
Detailed Answer: **109**

❏ A. Gina should call a team meeting and have the team perform a lessons-learned session on why the project is not going as planned.

❏ B. Talk to the sponsor and get referential authority to make the team perform the work.

❏ C. Techniques that work well in one phase of a project might not work well in other phases. Therefore, she might need a collaborative approach during initiation.

❏ D. All of the above.

14. The scheduling and coordinating of scarce resources is a challenge for a project manager, especially if the resources are committed to other projects or activities. Inputs to human resources planning include all of the following except

Quick Answer: **107**
Detailed Answer: **110**

❏ A. Templates

❏ B. Project interfaces

❏ C. Staffing requirements

❏ D. Constraints

15. The term *interface* is frequently used in a variety of situations that are related to your project. The definition of a technical interface, with regard to human resources management, is which of the following?

Quick Answer: **107**
Detailed Answer: **110**

❏ A. A method of moving data between organizational units

❏ B. Formal or informal reporting relationships between different technical disciplines, such as design and tooling

❏ C. The actual reporting relationship between two individuals in an organization

❏ D. Technical interfaces do not exist between human resources; this is a systems term

16. Fast Auto Supply has hired Edward Thomas, also known as E.T. to his friends, to finish the development of a new radio product. E.T. is reviewing the documents his predecessor has created. He comes across a list of job skills and competencies, and the time frame in which these would be needed. What is E.T. reviewing?

   - ❏ A. Resource requirements
   - ❏ B. Staffing requirements
   - ❏ C. Team evaluations
   - ❏ D. A preliminary project plan

Quick Answer: **107**
Detailed Answer: **110**

17. Ron is given an assignment to run a project to develop a new ice cream flavor. He is told that he must use Rick, a chemist in the food products department, on this project. This is an example of what?

   - ❏ A. Management preferences
   - ❏ B. An expected staff-assignment constraint
   - ❏ C. Poor management practices because the project has not been chartered or scoped
   - ❏ D. A collective-bargaining agreement

Quick Answer: **107**
Detailed Answer: **110**

18. It is good to have cohesiveness within a team. However, group think is dangerous in a project environment because

   - ❏ A. It inhibits appropriate problem solving.
   - ❏ B. It tends to enable groups to consider unpopular alternatives.
   - ❏ C. It allows for the use of outside expertise, undermining the project team.
   - ❏ D. It requires a sizeable amount of time to survey warning signals from other groups and organizations.

Quick Answer: **107**
Detailed Answer: **110**

19. Providing support and enthusiasm to team members and stakeholders is a valuable ingredient for a successful project manager. Coaching is considered what type of human resources technique?

   - ❏ A. Corrective
   - ❏ B. A role on the organizational chart
   - ❏ C. A practice designed to facilitate managing
   - ❏ D. A type of stakeholder analysis

Quick Answer: **107**
Detailed Answer: **110**

20. The corporate "grapevine" is considered what form of communication?
    - ❏ A. Accurate, especially for project information
    - ❏ B. An informal channel that might or might not have truthful information that should be considered by a project manager
    - ❏ C. Inappropriate
    - ❏ D. A "real world" communications method

Quick Answer: **107**
Detailed Answer: **110**

21. As the project develops through the planning phase, various deliverables are constructed that are inputs to other parts of the project. One of these deliverables is a responsibility assignment matrix (RAM), which is used for what part of human resources planning?
    - ❏ A. Role and responsibility assignments as an output of planning
    - ❏ B. A resource pool description
    - ❏ C. In conjunction with large, noncollocated groups to facilitate meeting management
    - ❏ D. To govern certain portions of a project

Quick Answer: **107**
Detailed Answer: **110**

22. Surrounding yourself with the right people at the right time is a form of resource leveling that will be beneficial in the long run and might reduce variances to your budget. What is one of the key elements of a staffing management plan?
    - ❏ A. How staff will be released from a project when they are no longer needed
    - ❏ B. A resource histogram
    - ❏ C. Details about resource skill sets
    - ❏ D. All of the above

Quick Answer: **107**
Detailed Answer: **110**

23. An experienced project manager once said, "Projects would run incredibly well if people's agendas did not get in the way." This statement summarizes one of the human resource challenges that a project manager must cope with throughout the entire project. Human resource planning produces all but which of the following artifacts?
    - ❏ A. Performance evaluation
    - ❏ B. Organization chart
    - ❏ C. A staff management plan
    - ❏ D. RAM

Quick Answer: **107**
Detailed Answer: **111**

24. You are developing a network diagram using an activity on arrow (AOA) format. While you are formatting the drawing, you show how the activities are linked together by using circles. These circles are known as

Quick Answer: **107**
Detailed Answer: **111**

- ❑ A. Data
- ❑ B. Events
- ❑ C. Predecessors
- ❑ D. Loops

25. Rick is working in a functionally organized company and is attempting to staff his project. Working in this environment can be a constraint to his resource planning. He does not have a preassigned group, nor does he have the money to obtain outside resources. What can Rick do?

Quick Answer: **107**
Detailed Answer: **111**

- ❑ A. Use the stage gate technique to stop the project until staffing issues are resolved.
- ❑ B. Negotiate with functional managers and other project managers for staffing on his project.
- ❑ C. Attempt to do the project himself, and lengthen the time for delivery.
- ❑ D. Consult the organizational policies for recruitment.

26. A staffing pool description provides which of the following pieces of information?

Quick Answer: **107**
Detailed Answer: **111**

- ❑ A. Employee's past performance reviews
- ❑ B. Employee competencies
- ❑ C. Employee age
- ❑ D. Employee bill rate

27. The process of interviewing and hiring personnel is a time- and resource-consuming part of the staff acquisition process. Therefore, many companies are outsourcing this human resource function to other organizations so they can focus on their core competencies instead. The outputs of staff acquisition are which of the following?

Quick Answer: **107**
Detailed Answer: **111**

- ❑ A. Assignment characteristics
- ❑ B. Contracts for outsourced staff
- ❑ C. Staff assignments and project team directory
- ❑ D. All of the above

Quick Check

28. Arnie and Jeff are project managers who are having lunch and discussing their respective projects and the risks associated with each.

    "I just don't know what I don't know!" says Arnie, frustrated.

    "Do a SWOT," Jeff offers.

    What is Jeff talking about?

    ❑ A. An analysis of security, work breakdown structure (WBS), objectives, and tactics

    ❑ B. A strategic waterfall opportunity template

    ❑ C. Jeff's mouth was full—he meant to say "SWAG"

    ❑ D. An evaluation of the strengths, weaknesses, opportunities, and threats that might affect Arnie's project

Quick Answer: **107**
Detailed Answer: **111**

29. Risk identification can be defined as

    ❑ A. Identifying all the risks on a project

    ❑ B. Determining which risks might affect a project and recording their attributes

    ❑ C. Identifying key risks by performing a Pareto analysis

    ❑ D. Knowing when to label issues as risks for mitigation purposes

Quick Answer: **107**
Detailed Answer: **111**

30. Cara is having regular team meetings on her new footwear product. She has had the team do a first cut on its view of what risks affect the project. What should she do next?

    ❑ A. Document the risks and file them in the project folder.

    ❑ B. Involve stakeholders in a second review and then file in the project folder.

    ❑ C. Involve stakeholders in a second review and then individuals who are not project team members for a final, unbiased review.

    ❑ D. Develop risk responses.

Quick Answer: **107**
Detailed Answer: **111**

31. Boyd works in the pharmaceutical industry and is involved in a new drug release to help individuals who suffer from chronic depression. He is aware of a potential new change in the way the FDA allows new drug products to come to market, but he is not sure whether his product will be "grandfathered." This is an example of which of the following?

    ❑ A. An internal risk

    ❑ B. A technical risk

    ❑ C. Iterative product development

    ❑ D. An external risk

Quick Answer: **107**
Detailed Answer: **112**

32. Surfer Joe lives and works in Los Angeles, an earthquake-prone area, and is a manager of IT operations for a health food distributor. He is working on developing a business continuity site for his computer room, outside of the earthquake zone. What type of risk is Joe trying to mitigate?

    ❑ A. An external risk
    ❑ B. An organizational risk
    ❑ C. *Force majeure*
    ❑ D. A Project Management risk

Quick Answer: **107**
Detailed Answer: **112**

33. A golf club manufacturer is beginning a project to develop a new club head out of a titanium alloy using an unproven high heat and cooling method. The product will have embedded "flex beads," and is expected to revolutionize the industry, according to management. As the project manager for the new product development, which of the following concerns you most?

    ❑ A. Lack of prior experience in product development
    ❑ B. The technical risks associated with the new manufacturing method
    ❑ C. Other companies getting the process developed first
    ❑ D. Sufficiency of the budget to cover experimentation

Quick Answer: **107**
Detailed Answer: **112**

34. Your company has decided to develop a Project Management Office (PMO) specifically to address the new rapid development methodologies available in IT. As the project manager for the development and deployment of the methodology, you are concerned because your boss, the CIO, has said she wants it to be available in two months and you have no staff to help. What type of risk is this?

    ❑ A. Both project and organizational
    ❑ B. External
    ❑ C. Technical
    ❑ D. Job

Quick Answer: **107**
Detailed Answer: **112**

35. You are trying to gain consensus on issues associated with a merger between your company, which produces egg rolls, and a new startup in the egg roll business. You have sent questionnaires to legal, marketing, and manufacturing and have compiled the results. You are now about to send out the compilation for a new round of feedback. What technique are you using?

    ❑ A. Brainstorming
    ❑ B. Interviewing
    ❑ C. Delphi
    ❑ D. Assumption analysis

Quick Answer: **107**
Detailed Answer: **112**

Quick Check

36. As a project manager, you want to solicit information from experts, but do not want a single individual to have undue influence over the results. You are looking for the most unbiased data possible. What technique should you use?

   ❏ A. Brainstorming
   ❏ B. Interviewing
   ❏ C. Delphi
   ❏ D. Assumption analysis

Quick Answer: **107**
Detailed Answer: **112**

37. An Ishikawa diagram is useful for all but which of the following processes?

   ❏ A. Quality control
   ❏ B. Risk identification
   ❏ C. Quality planning
   ❏ D. Activity sequencing

Quick Answer: **107**
Detailed Answer: **112**

38. There are various methods to graphically depict the logic of a project. Which of the following diagramming techniques is not used as a tool of risk identification?

   ❏ A. System process
   ❏ B. Fishbone
   ❏ C. WBS
   ❏ D. Influence

Quick Answer: **107**
Detailed Answer: **113**

39. You are driving down the highway and going above the speed limit. Behind you, you see a state trooper car with its lights flashing. The state trooper car is an example of what?

   ❏ A. Poor judgment
   ❏ B. A cause and effect
   ❏ C. A risk trigger
   ❏ D. A risk

Quick Answer: **107**
Detailed Answer: **113**

40. Jane has been working long hours on her project. Many of her team members have been coming down with the Asian flu, and causing project delays. As a key project team member, Jane has now listed the Asian flu as a minor project risk, in case she gets it. Jane, sitting alone at her desk, begins to cough and feel chilled. What has happened?

   ❏ A. A risk response
   ❏ B. A cause and effect
   ❏ C. A risk trigger
   ❏ D. A risk

Quick Answer: **107**
Detailed Answer: **113**

41. Risk identification, analysis of risks, and development of miti-gation strategies are vital steps in the success of a project. Assessing the impact and likelihood of identified risks is known as

- ❏ A. Risk management
- ❏ B. Quantitative risk analysis
- ❏ C. Qualitative risk analysis
- ❏ D. Risk assessment

Quick Answer: **107**
Detailed Answer: **113**

42. Because project managers spend a large percentage of their time communicating with other team members and stakehold-ers, being timid is usually not a virtue for success. Interviewing is a technique identified by PMI that can be used in a number of processes to gather information that might be vital to the project. Which process does not use interviewing?

- ❏ A. Qualitative risk analysis
- ❏ B. Quantitative risk analysis
- ❏ C. Risk identification
- ❏ D. Risk management

Quick Answer: **107**
Detailed Answer: **113**

43. Weighing of risks and risk outcomes should impact the project selection process as an organization decides what projects should be added to its project portfolio. What factor can mag-nify the importance of a particular risk?

- ❏ A. Time criticality of risk-related actions
- ❏ B. Quality of information
- ❏ C. Mitigation strategies
- ❏ D. Prioritization

Quick Answer: **107**
Detailed Answer: **113**

44. Determining the validity of information and the probability of outcomes can be a guessing game in some circumstances and can lead to ambiguity and chaos. Data precision is an input to assessing the impact and likelihood of an identified risk. What does data precision provide?

- ❏ A. Information on the extent to which a risk is known, the data available, and the quality of the data about the risk
- ❏ B. A probability rating for the risk
- ❏ C. The extent to which assumptions are used in evaluating risks
- ❏ D. The risk priority

Quick Answer: **107**
Detailed Answer: **113**

45. Aaron is developing a project plan and assessing risk. He realizes he has a noncollocated project team, multiple functional departments involved, and multiple IT teams programming, using a new unproven web tool. James, on the other hand, is working on a project that is using a single, proven technology with one team. What is their relative project risk based on project type?

- ❑ A. James has a relatively high-risk project because his team is noncollocated.
- ❑ B. Aaron has a relatively low-risk project type because there are many experts involved.
- ❑ C. James has a highly complex project using state-of-the-art technology, and is therefore in a project with more uncertainty.
- ❑ D. Aaron has a highly complex project using state-of-the-art technology, and is therefore in a project with more uncertainty.

Quick Answer: **107**
Detailed Answer: **113**

46. Craig needs to decide what projects should be added to the project review board agenda for the meeting next week. He has a list of over 20 projects that have various degrees of risk and return on investment (ROI). Therefore, he ranks the projects according to their probability of success and ROI. A risk probability is defined as

- ❑ A. A rating of high, medium, or low
- ❑ B. The impact of a risk to the project
- ❑ C. The effect on project objectives if the risk occurs
- ❑ D. The likelihood that a risk will occur

Quick Answer: **107**
Detailed Answer: **114**

47. During the planning phase of a project, you should do a risk analysis for your project. Attributing a quantitative measurement to risks can be a challenge because different people might have different opinions of which attributes are the most important. A risk impact scale that is high, medium, or low is known as

- ❑ A. A probability scale
- ❑ B. An ordinal scale
- ❑ C. A cardinal scale
- ❑ D. Nonlinear

Quick Answer: **107**
Detailed Answer: **114**

48. Utilization of best practices in Project Management requires the retainment of archives for future reference. Part of these archives should include risk analysis–related deliverables so they can be reviewed for future projects. Assessing risk probability is difficult because

    ❏   A. Probability assessment is a mathematical process that requires a mathematician.
    ❏   B. Data precision is unknown.
    ❏ , C. At the beginning of a project, risk is higher.
    ❏   D. It often requires expert judgment, and is often done without the benefit of historical information.

Quick Answer: **107**
Detailed Answer: **114**

49. Data precision ranking uses all of the following except

    ❏   A. Extent of understanding of the risk
    ❏   B. Quality of the data about a risk
    ❏   C. A probability impact matrix
    ❏   D. Reliability and integrity of the data about a risk

Quick Answer: **107**
Detailed Answer: **114**

50. Rachel has been working on the qualitative risk analysis for her canning machinery rebuild project. She notices that her data precision rankings for most of her risks are very low. What should she do?

    ❏   A. Revisit the rankings with the project team.
    ❏   B. Accept the data as it is. The rankings are intended to be a guideline to develop risk responses.
    ❏   C. See whether she can gather more accurate data.
    ❏   D. Consult an expert.

Quick Answer: **107**
Detailed Answer: **114**

51. Outputs of qualitative risk analysis include all of the following except

    ❏   A. Overall risk ranking for the project
    ❏   B. Risk triggers
    ❏   C. List of prioritized risks
    ❏   D. List of risks requiring additional analysis and management effort

Quick Answer: **107**
Detailed Answer: **114**

52. The ability to research the project risks and capture them for future reference helps to show a relationship to the success of a project. Quantitative risk analysis and qualitative risk analysis differ in what ways?

Quick Answer: **107**
Detailed Answer: **114**

- ❏ A. Qualitative risk analysis assesses the impact and likelihood, whereas quantitative risk analysis assesses the consequence on specific project objectives.
- ❏ B. Quantitative risk analysis assesses the impact and likelihood, whereas qualitative risk analysis assesses the consequence on specific project objectives.
- ❏ C. They are essentially the same and generally done at the same time.
- ❏ D. Qualitative risk analysis uses the risk management as input whereas quantitative risk analysis does not.

53. There are numerous objectives of the risk analysis process that can contribute to the development of the change control management process. One of the objectives of quantitative risk analysis is to

Quick Answer: **107**
Detailed Answer: **114**

- ❏ A. Develop a probability of project success.
- ❏ B. Quantify the risk exposure of a project and determine the size of reserves needed.
- ❏ C. Perform sensitivity analysis.
- ❏ D. Use the Monte Carlo technique.

54. Unfortunately, risk analysis is not done regularly on many projects at many companies. A lot of time should be spent on risk analysis during the planning phase as a key ingredient to the success of a project by proactively identifying and isolating known risk occurrences. Randy is evaluating a number of risk options and the probabilities as well as costs associated with each option. He wants to provide the highest expected value for his choice. What tool should he use?

Quick Answer: **107**
Detailed Answer: **114**

- ❏ A. Critical path method (CPM)
- ❏ B. Decision tree analysis
- ❏ C. Sensitivity analysis
- ❏ D. Expert judgment

55. Dylan has formed his new IT team and looks forward to planning his first project. His mentor has emphasized that he needs to develop a risk response plan to help show the IT governance board that he is forward thinking in his project plan development. Which of the following is not true of risk response planning?

  ❏ **A.** It must be timely.

  ❏ **B.** It must be cost effective.

  ❏ **C.** It is decided by the project manager.

  ❏ **D.** It must be owned by a responsible person.

Quick Answer: **107**
Detailed Answer: **115**

56. The ability to be creative and open minded about new ideas will have a positive impact upon your risk response plan development and can lead to other opportunities as others realize your capabilities. Risk response planning involves which of the following?

  ❏ **A.** Developing options and assigning individual responsibility for risk responses

  ❏ **B.** Identifying risks requiring the most attention

  ❏ **C.** Determining whether a risk trigger has occurred

  ❏ **D.** Reducing threats to the project

Quick Answer: **107**
Detailed Answer: **115**

57. You are creating your risk response plan and are deciding to change your project plan resources to protect your project from the impact of a key resource needing to use the Family Leave Act. What type of risk response strategy are you using?

  ❏ **A.** Acceptance

  ❏ **B.** Mitigation

  ❏ **C.** Transference

  ❏ **D.** Avoidance

Quick Answer: **107**
Detailed Answer: **115**

58. Jessica is developing a project plan for a project with a new technology and realizes the in-house programmers do not have the experience to do the work, which could potentially cause the project schedule to be delayed significantly during their learning curve. As a consequence, Jessica has decided to use a contracting firm with a fixed-price bid to address the coding risk. What type of risk strategy is she using?

  ❏ **A.** Acceptance

  ❏ **B.** Mitigation

  ❏ **C.** Transference

  ❏ **D.** Avoidance

Quick Answer: **107**
Detailed Answer: **115**

59. A1 company wants you to develop a new web front end to a legacy system. The functionality of the entire development involves more than 1,000 transactions. You are expected to deliver the new system in one year. As you develop the project plan, you realize the risk of delivering a year out might hide problems in terms of the complexity of the project and you decide to propose delivery of small, frequent packages of functionality in one-month intervals. What type of risk strategy are you using?

Quick Answer: **107**
Detailed Answer: **115**

    ❑   A. Agile programming techniques
    ❑   B. Mitigation
    ❑   C. Transference
    ❑   D. Avoidance

60. Some people indicate that Project Management adds too much paperwork and documentation to the project and does not have a perceived value. By providing value-added deliverables such as a risk analysis and a risk register, a project manager allows stakeholders to have a full understanding of the issues that could add to the timeline and/or costs of the project. A risk register is also known as

Quick Answer: **107**
Detailed Answer: **115**

    ❑   A. A risk threshold
    ❑   B. A risk management plan
    ❑   C. A list of prioritized risks
    ❑   D. A risk response plan

61. Being prepared to respond to adverse conditions is part of many healthcare workers' jobs. Increasing numbers of clinical personnel are realizing how Project Management risk response planning can be incorporated into their operations to handle these adverse situations. A risk response plan should include all of the following except

Quick Answer: **107**
Detailed Answer: **115**

    ❑   A. Risk owners and responsibilities
    ❑   B. Specific actions to implement
    ❑   C. Contractual agreements
    ❑   D. Budgets and time frames for responses

62. A residual risk is defined as

Quick Answer: **107**
Detailed Answer: **115**

    ❑   A. A risk that arises as a direct result of a risk response
    ❑   B. A risk that remains as an accepted or unaddressed risk
    ❑   C. A risk that is not properly mitigated, and therefore remains
    ❑   D. A risk that must be incorporated into the project plan

. . . .

63. The process to acquire capital goods can be time consuming, especially if numerous approvals are needed and there is a lack of urgency from the departments involved in the purchase order process. Determining when to obtain products and services from outside the organization for a project should be done during which process?

    ❑ A. Activity cost estimating
    ❑ B. Procurement planning
    ❑ C. Scope definition
    ❑ D. Activity definition

64. Ray has a technical problem with his project implementing the infrastructure needed for a voice response unit. He is considering an outside vendor for help, and knows that because he is late in the planning process, he will only have a limited budget to engage help. He also knows the system he is implementing is only supported by one firm in his city. What factors are most likely to influence his procurement planning?

    ❑ A. Market conditions
    ❑ B. His project scope statement
    ❑ C. Contract type
    ❑ D. Other units in his organization

65. Ron is running a construction firm, and working on a business building in the downtown area. He realizes he will need an extra dump truck to make the schedule for clearing the lot. In general, Ron has sufficient trucking capacity, but he might be getting more downtown work. He is considering procuring another truck, but isn't sure whether he should rent or buy. How should Ron approach the issue?

    ❑ A. Perform a cost benefit analysis.
    ❑ B. Determine the indirect and direct costs of each option, and estimate the portion allocated to the project for a purchase.
    ❑ C. Consider double shifts on the trucks he has.
    ❑ D. Contact a consultant.

Quick Check

Quick Answer: **107**
Detailed Answer: **116**

Quick Answer: **107**
Detailed Answer: **116**

Quick Answer: **107**
Detailed Answer: **116**

66. Josh wants to transfer risk to another entity in order to reduce the risk for his "hole-in-one" celebrity golf tournament project. Because this generally involves a cost, it will be necessary for documents to be created that outline the obligations of both parties. Which contract type moves risk to the seller most effectively?

   ❏ A. Fixed price
   ❏ B. Cost-reimbursable
   ❏ C. Cost plus
   ❏ D. Time and material

67. Rhonda has decided to outsource a particular deliverable on her construction project. She has described the product and services in detail and has included the necessary reporting requirements. What has Rhonda prepared?

   ❏ A. A statement of work (SOW)
   ❏ B. A contract
   ❏ C. A procurement management plan
   ❏ D. A scope definition

68. New project managers are frequently perplexed by the proliferation of various terms in the Project Management field. Two areas frequently confused include *procurement* and *solicitation*. The difference between procurement planning and solicitation planning is

   ❏ A. Procurement planning develops the procurement management plan, whereas solicitation planning develops the SOW.
   ❏ B. Procurement planning involves preparing the documents to support solicitation, whereas solicitation planning identifies which project deliverables can be best met by an outside organization.
   ❏ C. Procurement planning identifies which project deliverables can be best met by an outside organization, whereas solicitation planning involves preparing the documents to support solicitation.
   ❏ D. Procurement planning develops the evaluation criteria for vendors, whereas solicitation planning determines the SOW.

69. Companies spend millions of dollars annually by moving employees from cubicle to cubicle and office to office. Ellen is setting up a meeting to talk about her requirements to all prospective companies hoping to provide the moving service for her office move project. What type of meeting is Ellen having?

- ❑ A. A project kickoff meeting
- ❑ B. An illegal one—discussion with prospective sellers before a contract is unethical
- ❑ C. A prebid conference
- ❑ D. An advertising meeting

70. During procurement planning, Jeff is considering the items he needs to outsource, and the vendors who could potentially be involved. Why is it important for Jeff to consider potential vendors?

- ❑ A. To create the qualified seller list
- ❑ B. In order to exercise some degree of control over contracting decisions
- ❑ C. Jeff doesn't need to consider vendors; that task is done in solicitation planning and the actual solicitation process
- ❑ D. Because vendor capability is a risk to be factored into his planning

71. From the following table, what is the total slack for Event 1?

Activity	Duration Estimate (Days)	Earliest Start	Earliest Finish	Latest Start	Latest Finish	
Event 1	20	10	30	35	55	25
Event 2	2	14	16	23	25	9
Event 3	13	27	40	79	92	52
Event 4	8	13	21	88	96	75

- ❑ A. 10
- ❑ B. 25
- ❑ C. 30
- ❑ D. 20

34
52
75
161

. . . .

Quick Check

72. From the table in Question 71, which event has a negative slack?

Quick Answer: **107**
Detailed Answer: **117**

- ❏ A. Event 3
- ❏ B. Event 2
- ❏ C. Event 1
- ❏ D. None

73. From the table in Question 71, what is the total slack for the project?

Quick Answer: **107**
Detailed Answer: **117**

- ❏ A. 20
- ❏ B. 161
- ❏ C. 268
- ❏ D. 88

74. Budiono is excited to be involved with his new international project in Indonesia but is trying to determine the critical path for his project because several of the tasks have long durations. In doing forward pass and backward pass calculations, it is important for him to identify and focus on paths of tasks that have a _____ slack for the project.

Quick Answer: **107**
Detailed Answer: **117**

- ❏ A. negative
- ❏ B. zero
- ❏ C. positive
- ❏ D. delayed

Quick Check

75. Norma has been doing Project Management for over 20 years and has never heard of PMI. Now she is overwhelmed with all the new terminology that she has to learn from the PMBOK for tasks that she used to take for granted. She is surprised to find out that the longest path of activities from the beginning to the end of the project is called the

Quick Answer: **107**
Detailed Answer: **117**

   ❑ A. Path with positive slack
   ❑ B. Relative difference
   ❑ C. Critical path
   ❑ D. Schedule variance

76. While evaluating the network diagram for the town hall expansion project, Jeff looks at the relationship between the facility management timelines and the construction contractors. He realizes the earliest start and the earliest finish times for the tasks are determined by calculating _____ through the diagram.

Quick Answer: **107**
Detailed Answer: **118**

   ❑ A. forward
   ❑ B. backward
   ❑ C. progressive elaborations
   ❑ D. consistently

77. Using backward pass calculations, what is the latest start time of a task if the duration is 37 days, the required completion is 219 days, the latest finish is 245 days, and the estimated completion is 205 days?

Quick Answer: **107**
Detailed Answer: **118**

   ❑ A. 208
   ❑ B. 14
   ❑ C. 40
   ❑ D. 450

dur.
A   37   LS   LF
                            208   245

Use the following network diagram logic to answer Questions 78 and 79:

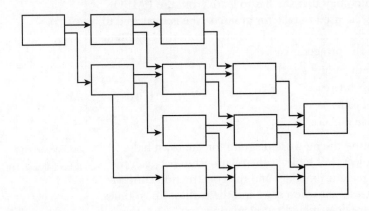

78. Sara has never seen a network diagram before, but she must explain the concept to the shareholders at next week's steering committee meeting, and get their buy-in for the schedule of a software development project that she is working on. This diagram is an example of

  ❑   A.   Activity on arrow formatting

  ❑   B.   Looping

  ❑   C.   Serial processing

  ❑   D.   Laddering

Quick Answer: **107**
Detailed Answer: **118**

79. What type of formatting is it?

  ❑   A.   Activity on arrow

  ❑   B.   Activity in box

  ❑   C.   Work breakdown structure

  ❑   D.   Responsibility assignment matrix

Quick Answer: **107**
Detailed Answer: **118**

80. With the development of a new space shuttle landing protocol, you need to make some decisions about the duration estimates that you are to provide at the kickoff meeting with the heads of the aerospace division. By following a beta probability distribution with three estimates and utilizing a network diagram, calculate the expected duration with the following probabilities:

T (Optimistic) = 7 days

T (Most Likely) = 10 days

T (Pessimistic) = 22 days

  ❑   A.   7 days

  ❑   B.   17 days

  ❑   C.   12 days

  ❑   D.   32 days

Quick Answer: **107**
Detailed Answer: **118**

Quick Check Answer Key

1. A	**28.** D	**55.** C
2. D	**29.** B	**56.** A
3. B	**30.** C	**57.** D
4. C	**31.** D	**58.** C
5. B	**32.** C	**59.** B
6. C	**33.** B	**60.** D
7. A	**34.** A	**61.** C
8. B	**35.** C	**62.** B
9. A	**36.** C	**63.** C
10. C	**37.** D	**64.** A
11. A	**38.** D	**65.** B
12. B	**39.** C	**66.** A
13. C	**40.** C	**67.** A
14. A	**41.** C	**68.** C
15. B	**42.** A	**69.** C
16. B	**43.** A	**70.** B
17. B	**44.** A	**71.** B
18. A	**45.** D	**72.** D
19. C	**46.** D	**73.** B
20. B	**47.** B	**74.** A
21. A	**48.** D	**75.** C
22. A	**49.** C	**76.** A
23. A	**50.** C	**77.** A
24. B	**51.** B	**78.** D
25. B	**52.** A	**79.** B
26. B	**53.** B	**80.** C
27. C	**54.** B	

Answers and Explanations

1. **Answer A** is the best answer. This is the PMI-defined reason for the differences between core and facilitating processes. Answer B is incorrect because facilitating processes are not optional. Answer C is tempting because it is generally true, but not the best answer. Answer D is incorrect because the quantitative risk analysis involves measuring.

2. **Answer D** is the PMI definition of quality planning. Answer A is incorrect because it is the definition of quality assurance. Answer B is incorrect because it is the definition of quality. Answer C is incorrect because it is the definition of quality control.

3. **Answer B** is the best answer because it codifies the overall intentions of the Jumping Gymboree organization with regard to quality. Answer A may be true, but it is not the best answer. Answer C would be appropriate if her new site were launched. Although Answer D is tempting, it does not provide the focus on quality.

4. **Answer C** is correct. Jeff provides fewer services or features than Ralph; therefore, he provides a lower-grade service. However, Jeff's service meets or exceeds the expectations and is therefore a high-quality service, whereas Ralph's service is inconsistent. Ralph will not continue to get more business if his quality remains poor; however, Jeff would be smart to consider adding a service or two. Answers A, B, and D are incorrect because they do not accurately reflect the facts in this explanation because Jeff's service is low grade and high quality.

5. **Answer B** is correct. The costs of quality are the total cost of all efforts to achieve quality, including work to conform and rework due to nonconformance. Answer A is incorrect because, although it touches on appraisal costs (quality control) and failure, it does not mention prevention costs. Answer C is incorrect because internal and external costs are related to failure costs, and stakeholder satisfaction relates to conformance costs, but appraisal costs are missing. Answer D is incorrect because these are tools and techniques for quality planning related to appraisal, but do not include the other items in the definition of cost of quality.

6. **Answer C** is correct. The quality management plan must address the project quality system, including the procedures and processes needed to implement the process. Answer A is incorrect because a quality management plan may be informal or formal, highly detailed or broadly framed, depending on the project. Answer B is tempting because, ideally, the quality management plan will address industry standards, but these are inputs to the quality planning process. Answer D is incorrect because a checklist is another output of the quality planning process, but not the quality plan. Federal approval is a red herring.

7. **Answer A** is the best answer. Understanding the complexity of the audience and the communications requirements is the first input to communications planning. Answers B and C may take place during the stakeholder analysis, but are not what needs to be compiled first. Answer D is often an option chosen in projects that get into trouble. Not considering all stakeholders in communications can lead to lack of acceptance in a project.

8. **Answer B** is correct. Allen has considered the availability of technology, the expected expertise of the recipient, and the possibility that the technology will change during the project. This is tricky because Answer A would be a logical route to pursue, and Answer C would be a factor to consider in the communication content, but not the method. Answer D is also tempting but not the best answer because other stakeholders do matter, but the method can be tailored to their needs as well.

9. **Answer A** is correct. The broadly framed statement does not mention data collection or storage. Answer B is incorrect because the project control board will assess information between scheduled communications. Answer C is incorrect because the project control board would also serve the function of modifying the plan if necessary. Answer D is incorrect because a communications matrix is the production schedule of when each type of communication will be produced.

10. **Answer C** is the best answer. Communications plans must be devised to avoid wasting resources with inappropriate technology or unnecessary information. Answer A addresses the unnecessary information portion of the problem, but not the inappropriate technology issue. Although Answer B might be more and more true in society, it is not stated in the question. Answer D would be true if the technology choice were appropriate.

11. **Answer A** is correct and includes all stakeholders. Answers B and C are incorrect because they are missing stakeholders. Answer D is incorrect because it is the definition of organizational planning.

12. **Answer B** is the correct answer. Answer A is incorrect because her past autocratic techniques might not work in a temporary environment. Answer C is probably true, but it is not the best answer. Answer D, the X theory of management, is another term used for an authoritarian management style.

13. **Answer C** is correct. Gina's detail orientation might not be helping to develop buy-in from the rest of the team members. Answer A is incorrect because it is not the best answer, although at times a lessons-learned session in an early stage of a project can help. Answers B and D are incorrect because requesting referent power will not likely resolve this situation. Referent power involves borrowing of authority from a functional manager, which could actually make the situation worse, if not utilized correctly.

14. **Answer A** is correct. Answers B, C, and D are all inputs to human resources planning. Templates are a tool used in HR planning.

15. **Answer B** is correct, according to PMI's definition of project interface inputs into organizational planning. Answers A, C, and D are incorrect because they are not the correct definition according to the PMBOK. This is a straightforward memorization-type question.

16. **Answer B** is correct and is PMI's definition of staffing requirements. Answer A is incorrect because resource requirements may also include materials and supplies. Answer C is incorrect because there is no evaluation material mentioned in the question. Answer D is tempting, but the information does not include dependencies, and is therefore not a project schedule. Further, PMI depicts the project plan as a grouping of planning documents, not the project schedule.

17. **Answer B** is correct. Although Answer A is tempting, the better answer is that it is a constraint. Answer C is incorrect because the project's scope is clearly to deliver a new ice cream flavor. Answer D is incorrect, although the constraint could be a result of a labor agreement.

18. **Answer A** is correct. Group think can cause collective rationalization, and pressures for conformity that are counterproductive to good problem solving. Answers B, C, and D are incorrect because they are techniques for avoiding group think.

19. **Answer C** is correct. Coaching is an HR practice listed as a tool and technique within organizational planning. Answer A is tempting because often coaching does occur as a corrective action. Answer B is incorrect because coaches are usually managers on organizational charts. Answer D is incorrect because coaching is not related to stakeholder analysis.

20. **Answer B** is correct. Project managers need to be aware of the effect of the corporate grapevine, either good or bad, because it can influence morale on a project. Answer A is incorrect because often grapevine information is incorrect. Answers C and D may be true, but are not the best answers.

21. **Answer A** is correct. The responsibility assignment matrix (RAM) is used to link role assignments closely to scope and the WBS. Answer B is incorrect because a resource pool description is an input to schedule development. Answers C and D are nonexistent artifacts.

22. **Answer A** is correct. PMI states that particular attention should be paid to how staff are released from a project. It is also possible to improve morale by reducing uncertainty with continual communication. Answer D is tempting because all items are elements of a staffing management plan, but Answer A is the best answer. Answers B and C are incorrect because they would not likely resolve the entire situation.

23. **Answer A** is correct. Performance evaluations are not an output of human resources planning. Answers B, C, and D are outputs of the human resource planning process and therefore incorrect answers to this question.

24. **Answer B** is correct. Whenever using the activity on arrow format, the activities are linked by circles that are known as *events*. The event is used to show the finish of activities entering into it and the start of activities that are going out of it. Answer A is incorrect because it does not fully answer the question. Answer C is incorrect because predecessors only describe the activities that occur before the event. Answer D is incorrect because network loops are perpetually repeating relationships among activities and cannot occur in a network diagram.

25. **Answer B** is correct. Rick's only real choice here is to negotiate. Answer A could be employed, if his negotiations fail, but it is not the best answer. Answer C is incorrect because we do not know the scope of the project, and whether it can be done by one person. Answer D is incorrect because Rick has no authority for outside recruitment.

26. **Answer B** is correct. Employee competencies, previous experience, personal interests, availability, and characteristics are all part of the staffing pool description. Answer A is incorrect; although past performance is considered, the performance reviews are not part of the description. Answer C is generally illegal to include. Answer D is incorrect because billing rate is not part of the description.

27. **Answer C** is correct. Answers A and B are not outputs of staff acquisition. Answer D is incorrect because Answers A and B are not included.

28. **Answer D** is correct. A SWOT analysis is a technique for risk identification. Answers A, B, and C are incorrect acronyms.

29. **Answer B** is correct, and the definition of risk identification from PMI. Answer A is incorrect, but a hoped-for goal on all projects. Answer C is incorrect because a Pareto analysis would be part of quantitative risk analysis. Answer D is incorrect, but a good skill for a project manager to have.

30. **Answer C** is correct. Involving stakeholders and nonproject team members is key to developing an unbiased analysis of risk. Answer A is incorrect because it does not iterate through another pass of evaluation. Answer B is tempting, and often where many project managers end, but it is not the best answer. Answer D is not done until after risk qualification and quantification are done.

31. **Answer D** is correct. FDA rulings and regulations are an example of an external risk. An example of an internal risk might be lack of funding for a project. A technical risk is the capability of producing the product with a new process. Iterative product development is not associated with risks. Answer A is incorrect because an internal risk would likely be generated within his own company and not an organization such as the FDA. Answer B is incorrect because this example does not involve a technical risk. Answer C is incorrect because iterative product development involves the different stages that a product evolves into over time and is not applicable to this situation.

32. **Answer C** is correct. A *force majeure* is an external risk, such as a flood or an earthquake that generally requires disaster recovery rather than risk management. Answer A is tempting because an earthquake is a type of external risk, but it is not the best answer. Answer B is incorrect because organizational risks involve scope time or cost. Answer D is incorrect because Project Management risks involve poor planning.

33. **Answer B** is correct. The technical risks associated with the product development should concern you because they are unproven. Answer A is incorrect because the golf manufacturer has clearly developed products in the past. Answers C and D might concern you, but they are not the best answers.

34. **Answer A** is correct. The risks posed are both inadequate planning and inadequate funding in scope, time, and resources. Answer B is incorrect because the source of the risk is internal: the CIO. Answer C is incorrect—although the rapid development concept is relatively new, there is no new technology in creating a methodology. Answer D may be true, but it is not a risk category identified by PMI.

35. **Answer C** is correct. The Delphi technique is a way to reach consensus with experts via questionnaire. Answer A is incorrect because brainstorming is generally not done by questionnaire, but in a facilitated session. Answer B is incorrect because a questionnaire is being used. Interviewing involves one-on-one conversations. Answer D is incorrect because assumption analysis is not a technique identified by PMI.

36. **Answer C** is correct. The Delphi technique is useful because participation is anonymous, and the multiple iterations generate a consensus without undue bias. Answers A, B, and D are incorrect because they do not allow the source to be anonymous. This anonymity will likely lead to the least-biased results.

37. **Answer D** is correct. Ishikawa, fishbone, or cause-and-effect diagrams are used in all the quality processes as well as risk identification. Answers A, B, and C are incorrect because Ishikawa is not used in quality control, quality planning, or activity sequencing.

38. **Answer D** is correct. The WBS is not a diagramming technique; however, it is an input to risk identification. Answers A, B, and C are incorrect because system processes diagrams, fishbone diagrams, and influence diagrams are all diagramming techniques that can be used in risk identification and therefore are incorrect answers to this question.

39. **Answer C** is correct. The state trooper lights are a risk trigger, or a warning sign or indication that a risk is about to occur. It isn't definite because you don't know yet whether the state trooper car is after you. Answers A and B may be true to a certain extent, but are not the best answers to this question. Answer D is incorrect because the state trooper car is not the risk.

40. **Answer C** is correct. Jane's coughing and chills are a risk trigger and could be an indicator that she might have the Asian flu. Answer A is incorrect because the risk response is not stated in the question. Answer B is incorrect because there has not been a cause-and-effect relationship developed in this situation. Answer D is incorrect because she has not actually been diagnosed as having the flu.

41. **Answer C** is correct, and the definition of qualitative risk analysis. Quantitative risk analysis is defined as the numeric analysis of probability of each risk. Risk management is the overall set of risk activities. Risk assessment is not a PMI term. Answers A, B, and D are incorrect because they do not involve assessing the impact and likelihood of identified risks.

42. **Answer A** is correct. Qualitative risk analysis focuses on probability, and does not use interviewing as a technique. Risk identification and quantitative risk analysis do use interviewing as a technique. Answers B, C, and D are correct reasons for interviewing and therefore are incorrect for this question.

43. **Answer A** is correct. The time criticality of a risk-related action can increase the importance of a risk. Answer B is incorrect because quality of information can actually reduce risk. Answer C is incorrect because mitigation strategies do not magnify a risk. Answer D is incorrect because prioritization is a tool that is used in risk response development.

44. **Answer A** is correct. Data precision is defined as the information about a risk. Answer B is incorrect because the probability and impact are a technique of qualitative risk analysis. Answer C is incorrect because assumptions are another input. Answer D is incorrect because prioritization is an output of qualitative risk analysis.

45. **Answer D** is correct. Aaron's project spans multiple departments and locations and is using an unproven technology; therefore, the project has a higher risk profile. Answer A is incorrect because James's team is collocated. Answer B is incorrect because, even with experts, the complexity of his project makes it risky. Answer C is incorrect because James is using proven technology.

46. **Answer D** is correct. Answer A is incorrect because it describes the actual qualitative ratings. Answers B and C are incorrect because they are risk consequences.

47. **Answer B** is correct. An ordinal scale is rank-ordered values. Answer A is incorrect because a probability scale is between 0 and 1. Answer C is incorrect because a cardinal scale assigns values to impacts. Answer D is incorrect because linear and nonlinear values are used in cardinal scales.

48. **Answer D** is correct. Answer A is incorrect, and generally not true. Probability does not require a mathematician. Answer B is incorrect because data precision is an input to qualitative risk analysis. Answer C is true, but not the best answer for this question.

49. **Answer C** is correct. Answers A, B, and D are all items to consider when ranking data precision. A probability impact matrix is a tool in qualitative risk analysis, separate from data precision ranking.

50. **Answer C** is correct. Low precision rankings mean there might be a lack of understanding about the risk, and therefore more data is needed for useful qualitative analysis. Answer A is incorrect because the analysis most likely included the project team. Answer B is incorrect because the low rankings point to a need for further information. Answer D is tempting, but also incorrect for this question.

51. **Answer B** is correct. Answers A, C, and D are all outputs of qualitative risk analysis. Answer B is an output of risk identification.

52. **Answer A** is correct. Answer B is incorrect because it is the opposite of Answer A. Answer C is tempting because it is often true that they are done at the same time; however, the objectives of the two functions are different. Answer D is not true because both processes use the risk management plan as inputs.

53. **Answer B** is correct. Answer A is incorrect because quantitative analysis focuses on the probability of achieving the cost and time objectives, not necessarily the entire project's success. Answers C and D are tools used in quantitative risk analysis, not objectives of the process.

54. **Answer B** is correct. A decision tree focuses on the probability and cost outcome of a particular decision path and provides the means to analyze which decision would provide the highest expected value. Answer A is the critical path method and is used in scheduling, not risk analysis. Answer C is incorrect because sensitivity analysis is used to determine what risks have the most impact on the project. Answer D is tempting because expert judgment is used so often in projects, but it is not the correct answer.

55. **Answer C** is correct. A risk response plan must be agreed upon by all parties involved. Answers A, B, and D are attributes of risk response planning.

56. **Answer A** is correct. Answer B is incorrect because it is an objective of quantitative risk analysis. Answer C is incorrect because it is a part of risk control and monitoring. Answer D is tempting, but incorrect, because risk response planning doesn't reduce a threat; it determines actions to take to reduce a threat or enhance an opportunity.

57. **Answer D** is correct. By changing your project plan, you are attempting to avoid or eliminate the risk entirely. Answers A, B, and C, use different tactics to mitigate risk, and are therefore incorrect.

58. **Answer C** is correct. By using contractors with a fixed price, she is transferring the risk of the new technology and coding schedule performance to the contract company. Answers A, B, and D are not this type of risk strategy.

59. **Answer B** is correct. By taking action to reduce the probability of hidden problems by delivering more frequently, you are mitigating the possibility of the problems. This is not to say that some might still exist. Answer A is tempting because agile programming is, in effect, the mitigation strategy. Answers C and D are different risk strategies.

60. **Answer D** is correct. Answers A, B, and C are inputs to risk response planning.

61. **Answer C** is correct. Risk response plans do not include contractual agreements, although they are an output of risk response planning. Answers A, B, and D are all elements that should be included in the risk response plan.

62. **Answer B** is correct. Answer A is incorrect, and is the definition of a secondary risk. Answer C is tempting because of the word *residual*, but it is not true. Answer D is an output of risk planning and would involve other risk response plans.

63. **Answer C** is correct. Procurement planning should be done during the scope definition effort, according to the PMBOK. Answer B is tricky because the question defines procurement planning—but this is the process, not the timing of when to do it. Answers A and D are not the appropriate processes during which procurement planning should take place.

64. **Answer A** is correct. Ray is in need of specialized services from a single firm. Depending on who else happens to need their services, he might or might not be able to afford them. Answer B is incorrect because it is an input to procurement planning, but not a factor that will influence Ray's planning. Answers C and D are incorrect because they are tools and techniques of procurement planning.

65. **Answer B** is correct. Ron needs to do a make-or-buy analysis, which involves determining the lowest cost. Answer A is tempting but it is not the appropriate tool for this issue. Answer C may be true, but it is not the best answer. Answer D is incorrect because contacting a consultant would not provide him with any new information he does not have.

66. **Answer A** is correct. Fixed-price contracts put the burden on the seller to produce the product or deliverable within the specified time for a specified cost. Answer B is incorrect because the costs are recoverable by the seller, so if they go over budget, costs are still recovered. Answer C is incorrect because cost plus enables the seller to achieve a profit in addition to all the costs associated. Cost plus is another form of cost reimbursable. Time and material contracts shift the risk entirely to the purchaser. Answer D is incorrect because time and material pricing puts the burden on the buyer because the seller does not have an incentive to keep costs low.

67. **Answer A** is correct. A statement of work requires sufficient detail for the prospective seller to determine whether he can and wants to do the work required. Answer B is incorrect because a contract involves pricing and timing and sometimes performance incentives. Answer C is incorrect because the procurement management plan describes how the remaining procurement processes will be governed. Answer D is tempting because, in essence, an SOW is a scope definition; however, this is not the best answer.

68. **Answer C** is correct. Answer A is incorrect because the SOWs are developed in procurement planning. Answer B is incorrect because it is the opposite of Answer C. Answer D is incorrect because evaluation criteria are an output of solicitation planning.

69. **Answer C** is correct. A meeting with prospective vendors is called a bidding conference, or a prebid conference. Answer A is incorrect because kickoff meetings involve all stakeholders, and are associated with the project, not solicitation. Answer B is incorrect because bidder conferences, as long as all bidders are on equal footing, are perfectly legal and good practice. Answer D is incorrect but tempting because it is also a tool and technique of solicitation planning.

70. **Answer B** is correct. PMBOK states that considering potential vendors during the procurement planning may help exercise influence over the contract. Answer A is incorrect because the qualified seller list is an input to solicitation. Answer C is incorrect but tempting because vendors are considered during solicitation planning and solicitation. Answer D may be true, but it is not the best answer.

71. **Answer B** is the correct answer. The calculation is

    Latest Finish (55)–Earliest Finish (30)=Slack (25)

    Therefore, Answers A, C, and D are incorrect.

72. **Answer D** is the correct answer. None of these events has a negative slack. The calculations are

    Event 1 Latest Finish (55)–Earliest Finish (30)=Slack (25)

    Event 2 Latest Finish (25)–Earliest Finish (16)=Slack (9)

    Event 3 Latest Finish (92)–Earliest Finish (40)=Slack (52)

    Event 4 Latest Finish (96)–Earliest Finish (21)=Slack (75)

    Therefore, Answers A, B, and C are incorrect.

73. **Answer B** is the correct answer. The calculation is

    Event 1 Latest Finish (55)–Earliest Finish (30)=Slack (25)

    Event 2 Latest Finish (25)–Earliest Finish (16)=Slack (9)

    Event 3 Latest Finish (92)–Earliest Finish (40)=Slack (52)

    Event 4 Latest Finish (96)–Earliest Finish (21)=Slack (75)

    Total Slack (161)=Slack 1 (25)+Slack 2 (9)+Slack 3 (52)+Slack 4 (75)

    Therefore, Answers A, C, and D are incorrect.

74. **Answer A** is the correct answer. In addition to identifying the paths that have potential slippage and the critical path for the project, the project manager needs to look for paths that have negative slack. Answer B is incorrect because zero slack is not necessarily bad unless you anticipate some events that were not identified in the estimates and could cause delays. Answer C is incorrect because a positive slack is advantageous to the project manager as a contingency, who uses it for unidentified issues that arise. Answer D is incorrect because there is no Project Management concept that would have a delayed slack effect for the project.

75. **Answer C** is the correct answer. Answer A is incorrect because paths with zero or negative values (not positive slack) are referred to as *critical paths*. Answer B is incorrect because it is an incorrect term for this question. Answer D is incorrect because a schedule variance is the difference between the actual schedule and the budgeted schedule.

76. **Answer A** is the correct answer. Earliest start and finish times are calculated by working through the network diagram from the first task to the last task. Answer B is incorrect because the backward pass calculation is formulated by working from the end of the project to the beginning of it. Answer C is incorrect because progressive elaborations are not associated with forward or backward pass calculations. Answer D is incorrect; however, it might sound correct because of questions on the test that use common everyday words to simplify complex concepts.

77. **Answer A** is the correct answer. The calculation is

    Latest Start (208)=Latest Finish (245)–Duration (37)

    Therefore, Answers B, C, and D are incorrect.

78. **Answer D** is the best answer. Laddering is done to show how a subject matter expert can complete one task and then go forward to complete the same task as another subject matter expert begins the second task that had a dependency upon the first task (for example, trimming and then painting rooms in a house). Answer A is incorrect because Activity on Arrow is another type of formatting that uses arrows to show relationships between tasks. Answer B is incorrect because looping in a network diagram is not possible because the task would perpetually repeat itself without being completed. Answer C is correct because serial processing is the sequential completion of tasks throughout a network diagram; however, it is not the best response because the diagram has multiple sequences going on simultaneously.

79. **Answer B** is the correct answer. This network diagram is formatted in activity in box formatting. Answer A is incorrect because AOA is activity on arrow, which is a different type of formatting. Answer C is incorrect because a work breakdown structure is not a network logic type of formatting. Answer D is incorrect because a Responsibility Assignment Matrix (RAM) is a reporting deliverable that is not associated with type of network diagram.

80. **Answer C** is the correct answer. The calculation is

    T (Duration Estimate)=Estimate (Optimistic)+4 (Most Likely)+ Estimate (Pessimistic)"6

    Therefore, (7+4[10]+22)"6= 11.5 rounded to 12

    Therefore Answers A, B, and D are incorrect.

Project Execution

Exam Prep Questions

1. Because the project execution phase requires the most time and resources of any phase of a project, there is a heavy emphasis on these processes in regard to the management of a project. The Project Management executing processes include all of the following except

   ❏ A. Source selection and team development
   ❏ B. Project plan execution and solicitation
   ❏ C. Quality assurance and contract administration
   ❏ D. Information distribution and staff acquisition

2. Margie is working on a project for a new military facility on the East Coast but she does not have a firm understanding of the milestones and timelines for the project. According to the PMBOK, an approved, formal document that is used to manage the execution of a project is known as

   ❏ A. A project plan
   ❏ B. A project notebook
   ❏ C. A scope document
   ❏ D. An organizational policy

3. Government regulations, organizational policies, and company guidelines are constraints that a project manager must be aware of whenever she is executing a project plan. Because these limitations can affect the options for the project and the responses to situations, some risk migration might be necessary. Inputs to the project plan execution to migrate these risks include

   ❏ A. Budgets
   ❏ B. Preventative actions
   ❏ C. Training plans
   ❏ D. Skills analysis reports

4. Marilyn is a senior project manager who is working on a project that has a duration of three years and is developed in three phases. During the project, she uses some project execution tools and techniques while intertwining skills that are routinely used for various types of management, such as leadership and communication. These execution tools and techniques are types of skills that are commonly referred to as

Quick Answer: **135**
Detailed Answer: **136**

- ❏ A. Supervisory skills
- ❏ B. Organizational skills
- ❏ C. General management skills
- ❏ D. Expert power skills

5. Greg realizes that he must do a lot of communicating in order for his project for the new elementary school system to be successful and to keep everyone informed as the project proceeds. The interactive processes that occur during the evolution of a project are known as

Quick Answer: **135**
Detailed Answer: **136**

- ❏ A. PMIS
- ❏ B. WBS
- ❏ C. EV
- ❏ D. BAC

6. Proactive planning will directly affect the execution of a project in numerous ways. Therefore, many project managers appreciate the opportunity to be involved with a project from the initiation of the project. One of the inputs to the project plan execution includes anything that is done to bring the project back in-line. This input completes the feedback loop and is known as a

Quick Answer: **135**
Detailed Answer: **136**

- ❏ A. Change control
- ❏ B. Communication plan
- ❏ C. Status report
- ❏ D. Corrective action

7. John is hard at work on a $5 million telecommunications project that utilizes interactive voice response units to automate several processes that are currently being done by humans. His extensive project plan can be described as all of the following except

Quick Answer: **135**
Detailed Answer: **137**

- ❏ A. A method to identify milestones
- ❏ B. A document or collection of documents that change over time
- ❏ C. Formal and approved
- ❏ D. Only used by the project manager to execute the project

8. Ken is brought in as a consultant to work on a project execution that is having scope problems and unrealistic stakeholder expectations. Which of the following statements is not true about the project execution?

- ❑   A.   The project performance will be measured against the project plan.
- ❑   B.   The majority of the budget is spent.
- ❑   C.   Decisions on when and with whom to communicate are made.
- ❑   D.   The product of the project is actually produced.

9. Sadie is leading a market research project that is being conducted through an educational grant from an international think tank. Her project's purpose is to define the buying habits of the typical consumer of various demographics and geographic locations. Therefore, she wants to use different types of root cause analysis techniques that may include all of the following except

- ❑   A.   Excel spreadsheets
- ❑   B.   Process flow diagrams
- ❑   C.   Fishbone
- ❑   D.   Ishikawa

10. You have been faced with corporate bureaucracy ever since you started your project earlier this year. Guidelines and rules of a company or organization can cause bottlenecks for timelines and require escalation to the appropriate levels of an organization. It is your responsibility as the project manager to be aware of which project execution tools and techniques can positively impact your project. Which of the following is a project execution tool that you can use?

- ❑   A.   Corporate hierarchies
- ❑   B.   Organizational procedures
- ❑   C.   Product skill and knowledge
- ❑   D.   Project review board

11. A project plan is a constant source of information for the project manager and is used for systems integration. This integration plays a vital part in the performance attributes of a project. Which of the following statements does not describe an objective of systems integration?

- ❑   A.   Performance
- ❑   B.   Effectiveness
- ❑   C.   Cost
- ❑   D.   Autonomy

. . . .

Quick Answer: **135**
Detailed Answer: **137**

12. The project plan must contain certain elements that are vital to the project. These include all of the following except
   - ❑ A. Potential problems and contractual aspects
   - ❑ B. Personnel information and schedules
   - ❑ C. Evaluation methods and general approach
   - ❑ D. Schedules and forward pass calculations

Quick Answer: **135**
Detailed Answer: **137**

13. Linear responsibility charts can be used for all of the following except
   - ❑ A. Keeping track of who must approve what items
   - ❑ B. Critical interfaces
   - ❑ C. Project timelines
   - ❑ D. Determining who is responsible for what task

Quick Answer: **135**
Detailed Answer: **138**

14. This project execution tool is usually triggered by a written or verbal approval to begin the activities and encourages control of the work processes. It is known as the
   - ❑ A. Work authorization system
   - ❑ B. Change control system
   - ❑ C. Communication plan
   - ❑ D. Project Management information system

Quick Answer: **135**
Detailed Answer: **138**

15. You feel that you need to micromanage certain parts of the project, but you do not want to alienate your team. How often should a project plan be monitored?
   - ❑ A. Weekly
   - ❑ B. Monthly
   - ❑ C. At the end of the project
   - ❑ D. Continuously

Quick Answer: **135**
Detailed Answer: **138**

16. You have a laundry list of tasks and you are overwhelmed by the ambiguous details due to the large number of deliverables that are required in the next two weeks. Following up to make sure that everything is done correctly and fulfills the requirements of the project is known as
   - ❑ A. Quality measurement
   - ❑ B. Quality assurance
   - ❑ C. Variance monitoring
   - ❑ D. Triple constraints

17. Events such as project schedule alterations and scope creep can impact the work results and activities related to the project and therefore require a response from the Project Management team. This response might require an approval for implementation. _____ generally has a direct impact upon the work results.

Quick Answer: **135**
Detailed Answer: **138**

- ❑ A. A change request
- ❑ B. A budget decrease
- ❑ C. An execution output
- ❑ D. A GNP increase

18. There are many tools and techniques that are used throughout a project that are affiliated with inputs and outputs of various processes. Some of these aspects include quality planning and quality control. The costs of nonconformance and its impact on quality can be postponed until the end of the project if

Quick Answer: **135**
Detailed Answer: **138**

- ❑ A. The team says
- ❑ B. You have a risk mitigation plan
- ❑ C. The budget has anticipated that the costs of nonconformance increases over time
- ❑ D. Quality planning involves auditing the project

19. Marcie has accepted a consulting assignment with a Fortune 500 publishing company for the development of a line of children's books, and she wants a strong quality policy. Because she is responsible for quality assurance during the project execution, she wants to learn more about the subject. What is the difference between quality planning and quality assurance?

Quick Answer: **135**
Detailed Answer: **138**

- ❑ A. None. Prior to ISO 9000, they were considered the same thing.
- ❑ B. Quality planning uses the tools and techniques of cost-benefit analysis, benchmarking, flowcharting, and design of experiments to determine how quality should be assessed. Quality assurance does not use these.
- ❑ C. Quality assurance is the totality of characteristics of an entity that bear on its capability to satisfy stated or implied needs. Quality planning is planning those characteristics.
- ❑ D. Quality planning focuses on identifying which quality standards to use, whereas quality assurance focuses on planned and systematic activities to ensure the standards.

20. Some of the Project Management processes have multiple inputs and outputs. The only output to quality assurance is

Quick Answer: **135**
Detailed Answer: **139**

❏ A. A performance variance
❏ B. A change control document
❏ C. Re-baselining the project plan
❏ D. Quality improvements

21. Team development involves the growth of competencies to increase the performance of the project. This can include individuals, stakeholders, or groups that have a vested interest in the project. Inputs into team development include all of the following except

Quick Answer: **135**
Detailed Answer: **139**

❏ A. Training
❏ B. External feedback
❏ C. Project staff
❏ D. Performance reports

22. The conflict that a team member feels whenever he has dual reporting responsibilities between a functional manager and the project manager is known as

Quick Answer: **135**
Detailed Answer: **139**

❏ A. A critical success factor
❏ B. Ambiguous jurisdiction
❏ C. Conflict resolution
❏ D. Portfolio project management

23. Quality assurance tools and techniques include all of the following except

Quick Answer: **135**
Detailed Answer: **139**

❏ A. Benchmarking
❏ B. Design or prototype
❏ C. Cost and benefit analysis
❏ D. Flowcharting

24. Susan is constantly plagued by frustrations in her projects. What is the best project team environment to work in?

Quick Answer: **135**
Detailed Answer: **139**

❏ A. A team in the same room that reports directly and only to the project manager
❏ B. A team that meets frequently face to face, but has other functional duties
❏ C. A loosely connected group of functional experts who help direct the project
❏ D. A team that resides offsite

25. The knowledge that the team and stakeholders gain by actually performing the project is known as

Quick Answer: **135**
Detailed Answer: **139**

   ❑ A. Team development
   ❑ B. Best practices
   ❑ C. Lessons learned
   ❑ D. Cumulative intellectual capacity

26. Rob and Larry are on the same project team and do not get along very well due to personality conflicts. Team development is important to the success of a project because

Quick Answer: **135**
Detailed Answer: **140**

   ❑ A. It forces people to get along with each other.
   ❑ B. It encourages people to participate with the other team members.
   ❑ C. It can lead to good friendships outside of work.
   ❑ D. It occurs throughout the entire project.

27. Providing positive reinforcement to your team can enhance its performance and lead to positive outcomes for the project. Traditional reward systems do not

Quick Answer: **135**
Detailed Answer: **140**

   ❑ A. Work in a functional organization
   ❑ B. Generally fulfill the requirements for a project
   ❑ C. Work in an autocratic management environment
   ❑ D. Encourage team member loyalty

28. Sam realizes that the collaborative environment is the most productive for his team. Which of the following is a good team-building technique?

Quick Answer: **135**
Detailed Answer: **140**

   ❑ A. Involving the team in the planning process
   ❑ B. Having a barbeque
   ❑ C. Doing a lessons-learned session
   ❑ D. Letting individual team members operate independently

29. Project managers generally have all of the responsibility and none of the authority to push their projects to completion. Therefore, they must rely upon _____ within a functional organization to get the support of the team and other stakeholders.

Quick Answer: **135**
Detailed Answer: **140**

   ❑ A. Expert power
   ❑ B. Coercive power
   ❑ C. Reward power
   ❑ D. Referent power

. . . .

30. You are the single point of contact (SPOC) for your projects and are frequently overwhelmed by the quantity of information and materials that you are required to disseminate to the team. What is the key purpose of distributing project information?

Quick Answer: **135**
Detailed Answer: **141**

- ❏   A.   To create an archive of project information that can be used by other projects
- ❏   B.   To inform stakeholders in a timely manner of work results
- ❏   C.   To make sure the project continues to have sponsorship
- ❏   D.   To resolve conflicts between project members

31. Valerie has begun her work as a contract services project manager at a military facility. She is well prepared to handle a multitude of different volatile circumstances to provide a positive outcome. She also knows when to become a hard-nosed manager. The utilization of force by a manager is known as

Quick Answer: **135**
Detailed Answer: **141**

- ❏   A.   Legitimate power
- ❏   B.   Coercive power
- ❏   C.   Reward power
- ❏   D.   Referent power

32. The close proximity that a team has to each other can have a positive impact on communication and productivity. This is an example of

Quick Answer: **135**
Detailed Answer: **141**

- ❏   A.   Synergy
- ❏   B.   Brainstorming
- ❏   C.   Collocation
- ❏   D.   Team building

33. Team development covers many facets of a project for Marge at XYZ Corporation. The outputs to team development are all of the following except

Quick Answer: **135**
Detailed Answer: **141**

- ❏   A.   An input to quality assurance
- ❏   B.   An input to performance appraisals
- ❏   C.   Increased efficiency
- ❏   D.   Lower defect rate

34. Formal management processes that utilize guidelines that promote or reinforce desired behavior are known as

Quick Answer: **135**
Detailed Answer: **141**

- ❏   A.   360-degree feedback forums
- ❏   B.   Reward and recognition systems
- ❏   C.   Peer evaluations
- ❏   D.   Team celebrations

35. Approaching a problem straight-on in order to discuss it for a win-win resolution is Michelle's approach to leading projects and working with her subordinates. This from-the-hip approach to problem solving has been very successful in her management development and interactions as she rises within the organization. This conflict resolution technique is commonly referred to as

   ❏ A. Buy-in
   ❏ B. Negotiation
   ❏ C. Fact finding
   ❏ D. Confrontation

36. DeVonne is familiar with temporary solutions to conflicts and not coming to a final resolution. This is inherent within the industry that she works in and is frequently called "putting it in the parking lot" or "putting it on the back burner." This _____ technique is not recommended for a long-term solution.

   ❏ A. Contingency
   ❏ B. Smoothing
   ❏ C. Procrastination ✗
   ❏ D. Project execution ✗

37. Maslow's Hierarchy is frequently discussed in college classes throughout the world and tends to still be relevant in today's business settings. What is it?

   ❏ A. A pyramid of needs
   ❏ B. The hierarchy order of the British royal family
   ❏ C. Self-actualization
   ❏ D. A philosophy that is similar to Deming's work

38. Fredrick Herzberg postulated a theory that people are motivated by factors that deal with the work and the satisfaction that people get by performing the actual functions of their jobs. This form of job satisfaction can be valuable to a project manager as she determines how to motivate team members and also maximize their efficiency. What did Herzberg call this theory?

   ❏ A. X Theory
   ❏ B. Hygiene Theory
   ❏ C. Y Theory
   ❏ D. Hawthorne Effect

39. After physical needs and security, what is the third-level need of Maslow's Hierarchy?

Quick Answer: **135**
Detailed Answer: **142**

❑   A.   Social needs

❑   B.   Self-esteem

❑   C.   Self-actualization

❑   D.   Safety

40. Susan works as the director of the Project Management Office (PMO) at an electrical supply company and she puts a premium on a good employee medical policy for her family. Benefits, pay, and work conditions are examples from Herzberg's Hygiene Factors Theory. The job satisfaction and challenge that Susan gets from her job by actually performing her work is known as

Quick Answer: **135**
Detailed Answer: **142**

❑   A.   A monetary expectancy

❑   B.   An intrinsic reward

❑   C.   A motivator

❑   D.   A satisfaction trigger

41. Charles has an autocratic type of management style that can sometimes offend subordinates if they do not understand his expectations. Many times, he uses formal power as a win-lose conflict resolution technique whenever his department does not want to participate in company initiatives. This technique is known as

Quick Answer: **135**
Detailed Answer: **142**

❑   A.   Confronting

❑   B.   Forcing

❑   C.   Coercion

❑   D.   Satisfaction trigger

42. Ted is up to his neck in paperwork for the new project that he just inherited from a previous employee of the company. He has just received requests for capital equipment and he decides that the event will be on the critical path for his project. The procurement process can be time consuming and laborious when you have to coordinate with all the purchase order–related paperwork and the individuals that process the documents. One step of the procurement process is known as solicitation. What is solicitation used for?

Quick Answer: **135**
Detailed Answer: **143**

❑   A.   Gathering requirements for a product purchase

❑   B.   Determining what vendors to buy from

❑   C.   Letting vendors know you have a need

❑   D.   Negotiating pricing

43. Joe gets up every day to work at a local office supply company and has done the same job for over 25 years. Because he only has 5 years to go before his retirement, he tends to lack enthusiasm about his career or about progressing within the company. He is motivated exclusively by the fact that he has bills to pay and anticipates that he will be paid for the work that he performs on a daily basis. Theorists would describe Joe's performance is most closely aligned with

- ❏ A. Expectancy Theory
- ❏ B. Contingency Theory
- ❏ C. Glass Ceiling Theory
- ❏ D. Achievement Theory

44. As a project manager, you will encounter numerous problems with resources that are overworked and do not seem to have enough time to help you with any projects. Sometimes these resources can become frustrated and use a passive-aggressive approach to new requests. Job attributes that help prevent job dissatisfaction are known as

- ❏ A. Motivators
- ❏ B. Expectations
- ❏ C. Social needs
- ❏ D. Hygiene factors

45. Juanita realizes that she must get participation in order to gain commitment on her project. Consequently, common sense mandates that she utilize different management styles during the project life cycle in order to meet the project's objectives and timelines. She understands that one management and team development style emphasizes a participatory environment and puts value on getting the team's involvement while soliciting feedback to enhance the performance of the team. This management style and philosophy are most closely related to what team development theory?

- ❏ A. Kerzner's Affiliation Theory
- ❏ B. McGregor's Y Theory
- ❏ C. Herzberg's Motivation-Hygiene Theory
- ❏ D. Meredith and Mantel's Expectancy Theory

Quick Check

Quick Answer: **135**
Detailed Answer: **143**

46. Modern Tool, Inc. is developing a new Project Management office based upon a five-year government contract that it just signed with the military. Because the team members for this new project are scattered around the world, keeping everyone informed will be a challenge for Ronak, the newly appointed international director of the office. The communication system that will develop during this project to assimilate information horizontally and vertically throughout the organization is known as the

❏ A. Corporate hierarchy

❏ B. Sender/receiver system

❏ C. Feedback loop

❏ D. Project Management Information System (PMIS)

Quick Answer: **135**
Detailed Answer: **144**

47. When looking at how much money will be spent on his nuclear reactor decommission project, Michael has allocated $200,000 to the initiation phase; $2,000,000 to the planning phase; $2,000,000 to the execution phase; and $300,000 to the closing phase. If you were analyzing Michael's budget, what would you say?

❏ A. The budget sounds good, but you need to beware of scope creep and how it can impact the budget.

❏ B. He needs to allocate monies for the control phase of the project.

❏ C. He does not have enough money for a project this big.

❏ D. Regardless of how much money he spends, the execution phase will use the most money.

Quick Answer: **135**
Detailed Answer: **144**

48. Your company has decided that it wants to install a new data center. You have contacted various contactors and facilities personnel to conduct studies about how much the data center expansion will cost. A contract between buyer and seller is created at what point in the procurement process?

❏ A. During procurement planning, based on the policies and procedures of the company

❏ B. During solicitation, when a proposal from a vendor is received

❏ C. During contract administration, when the vendor is actually producing the work requested

❏ D. During source selection, based on evaluation criteria, procurement policies, and supplier history

49. Paula is the accountant for Honorable Corporation and is responsible for the financial aspects of the community rehab project that began last year. The project is in the execution phase. She has recently noticed there is a budget variance that is due to the vice president going to Las Vegas for the weekend and charging it against the rehab project. What should she do?

   ❑ A. Bring it up at the next team meeting.
   ❑ B. Confront the vice president.
   ❑ C. Immediately advise the project manager.
   ❑ D. Sell her story to the local newspaper.

50. The mutual consent of a legally binding agreement is frequently part of the procurement process. This allows the review and weighing of various attributes while soliciting bids for various products and services. What is the purpose of contract administration?

   ❑ A. To manage the interfaces among various providers
   ❑ B. To ensure the seller's performance meets the contractual requirements
   ❑ C. To avoid change requests
   ❑ D. To provide payment to the vendor

51. In the reconstruction of New York City's World Trade Center area, there will be numerous opportunities for effective Project Management to enhance a productive work environment. This effective management style will enable the team to achieve the various milestones and meet deadlines by utilizing strong change control management techniques. As an output of the various control processes, anything that is done to bring expected future project performance back in-line with the project plan is known as a

   ❑ A. Change request
   ❑ B. Stratified opportunity
   ❑ C. Preventive action
   ❑ D. Corrective action

52. Carlos has accepted a recent highway construction project that has a tight 30-day time frame in order to get a major intersection re-engineered and construction completed. Therefore, people will need to be trained on language lessons and some new modern construction techniques that will increase their efficiency. This training, combined with additional human resources, will also increase productivity as the crews rotate through 24-hour shifts. From a Project Management standpoint, this employee training would be considered a

- ❑ A. Capital expense
- ❑ B. Work result
- ❑ C. Scope expansion
- ❑ D. Cost center debit

53. A project notebook is an excellent resource to provide a comprehensive overview of the project and provide archive materials for the team to reference as it progresses along the timeline. The notebook also provides an excellent repository for the project communications. Information distribution for the project has all of the following outputs except

- ❑ A. Change requests
- ❑ B. Status reports, deliverables, and formal documents
- ❑ C. Information and documents
- ❑ D. Presentations in formal and informal settings

54. As Rita develops an action plan for her project, she begins to itemize the keys that will lead to her future success. Because she is a PMP and is very familiar with PMI methodologies, she realizes that quality planning tools and techniques can also be used for quality assurance on her project. Therefore, she would like to try the use of flowcharting, such as Ishikawa diagrams or fishbone diagrams, for her new project. How are these tools used in relation to quality assurance?

- ❑ A. They show how various factors might be linked to potential problems.
- ❑ B. They are used in collaboration with a work breakdown structure (WBS).
- ❑ C. They determine kill points for a project.
- ❑ D. They utilize network logic to provide a forward pass calculation.

55. As the world evolves into a more energy-conscious environment, engineers will need to adapt to new constraints in quality to fulfill their end users' requirements. When electronic component designers want to determine what combination of features will provide reliability and functionality, they might use a statistical method that helps identify which factors will influence specific variables. This utilization of "what if" scenarios can be described as a

- ❑ A. Procurement plan
- ❑ B. Cost of quality
- ❑ C. Design of experiments
- ❑ D. System flowchart

Quick Answer: **135**
Detailed Answer: **145**

56. Someone once said, "Projects would run incredibly well if people did not get in the way," as a statement to illustrate how personal agendas and conflicts can complicate a project and impact the timeline. Team development on a project becomes more challenging when the functional and project managers are both requesting a subject matter expert's (SME's) time and expertise on a project. This tends to give the SME a feeling of conflict that can be categorized as

- ❑ A. Ambiguous jurisdiction
- ❑ B. Internal conflict
- ❑ C. Referent power
- ❑ D. Autonomy

Quick Answer: **135**
Detailed Answer: **145**

57. Jeff wants to use collocation of team members to enhance the performance of the team and focus on the end results of the project. A common method of collocating a team is to

- ❑ A. Use frequent video conferencing.
- ❑ B. Hold weekly status meetings.
- ❑ C. Develop a reward and recognition system.
- ❑ D. Set up a war room.

Quick Answer: **135**
Detailed Answer: **146**

Quick Check

58. For the communications to over 100 stakeholders to be effective and informative, Darryl decides to draft a communication management plan for the project, have the team review it, and then get signoff for the implementation. All of the team is responsive to the changes that were suggested by the other stakeholders, and the final signoff comes within days after the kickoff meeting. A communication management plan provides all of the following details except

Quick Answer: **135**
Detailed Answer: **146**

- ❏ A. Methods to gather and store information
- ❏ B. Production schedules for communications
- ❏ C. To whom and by what methods that information will flow
- ❏ D. Lessons learned by the team

59. Suzanne realizes that she must be an excellent communicator in order to successfully migrate from a systems analyst position to a Project Management role in her career path. Communications planning is frequently allied with organizational planning because

Quick Answer: **135**
Detailed Answer: **146**

- ❏ A. They both use the same channels.
- ❏ B. The project's managerial configuration will impact the project's communication necessities.
- ❏ C. Both planning activities involve executive stakeholders and utilize similar deliverables.
- ❏ D. Organizational planning is an output of the communication planning process.

60. Takashi is going through the source selection process for a new library indexing system project that is in the initiation phase. He uses the following chart to track the vendors and selection criteria for the various vendors:

Quick Answer: **135**
Detailed Answer: **146**

	Vendor 1	Vendor 2	Vendor 3
Criteria A	No	No	Yes
Criteria B	Yes	Yes	No
Criteria C	No	Yes	No

Based upon feedback from the team, Takashi develops a weighted selection process and the following formula to assign weights to the various criteria:

$.9a + .5b + .3c$ = Weighted average

Based upon these three criteria, which vendor should Takashi select?

- ❏ A. Vendor 1
- ❏ B. Vendor 2
- ❏ C. Vendor 3
- ❏ D. Look at another vendor

Quick Check Answer Key

1. D	**28.** A	**55.** C
2. A	**29.** D	**56.** A
3. B	**30.** B	**57.** D
4. C	**31.** B	**58.** D
5. A	**32.** C	**59.** B
6. D	**33.** A	**60.** C
7. D	**34.** B	
8. C	**35.** D	
9. A	**36.** B	
10. B	**37.** A	
11. D	**38.** B	
12. D	**39.** A	
13. C	**40.** C	
14. A	**41.** B	
15. D	**42.** C	
16. B	**43.** A	
17. A	**44.** D	
18. C	**45.** B	
19. D	**46.** D	
20. D	**47.** D	
21. A	**48.** D	
22. B	**49.** C	
23. B	**50.** B	
24. A	**51.** D	
25. C	**52.** B	
26. B	**53.** A	
27. B	**54.** A	

Answers and Explanations

1. **Answer D** is correct because staff acquisition is not part of the Project Management executing processes. Staff acquisition is one of the Project Management planning facilitating processes. Answers A, B, and C are incorrect because all of these processes are included in the Project Management executing processes.

2. **Answer A** is correct. Answer B is incorrect because the project notebook is a repository for the documents associated with the project and notes used to execute the project. Answer C is incorrect because the scope document is not used to execute the project and it is developed before the executing phase of the project. Answer D is incorrect because a company's organizational policy is not used to execute the project.

3. **Answer B** is correct. Answer A is incorrect because budgets are not inputs into the project plan; however, they should be considered during the planning phase of a project. Answers C and D are incorrect because training plans and skills analysis are not inputs into the project plan execution process.

4. **Answer C** is correct because general management skills are one of the six tools and techniques that are utilized during the execution phase of a project. Answers A, B, and D are incorrect because they are not execution tools and techniques for a project.

5. **Answer A** is correct. A Project Management Information System (PMIS) is comprised of techniques and tools that are utilized to gather, integrate, and distribute the outputs of the project processes. Answer B is incorrect because a work breakdown structure (WBS) is used for the decomposition of tasks into work packets and not the distribution of outputs. Answer C is incorrect because earned value management (EVM) is a technique that is used to measure and report project performance throughout the entire project life cycle and is an input into the PMIS distribution process. Answer D is incorrect because the budget at completion (BAC) is a financial tool that is also an input into the information system.

6. **Answer D** is the best answer. Answer A is incorrect—although a change control management system can be used to manage a project and get it back in-line, it is not an input into the project execution processes. Answer B is incorrect because the communication plan is a tool that is the output of the planning phase of a project. Answer C is incorrect because the status reports are communication deliverables and do not directly affect the ability to bring the project back in-line. The status report advises the team about the steps to bring the project in-line and updates the stakeholders about the progress, action items, and timeline.

7. **Answer D** is correct. Project plans are used by the entire project team and help to communicate the tasks needed during the project time frame. Project plans are distributed to the project staff according to the communication plan. Consequently, a project plan is formal and approved. Answers A, B, and C are true statements and therefore incorrect answers.

8. **Answer C** is correct. Although some ad hoc communications and information requests are handled during the project execution, decisions on when, how, and with whom to communicate are defined in the planning phase of a communication plan. Answers A, B, and D are true statements and therefore incorrect answers.

9. **Answer A** is correct. Flowcharts, fishbone, and Ishikawa diagrams are all examples of root cause analysis techniques that might be effective when trying to determine why an event occurred and how it can be mitigated in the future. Because all of these techniques are applicable to this situation, Answer A is correct because Microsoft Excel spreadsheets would not likely be used as a root cause analysis tool but the other answers could be used for the analysis. Answers B, C, and D are correct answers and therefore incorrect responses to this question.

10. **Answer B** is the best answer. Organizational procedures and product skill/knowledge are the only two project execution tools and techniques that are listed. Therefore, Answers A and D are incorrect. Answer C is incorrect because product skill and knowledge involves how well you know your product and would not likely have an impact upon your ability to move through an organization quicker. Organizational procedures is the correct answer because a project manager should be aware and anticipate responses to organizational procedures because they are seen as constraints for the project and should be identified earlier in the project.

11. **Answer D** is correct. Autonomy is not one of the objectives of systems integration. Consequently, Answers A, B, and C are correct and therefore incorrect for this question. Answer A is incorrect because performance is what the system does. Answer B is incorrect because this objective is linked with the achievement of the desired performance in an optimal manner.

12. **Answer D** is correct. Forward pass calculations are generally not required parts of the project plan; however, they are valuable to the project manager as he develops the estimates for various tasks. Answers A, B, and C are elements that should be part of the project plan. A good project plan is more than just a Gantt chart and Microsoft spreadsheet.

13. **Answer C** is correct because project timelines are not associated with linear responsibility charts (also known as a responsibility assignment matrix). Answers A, B, and D are correct because they can be used for these purposes. Therefore, they are incorrect answers to this question.

14. **Answer A** is correct. The work authorization system (WAS) is the mechanism that triggers the work to be done and is a catalyst for pushing the project forward. Answers B, C, and D are incorrect because they are not triggers for the project processes to go forward.

15. **Answer D** is correct. Answers A and B are incorrect because, although some projects might have tasks that can be monitored monthly or weekly and depend on the project itself, the *best* answer per the PMBOK is *continuously*, so that a project manager can ensure budget adherence and timeliness of the project. Answer C is incorrect because a project plan is a "living" document and as such is modified often to reflect change within the project.

16. **Answer B** is correct. Answer A is incorrect because quality measurement is a method of monitoring quality without the follow-through that is associated with quality assurance. Answer C is incorrect because the monitoring of variances is not a specific answer that provides actions to fulfill the requirements. Answer D is incorrect because the triple constraints (scope, time, and budget) are attributes that are associated with the project and are not actions involved with making sure that everything is done.

17. **Answer A** is correct. Answer B is incorrect because a budget decrease would have to go through the change request process to impact the project. Otherwise, it has an indirect impact upon the work results. Answers C and D are incorrect because any execution output or GNP increase would not have a direct impact upon the project. They might have an indirect impact and require a change request if they can impact the project in some way.

18. **Answer C** is the best answer. The costs of nonconformance to quality standards tends to increase over time; therefore, the project manager should adhere to the quality conformance requirements of the project from the onset. Answer A is incorrect because the team should not make the final decision without determining the long-term implications while focusing on quality. Answer B is incorrect because a risk mitigation plan would not give you the flexibility to postpone nonconformance. Answer D is incorrect because auditing the project is a quality control technique for the project.

19. **Answer D** is correct. Answer A is a true statement, but it isn't the best answer and is therefore incorrect. Answer B is incorrect because both quality planning and quality assurance use the same tools and techniques. Answer C is the definition of *quality*, not quality planning or quality assurance, and is therefore incorrect for this question.

20. **Answer D** is the correct answer. Quality improvement involves any actions taken to improve the quality of the project in response to quality deficiencies or irregularities. Answer A is incorrect because a variance in performance is not an output to the Project Management processes. Answer B is incorrect because a change control document is affiliated with the change control management system and is an output of that tool. Answer C is incorrect because re–baselining the project plan would not be tied with quality assurance except that the project manager must calculate the time requirements that are needed for quality planning and assurance.

21. **Answer A** is the correct answer. Training is a tool and technique of team development, not an input to team development. Answers B, C, and D are all inputs to team development along with the project plan with the staffing management plan.

22. **Answer B** is the correct answer. The conflict that a team member feels when he reports to multiple people can be frustrating because he might have confusion as to whom he should provide support. Answer A is correct; however, it is not the best answer for this question. Answer C is incorrect because conflict resolution is the process that a person would go through in order to resolve this confusion about the dual reporting aspect of the project. Answer D is incorrect because portfolio Project Management is involved with the financial aspects of a project and is not associated with team member conflict.

23. **Answer B** is correct. Answers A, C, and D are Project Management quality assurance tools and techniques that are used during the execution phase of a project. Therefore, they are incorrect answers to this question.

24. **Answer A** is correct. Co-location and a projectized environment is the best situation for a project team. Although Answer B can work effectively, team members with other functional duties will have conflicts of priorities. Therefore, Answer B is incorrect. Answer C is the definition of subject matter experts; therefore, it is incorrect. Answer D is tricky because offsite team building is often encouraged in team literature. However, it's not the *best* answer and is therefore incorrect.

25. **Answer C** is correct. Lessons learned are important outputs of projects and can be used for historical data and to provide assistance for other projects. Answer A is incorrect because team building involves the activities that develop camaraderie in order to enhance team performance. Answer B is incorrect because best practices are those successful activities that a team wants to repeat in current or future projects. Answer D is incorrect because it is a fictitious term that is not related to Project Management.

26. **Answer B** is the best answer. Team development is important because it encourages people to participate well with others. Team development is a perpetual activity that an effective project manager must perform in order to develop cohesiveness within the team. Answer A is incorrect because team development does not force people to get along with each other, but it provides opportunities for team members to interact and potentially develop good working relationships. Answer C is incorrect because the purpose of team development is work related, although these relationships can lead to friendships outside of work. Answer D is incorrect because team development does not always extend over the duration of the project.

27. **Answer B** is the best answer. Reward systems do not generally work for a project because a project manager might not report to her functional manager and receive the positive rewards that are usually associated with employment. Answer A is incorrect because traditional reward systems do not generally work due to the reporting structure that is inherent within a functional organization. Answer C is incorrect because an autocratic work environment does not typically work well with projects and, frequently, the reward system is the only positive reinforcement that a team member receives from an autocratic type of manager. Answer D is correct; however, it is not the best answer to this question.

28. **Answer A** is correct. Involving the team in the planning of the project helps all members develop a better understanding of the project and helps to provide buy-in. Having a barbeque can be a team-building technique, but it isn't the *best* one. Therefore, Answer B is incorrect. Lessons-learned sessions are typically done at the end of phases or the end of a project. These can become team-building events by airing difficulties, but they are intended to correct project direction, not to build the team. Therefore, Answer C is incorrect. Allowing individuals to operate independently is a good management technique in general; however, without supervision or project control, it could actually cause team problems. Therefore, Answer D is incorrect.

29. **Answer D** is correct. "Borrowed" legitimate power that is transferred from a formal leader to a project manager is one source of influence for a project manager as he moves the project forward. Answer A is incorrect because expert power is based upon a person's knowledge or expertise. Answer B is incorrect because coercive power is based upon intimidation or use of force to push one's issue or decision. Answer C is incorrect because reward power is based upon the ability to provide or withhold rewards to or from a participant. Project managers are generally not involved with the distribution of rewards within an organization, although it is a good idea to provide some type of reward or reinforcement to a team, especially upon successful completion of a project.

30. **Answer B** is correct. Project information is important so that stakeholders and sponsors understand how well a project is meeting its goals. For sponsors, a project behind schedule might call for some type of intervention. Answer A is incorrect because, although it is important to create a project archive, it is not the purpose of distributing the information. Answer C is incorrect because project sponsorship should be resolved prior to project initiation. Occasionally, a project is canceled because it no longer meets the needs of the sponsors or company, but distributing the project information is not intended to keep sponsorship of the project. Answer D is incorrect because conflicts need to be managed by the project manager and resolved apart from reporting on the project.

31. **Answer B** is the correct answer. Coercive power is based upon the ability to use force or intimidation to push one's issues or decisions. Answer A is incorrect because legitimate power is power by formal authority or by functional title. Answer C is incorrect because reward power is based on the ability to provide or withhold rewards to or from a participant. Answer D is incorrect because referent power is borrowed, legitimate power that is transferred from a formal leader to a project manager.

32. **Answer C** is the best answer. Collocation occurs when team members are physically located within a close proximity of each other, which enhances communication, focus, and emphasis on project completion. Answers A, B, and D may be correct to some degree, but the concept of collocation is emphasized in the PMBOK.

33. **Answer A** is the correct answer. Quality assurance is not associated with team development. Answers B, C, and D are outputs to team development. Answers C and D are both types of performance improvements, which is an output to team development.

34. **Answer B** is the correct answer. Managers frequently use rewards and recognition in the workplace and understand the importance of providing positive feedback to their teams and stakeholders. Answer A is incorrect because 360-degree feedback is provided for employees during the evaluation process, and the output of these sessions can lead to rewards. Answer C is incorrect because rewards tend to have a stronger and longer lasting effect on reinforcing behavior than peer evaluations. Answer D is incorrect because it is not the exact definition in the PMBOK for the reward and recognition systems; however, team celebrations are a vital tool to reward your team for its participation on the project.

35. **Answer D** is correct. Confronting an issue is a technique that some project managers utilize to develop the best solution to a problem or issue. Answer A is incorrect because buy-in is more of a process of soliciting feedback and making a decision based upon the feedback. Answer B is incorrect because negotiation is the process that is used whenever you are trying to find a middle ground for mutual acceptance during the decision-making process. Answer C is incorrect because the fact finding does not generally involve a situation in which a win-win decision would need to be made concerning an issue.

36. **Answer B** is the correct answer. The conflict is downplayed for the time being until it reappears at a later time. This is a lose-lose resolution technique because the conflict does not get resolved or have closure. Answer A is incorrect; a contingency plan is involved with the planning and execution of the project as you look at the options that you have for your decision-making process. Answer C is correct; however, it is not the best response to this question. Procrastination makes your project planning and execution a challenging and awkward experience. Answer D is incorrect because project execution is not a smoothing technique.

37. **Answer A** is the correct answer. Maslow's Hierarchy of Needs is a pyramid of hierarchical needs, from basic physical needs to self-actualization. Answer B is incorrect because Maslow's Hierarchy is not associated with the royal family. Answer C is correct as one of the steps of Maslow's Hierarchy; however, it does not answer this question as well as Answer A. Answer D is incorrect because Maslow's Hierarchy is not related to Deming's Total Quality Management System that he successfully brought to cultures outside of the United States.

38. **Answer B** is the correct answer. The ability to get promoted and learn new skills are both examples of hygiene factors that contribute to why people enjoy their jobs and are motivated. Answers A and C are incorrect because they are McGregor's theories that are related to people's work ethic and approach to their job. Answer D is incorrect because the Hawthorne Effect is related to the increased productivity levels of workers that is correlated to the opportunity to provide feedback to management about working conditions.

39. **Answer A** is correct. This hierarchy is seen as a pyramid with the first level, physical needs, at the base of the pyramid. Answer B is incorrect because self-esteem is the fourth level of the pyramid. Answer C is incorrect because self-actualization is the fifth level of the pyramid. Answer D is incorrect because it is on the second level of the pyramid with security.

40. **Answer C** is correct. Motivators help provide job satisfaction, and hygiene factors are job attributes that help prevent job dissatisfaction. The necessity to keep your team satisfied is an important part of maintaining good productivity levels and team development. Answer A is incorrect because it is a fake term and not related to Project Management. Answer B is correct but not the best response for this question. Answer D is incorrect because it is a fake term.

41. **Answer B** is correct. The technique is best used when time is short or the conflict cannot be resolved through problem-solving techniques. Answer A is incorrect because confronting involves approaching a problem as a problem-solving activity that is used to discuss an issue for a win-win resolution. Answer C is incorrect because coercion is not a PMBOK-identified conflict resolution method. Answer D is incorrect because this term is not related to this topic and is not relevant to this question.

42. **Answer C** is correct. The solicitation process is the means by which you let vendors know what your requirements are. They then respond with a proposal on how they can meet your requirements. Answer A is incorrect because requirement gathering is done in the procurement planning stage. Answer B is incorrect because the actual determination of a vendor happens in the source selection phase. Answer D is incorrect because price negotiation happens in the source selection phase also.

43. **Answer A** is correct. Expectancy Theory asserts that people are motivated in their work with the expectation of being rewarded. Answer B is incorrect because Contingency Theory asserts that people strive to become competent and are motivated after the competency is developed. Answer C is incorrect because the Glass Ceiling Theory is not relevant to this question. Answer D is incorrect because Achievement Theory asserts that people are motivated by power, affiliation, or achievement.

44. **Answer D** is correct. Hygiene factors are hypothesized in Herzberg's Hygiene Theory, which states that an individual's motivation is based upon motivators and hygiene factors. Benefits, pay, and work conditions are examples of hygiene factors. Answer A is incorrect because motivators help provide job satisfaction and include the actual work and the satisfaction that you get from doing the work. These include new skills, getting promotions, and facing work-related challenges. Answer B is incorrect because expectations do not have a direct impact upon job satisfaction unless the expectations are not fulfilled. Answer C is incorrect because social needs are drawn from Maslow's Hierarchy of Needs and are not related to this question.

45. **Answer B** is correct. McGregor's Y Theory asserts that resources need limited supervision and want to positively contribute to an organization to help the project succeed. Answer A is incorrect because Kerzner does not have an affiliation theory. Answer C is incorrect because Motivation-Hygiene Theory is more related to attributes that motive people in the workplace rather than the management styles of team development. Answer D is incorrect because Meredith and Mantel were not the originators of Expectancy Theory, nor is the Expectancy Theory relevant to this question.

46. **Answer D** is the best answer. The Project Management Information System (PMIS) is a culmination of all of the communication tools and techniques that are used throughout the project to keep people informed. Answer A is incorrect because the corporate hierarchy is not a system that is used to communicate, although it is a tool that can assist with the communication and escalation processes. Answer B is correct; however, it is not the best answer for this question because the sender/receiver system is more involved with oral communication rather than all of the verbal and written communication for the project. Answer C is incorrect because a feedback loop is frequently used as a communication tool to provide communication back to an individual concerning issues or topics rather than being a communication system.

47. **Answer D** is the best answer. The execution phase of the project will use more money, time, and resources than the other phases of the project. Answer A is incorrect because the budget has not proportionately allocated money to the execution phase in comparison to the other phases of the project. Answer B may be correct, but it is not the best answer for this question. Answer C may be correct; however, we do not have enough information to make that conclusion with the limited information that we have in this question.

48. **Answer D** is correct. After the source selection is made, the end result is a contract to perform the requested activities. Answer A is partially correct because the corporate procurement policies do affect a contract, but that is not when it is created. Answer B is incorrect because the receipt of a proposal does not make a legal contract. Answer C is incorrect because a contract must be signed before work can be done. However, in certain circumstances, the actual act of work being produced can be considered a default contract. Project managers need to avoid this.

49. **Answer C** is correct. It is essential that team members bring up problems and issues as soon as possible and not ignore them. Problem resolution is part of our responsibility. Answer A is incorrect because delaying the issue until the next staff meeting could be detrimental if it is not resolved quickly. Answer B is not the best answer because the project manager is usually the single point of contact about the events surrounding the project, including expenses. Therefore, it is advantageous for the project manager to be aware of the expenditures and the impact upon the budget. The project manager can approach the vice president about the expenses. Answer D is incorrect because selling the story to a newspaper might be presumptuous of some problem without researching the matter further.

50. **Answer B** is correct. Contract administration involves all the execution phase tasks, including monitoring the project plan, performance reporting, and quality assurance. Answer A is incorrect because, although managing the interaction between various providers is a key element, it is not the purpose of contract administration. Answer C is incorrect because, although change requests are a normal part of most projects, avoiding them because of contractual concerns is inappropriate. Change requests should be managed according to the change control process. Answer D is incorrect because payment to the provider is part of contract administration, not the purpose of it.

51. **Answer D** is correct. Corrective actions are those activities that are a result of when the project is not going as planned and action needs to be taken to get the project back on track. Answer A is incorrect because a change request is the deliverable that triggers the corrective action. Answer B is incorrect because a stratified opportunity would not be associated with the corrective actions or the change control process. Answer C is incorrect because preventative actions are the proactive events that reduce the probability of risks materializing in a project.

52. **Answer B** is the best answer. Work results are the outcomes of the events that are performed to complete a project. This could include tangible work results, such as a highway infrastructure, or intangible work results, such as employee development and knowledge. Answer A is incorrect because training is not considered a capital expense. Answer C could be correct, but it is not the best response for this question. Answer D is not a correct term and is not applicable to this question.

53. **Answer A** is the correct answer. Change requests are the outputs of the project plan execution and therefore are not directly involved with the information distribution process. Answers B, C, and D are outputs that are correlated with records, reports, and presentations as the outputs of information distribution.

54. **Answer A** is the correct answer. Cause-and-effect diagrams, which are also known as fishbone or Ishikawa diagrams, provide details about how various factors might be correlated to potential effects or problems. Answer B is incorrect because the diagrams are not used with a WBS. Answer C could be correct but it is not the best response for this question because kill points are decision points in which the justification for the continued participation of the project might be required. Answer D is not correct because the diagrams are not involved with network logic or forward pass calculations in order to provide quality assurance.

55. **Answer C** is the correct answer. The design of experiments can also be applied to Project Management issues, such as schedule and cost trade-offs, to determine how various levels of expertise can influence the average workloads and costs of different skill sets. Answer A is incorrect because the procurement plan is a deliverable that is associated with the solicitation process, not the execution phase of the project. Answer B is incorrect because the cost of quality is the cost of all efforts to achieve the service and/or product quality combined with expenses resulting from nonconformance to quality standards. Answer D is incorrect because a system flowchart shows how various elements of a system interact with each other, such as a cause-and-effect diagram.

56. **Answer A** is the correct answer. Ambiguous jurisdiction is the feeling that a team member can get when he has to split his allegiance to the functional manager and the project manager so that he can provide support to both parties. Answer B may be correct; however, it is not the best answer to this question. Answer C is incorrect because referent power tends to give strength to a team member because the functional manager is providing the project manager with loaned power that originates from the functional title. Answer D is incorrect because autonomy is the feeling of freedom to make choices, on your own, to fulfill the project needs.

57. **Answer D** is the correct answer. Collocating involves the placement of the team members in the same physical location to enhance their performance. A war room is a location where the team can gather and review notes, project artifacts, and other project-related items. Answer A is incorrect because the use of frequent videoconferencing does not allow collocation of the team and lacks the close proximity that is needed for this technique to work effectively. Answer B is incorrect because status meetings only provide temporary collocation of the team members and do not have same sustained impact. Answer C is incorrect because a reward and recognition system reinforces desired behavior and is not related to the physical proximity of team members to each other.

58. **Answer D** is the correct answer. Lessons learned is involved during the close-out of a project when the team determines what knowledge and skills were developed as a result of the project. Answers A, B, and C are correct statements and can be part of the communication management plan. Consequently, they are incorrect answers for this question.

59. **Answer B** is the correct answer. The organization's structure determines who receives communications and in what format. Therefore, the organization can set constraints upon the communication if the correct people are not kept informed about the project status. Answer A is incorrect because there is not enough information in this statement to come to any conclusions. Answer C is incorrect because the planning activities for this example may or may not involve executive stakeholders, nor will they have similar deliverables. Answer D is incorrect because organizational planning is not an output of the communication planning process.

60. **Answer C** is the correct answer. The weighted average calculation for Vendor 3 is

    $.9(1) + .5(0) + .3(0) = .9$

    Answer A is incorrect. The weighted average calculation for Vendor 1 is

    $.9(0) + .5(1) + .3(0) = .5$

    Answer B is incorrect. The weighted average calculation for Vendor 2 is

    $.9(0) + .5(1) + .3(1) = .8$

    Answer D is incorrect because there is enough information to determine a vendor based upon these criteria.

Project Control

Exam Prep Questions

1. Change control management is an integral part of the success for a project. A goal of integrated change control is to make sure that product scope changes are reflected in the project scope definition. What is a useful tool or technique that can be used to aid integrated change control?

   ❑ A. Performance reports
   ❑ B. Project plans
   ❑ C. Change requests — ·//
   ❑ D. Configuration management

2. Sarah has been assigned to a high-profile project with several strong personalities that want to expand the scope of her project. She realizes that minimizing scope creep through change control can have a positive impact upon the timeline for the project. Which of the following is an input to integrated change control?

   ❑ A. Change control system
   ❑ B. Performance measurement
   ❑ C. Performance reports
   ❑ D. Lessons learned

3. You are a project manager and are concerned that certain project work tasks will either be duplicated by multiple team members or not completed at all. What type of procedure can you put into place to ensure that this does not occur?

   ❑ A. Work authorization system
   ❑ B. Formal work sign-off system
   ❑ C. Control charts
   ❑ D. Change control board

4. Indonesia Limited Corporation is in the process of implementing a PMO and change control process within its organization. At its first staff meeting, there is a heated discussion about why change control should be maintained within the PMO and numerous tools and techniques are debated. Which of the following is not a tool and technique recommended by the PMBOK in integrated change control?

- ❏ A. Change control system
- ❏ B. Performance measurement
- ❏ C. Additional planning
- ❏ D. Corrective action

5. The work breakdown structure is an important input to which of the following project scope management processes?

- ❏ A. Scope planning
- ❏ B. Scope definition
- ❏ C. Scope change control
- ❏ D. Initiation

6. As a high-profile project manager for nuclear power projects, Theodore has come to the realization that incorporating project changes into the schedule throughout the project is imperative if he is going to keep the project on schedule. By utilizing network diagrams, he is able to track the scheduling and execution of the various tasks throughout the process. When performing a backward pass analysis of a project schedule, he knows that it is important to identify and evaluate all of the paths of activities that have

- ❏ A. Negative slack
- ❏ B. Positive slack
- ❏ C. No slack
- ❏ D. A critical success factor

7. Scope change control can be time consuming because it requires a lot of communication with resources and buy-in from stakeholders. The PMBOK states that scope change control deals with all of the following except

- ❏ A. Preventing changes from occurring
- ❏ B. Influencing the factors that result in scope changes to ensure that changes are agreed upon
- ❏ C. Determining that a scope change has occurred
- ❏ D. Managing the true changes when and if they occur

8. Why is the project plan important in change control?

Quick Answer: **163**
Detailed Answer: **165**

❑ A. The project plan documents the baseline that changes are managed against.

❑ B. The project plan enables all required changes to be approved.

❑ C. The project plan will probably change as the project progresses.

❑ D. The project plan facilitates stakeholder communication.

9. All of the following are outputs of scope change control except

Quick Answer: **163**
Detailed Answer: **165**

❑ A. Scope changes

❑ B. Corrective action

❑ C. Adjusted baseline

❑ D. Change requests

10. Risk monitoring and control involves tracking known risks, identifying new risks, and executing risk plans. Which of the following answers are outputs of risk monitoring and control?

Quick Answer: **163**
Detailed Answer: **165**

❑ A. Risk response audits and risk reviews

❑ B. A risk management plan and a risk response plan

❑ C. Corrective action and a risk management plan

❑ D. Workaround plans and corrective action

11. Project quality control includes verifying that the results comply with related quality standards. Both product results and Project Management results are included in quality control. What are some inputs to quality control?

Quick Answer: **163**
Detailed Answer: **165**

❑ A. Work results and rework

❑ B. Work results and operational definitions

❑ C. Quality improvement and rework

❑ D. Control charts and Pareto diagrams

12. Earned value analysis (EVA) is the preferred performance reporting technique. Earned value involves calculating all of the following values except for

Quick Answer: **163**
Detailed Answer: **166**

❑ A. Budgeted cost of work scheduled (BCWS) PV

❑ B. Cost performance index (CPI)

❑ C. Planned value (PV)

❑ D. Actual cost (AC)

13. The triple constraints of Project Management are areas that project managers should focus upon to provide more reliable and positive outcomes on a project. Project success is based heavily upon the control of cost, time, and scope, as well as

Quick Answer: **163**
Detailed Answer: **166**

- ❑   A. The acceptance given by the customer
- ❑   B. The human resources of the customer
- ❑   C. The level at which the project was under budget
- ❑   D. Very few lessons learned

14. The Project Management Book of Knowledge (PMBOK) is an internationally known reference guide for project managers. How does the PMBOK define the work breakdown structure (WBS)?

Quick Answer: **163**
Detailed Answer: **166**

- ❑   A. A formal, approved document used to guide both project execution and project control.
- ❑   B. A document that obligates the seller to provide the specified product and for the buyer to pay for it.
- ❑   C. A document that defines the sum of the products and services to be provided through the project, which is utilized for making future project decisions.
- ❑   D. A deliverable-oriented grouping of project elements that organizes and defines the total work scope of the project. Each descending level represents an increasingly detailed definition of the project work.

15. As you evolve as a project manager, you will have the opportunity to interact with some very talented people. In your current position, you are a telecommunications project manager and the project sponsor of your Internet project has asked you to change the scope of the project. What should you do?

Quick Answer: **163**
Detailed Answer: **166**

- ❑   A. Tell him that the scope cannot be changed after the baseline is set.
- ❑   B. Prepare a scope change document.
- ❑   C. Adapt a passive-aggressive stance and do nothing.
- ❑   D. Advise him about the potential impact to the timeline and resource allocation.

Quick Check

16. Your project office has issued a Project Management methodology that emphasizes the importance of integrated change
control. It communicates that change requests can occur in all
the following forms except

Quick Answer: **163**
Detailed Answer: **166**

   ❑ A. Externally or internally initiated
   ❑ B. Legally mandated or optional
   ❑ C. Oral or written
   ❑ D. Formal or informal

17. You are assuming the role of project manager on an existing
project. You are in the process of examining all scope change
requests. To assess the degree to which the project scope will
change, you need to compare the requests to which project
document?

Quick Answer: **163**
Detailed Answer: **167**

   ❑ A. Work breakdown structure (WBS)
   ❑ B. Project plan
   ❑ C. Contract
   ❑ D. Scope management plan

18. Schedule control is an important tool used to avoid schedule
delays. Time management corrective action often involves
expediting certain activities to ensure that they are completed
with the least possible delay. To plan and execute schedule
recovery, corrective action frequently requires

Quick Answer: **163**
Detailed Answer: **167**

   ❑ A. Root-cause analysis
   ❑ B. Re-baselining the project plan
   ❑ C. Change requests
   ❑ D. Resource leveling

19. Some organizations do not allow for a timeline to be re-
baselined and others prefer that changes are reflected in a new
baseline for the project. If you must re-baseline the project
schedule, it is important that you do it carefully so that

Quick Answer: **163**
Detailed Answer: **167**

   ❑ A. Resource leveling isn't needed
   ❑ B. All stakeholder approvals are documented
   ❑ C. All management approvals are documented
   ❑ D. Historical data is not lost

Quick Check

Quick Answer: **163**
Detailed Answer: **167**

20. Marvin is a great asset for the company and has made the transition from being a subject matter expert to a well-rounded project manager. In his years of training, he has come to the opinion that a well-thought-out change control management system should be communicated to the stakeholders at the beginning of the project during the kickoff meeting. One benefit of a schedule change control system is that it includes

    ❑ A. Which types of schedule changes are allowed
    ❑ B. Required approval levels for the authorization of schedule changes
    ❑ C. Methods for measuring cost variations
    ❑ D. Methods for measuring schedule variations

Quick Answer: **163**
Detailed Answer: **167**

21. Keeping the budget and schedule in check is a challenging endeavor for an inexperienced project manager who is not detail oriented. If the cost variance and the schedule variance are the same and greater than zero, what does this mean?

    ❑ A. The schedule variance is the cause of the cost variance.
    ❑ B. The variance is not favorable to the project.
    ❑ C. The variance is favorable to the project.
    ❑ D. The cost variance is the cause of the schedule variance.

Quick Answer: **163**
Detailed Answer: **168**

22. Your Project Management Office (PMO) director tells you that if you do not start using some form of project indicator so that management knows what to expect from your project, you will be fired. In an effort to give upper management an effective indicator, you decide to focus on the complete performance index (CPI). What is the purpose of this index?

    ❑ A. To predict whether the project will be over budget
    ❑ B. To predict all probable change requests through the remainder of the project
    ❑ C. To determine the cost performance needed to complete the remaining work within management's financial goal for the project
    ❑ D. To determine the value of all projects being performed at an organization

Quick Answer: **163**
Detailed Answer: **168**

23. Your client continually asks for the project's bottom line profit "numbers." Which category of profit is he really interested in?

    ❑ A. Operating
    ❑ B. Gross
    ❑ C. True
    ❑ D. Expected

24. Which of the following is a tool in scope planning for analyzing a design, determining its functions, and assessing how to provide those functions cost effectively?

    ❑ A. Pareto diagram
    ❑ B. Monte Carlo analysis
    ❑ C. Value engineering
    ❑ D. Fast tracking

Quick Answer: **163**
Detailed Answer: **168**

25. Resource-constrained planning can sometimes impact a budget if a resource is not available during the time period that was originally planned and the cost cannot be reallocated to another section of the budget. The undistributed budget is part of

    ❑ A. Stakeholder reserves
    ❑ B. An overall program's budget
    ❑ C. Another project's budget
    ❑ D. Performance measurement baseline

Quick Answer: **163**
Detailed Answer: **168**

26. Learning all of the inputs, outputs, tools, and techniques in the PMBOK can seem overwhelming; however, they become more cohesive and make more sense as you progress through the materials. Which of the following is an input to scope change control?

    ❑ A. Scope change control
    ❑ B. Performance reports
    ❑ C. Performance measurement
    ❑ D. Additional planning

Quick Answer: **163**
Detailed Answer: **168**

27. Construction project managers generally like scope creep because it can positively impact their bottom line and profitability for a developed property. The change control process involves documenting anything that was not originally agreed to in the scope document. How can change requests impact the scope?

    ❑ A. Either expansion or shrinking of the scope
    ❑ B. Only expansion of the scope
    ❑ C. Only shrinking of the scope
    ❑ D. It depends on the original scope of the project

Quick Answer: **163**
Detailed Answer: **168**

Quick Check

Quick Answer: **163**
Detailed Answer: **168**

Quick Answer: **163**
Detailed Answer: **169**

Quick Answer: **163**
Detailed Answer: **169**

Quick Answer: **163**
Detailed Answer: **169**

28. Martin is trying to decide how to outsource some of his company's noncore business activities because he does not have the appropriate staff to maintain the current level of operations. He realizes that resource leveling can only occur if the resources have flexibility in their availability. This shifting of resources might require a change control document to be approved by the sponsor. A change control system is concerned with

- ❑ A. Preventing all changes from affecting project execution
- ❑ B. Influencing factors that cause change, determining a change has occurred, and managing the implementation of a change
- ❑ C. Ensuring the change control board is informed
- ❑ D. None of the above

29. Many Project Management experts have speculated about the pitfalls of large-scale, high-dollar projects and how the burnout of valuable resources can be an inherent risk to the project. Which phase of the project life cycle has the greatest degree of uncertainty?

- ❑ A. Initiating
- ❑ B. Planning
- ❑ C. Executing
- ❑ D. Controlling

30. Alberta spends most of her time focusing on noncritical path elements of her project and thinks that implementation of some system might help get feedback from her team members. She is doing some research on the Internet and finds the term *PMIS*. What is a PMIS?

- ❑ A. A repository used for project information so that future projects can learn from previous ones
- ❑ B. An output that is required in a project plan
- ❑ C. A PM certification similar to the PMP
- ❑ D. None of the above

31. The work breakdown structure provides a foundation for the project to develop a responsibility assignment matrix and allocate resources. Which of the following statements about a WBS is false?

- ❑ A. It is a key project-planning tool.
- ❑ B. It is one method used to build a project schedule.
- ❑ C. It provides a framework for ordering a project's tasks.
- ❑ D. It breaks a project into greater detail by level.

32. There are numerous ways to reduce the estimated duration of activities in order to have a positive impact upon your timeline. Many times, this can save money for the project. Some ways to reduce the duration of activities include all of the following except

    ❑ A. Scope reduction
    ❑ B. More experienced resources
    ❑ C. Crashing the schedule
    ❑ D. Re-baselining

Quick Answer: **163**
Detailed Answer: **169**

33. A change control system does not have

    ❑ A. Paperwork
    ❑ B. Referential authority
    ❑ C. Approval requirements
    ❑ D. Tracking mechanisms

Quick Answer: **163**
Detailed Answer: **169**

34. The aftermath of the 9/11 terrorist attacks required a tremendous cleanup work effort. During the inception of these project plans, there was a more narrow focus, which eventually expanded to include countless subprojects. In order to monitor and control these subprojects, a change control management system was required. Which of the following is a tool and technique used in scope change control?

    ❑ A. Adjusted baseline
    ❑ B. Lessons learned
    ❑ C. Scope changes
    ❑ D. Additional planning

Quick Answer: **163**
Detailed Answer: **169**

35. Enrique wants to focus on only the key elements of his highway expansion project so that he can stick to the tight timeline. He stresses to his supervisors that any schedule changes must immediately be reported to the shift supervisor so that corrective measures can be taken. Schedule control requires

    ❑ A. Assessment of the magnitude of variation to a schedule to determine whether corrective action is needed
    ❑ B. Re-baselining
    ❑ C. Weekly meetings to update tasks
    ❑ D. None of the above

Quick Answer: **163**
Detailed Answer: **169**

36. Rework must be done when

    ❑ A. Complete planning has been done
    ❑ B. A quality control finding deems it necessary
    ❑ C. A project resource has not been trained
    ❑ D. None of the above

Quick Answer: **163**
Detailed Answer: **169**

37. Balancing the triple constraints of scope, time, and budget is always a challenge and some organizations indicate that you can only realistically focus on two of the elements. Because many of them focus on their bottom financial line, they lose sight of other cost-cutting options that would not be detrimental to the project. Which of the following is not an input to cost control?

- ❑ A. Revised cost estimates
- ❑ B. Cost baseline
- ❑ C. Performance reports
- ❑ D. Cost management plan

38. Estimating projects can be a time-consuming activity that requires input from various stakeholders on a project. Which of the following is the way the PMBOK defines estimate at completion (EAC)?

- ❑ A. It is the same as AC.
- ❑ B. It is the same as EVA.
- ❑ C. It is a forecast of most likely total project costs based on previous projects' performance.
- ❑ D. It is a forecast of most likely total project costs based on project performance and risk quantification.

39. Identifying and learning from the outcomes in a project can help for future projects. What types of lessons learned should be documented?

- ❑ A. Positive outcomes
- ❑ B. Negative outcomes
- ❑ C. Negative and positive outcomes
- ❑ D. None of the above

40. The risk analysis process is frequently overlooked at Backward Thinking Corporation, and Valerie is trying to convince upper management about the potential positive implication of performing this analysis. She explains how risk monitoring is rarely done in her department, which impacts the timeline and quality of her project execution. Risk monitoring and control

- ❑ A. Only needs to occur at the start of a project
- ❑ B. Only needs to occur at the end of a project
- ❑ C. Keeps track of identified risks, monitors residual risks, identifies new risks, and ensures the effectiveness of risk plans at reducing risk to the project
- ❑ D. All of the above

Quick Check

41. Big Clock Company is developing a new line of water motion clocks that will be used in shopping malls and airports. Because it has not done one of these projects before, it is going to develop a baseline for the project so it knows what the original timeline estimates were for each phase of the project. It realizes that measuring anticipated and actual performance on this project will help keep it on course. The performance measurement baseline is the

- ❏ A. AC
- ❏ B. EV
- ❏ C. PV
- ❏ D. EVA

Quick Answer: 163
Detailed Answer: 170

42. Which of the following can be used to monitor the number of errors that have been identified and the number that still remain unidentified?

- ❏ A. Trend analysis
- ❏ B. Quality assurance test
- ❏ C. Quality audit
- ❏ D. Lessons learned

Quick Answer: 163
Detailed Answer: 170

43. The ordering of defects or errors that should be used to guide corrective action is the underlying principle of

- ❏ A. Lessons learned
- ❏ B. Pareto diagrams
- ❏ C. Bar charts
- ❏ D. Error ordering

Quick Answer: 163
Detailed Answer: 170

44. Changes to the project are common in certain types of projects, especially when they involve new technology. Project modifications should be reflected in the

- ❏ A. Project plan
- ❏ B. Quality control document
- ❏ C. Lessons learned document
- ❏ D. Quality control audit

Quick Answer: 163
Detailed Answer: 170

45. Your client would like a forecast of project costs for the next six months so that he can review the budget. Which of the following sources of information should you consider?

- ❏ A. Similar project cost estimates
- ❏ B. Pending change requests
- ❏ C. Project plan
- ❏ D. WBS

Quick Answer: 163
Detailed Answer: 170

46. Maintaining quality on a project can be a challenge when stakeholders are demanding results within a short time frame. When utilizing statistical quality control, it is important to understand

    ❑ A. How it was used on similar projects
    ❑ B. Statistical sampling
    ❑ C. Attribute sampling
    ❑ D. Special causes and random causes

Quick Answer: **163**
Detailed Answer: **170**

47. Mario works for HS Corporation and is required to monitor and manage the budget for his new Broadway musical project. This week, it encountered several unexpected costs due to a hurricane in one of the cities in which the production is playing. Because of these added costs, his budget might be in jeopardy, and he needs to implement a cost control plan. A cost change control system can be used to

    ❑ A. Define the procedures by which the cost baseline may be altered
    ❑ B. Determine why a cost variance exists
    ❑ C. Define the budget ceiling for a project
    ❑ D. Determine where excess project funds should be utilized

Quick Answer: **163**
Detailed Answer: **171**

48. NRG Enterprises is developing a new line of memory-enhancing products that have the potential to gain a significant market share. The owner of NRG, Ima Smart, enforces very strict scope management policies to keep the focus of the project on this product line. A project scope change control system

    ❑ A. Must be part of the project plan
    ❑ B. Must be part of the WBS
    ❑ C. Defines the procedures by which project scope may be altered, including the paperwork, tracking systems, and approval levels necessary for authorizing change
    ❑ D. All of the above

Quick Answer: **163**
Detailed Answer: **171**

49. Lessons learned are important to document because an organization can use them to improve future projects and the Project Management process. Therefore, in project closing procedures, it is helpful to review the

    ❑ A. Checklists for risk identification
    ❑ B. WBS
    ❑ C. Original contract
    ❑ D. Vendor audits

Quick Answer: **163**
Detailed Answer: **171**

50. Risk management should be incorporated into every project in order to absorb, minimize, or eliminate events that could impact your budget and timeline. As stated in the PMBOK, the purpose of risk monitoring is to determine whether

    ❏   A. Risk responses have been implemented as planned
    ❏   B. Project assumptions are still valid
    ❏   C. A risk trigger has occurred
    ❏   D. All of the above

Quick Answer: **163**
Detailed Answer: **171**

51. Because projects tend to be the most risky at the beginning of the project life cycle, risk analysis can help a project manager acknowledge that no project is without a certain amount of risk. Which of the following is an input to risk monitoring and control?

    ❏   A. Risk management plan
    ❏   B. Risk response plan
    ❏   C. Project communication
    ❏   D. All of the above

Quick Answer: **163**
Detailed Answer: **171**

52. Periodic project risk reviews are considered to be

    ❏   A. An output of risk monitoring and control
    ❏   B. A tool and technique for risk monitoring and control
    ❏   C. An input to risk monitoring and control
    ❏   D. Not necessary

Quick Answer: **163**
Detailed Answer: **171**

53. High Water Septic Systems is dealing with pollution problems in one of its local rivers that is used as an overflow for its treatment plant. Therefore, the government has mandated that it develop a schedule for resolving the overflow problem and getting the river back to EPA standards. The project schedule is an output of schedule development. It is utilized as an input to

    ❏   A. Activity definition
    ❏   B. Activity sequencing
    ❏   C. Schedule control
    ❏   D. Activity duration estimating

Quick Answer: **163**
Detailed Answer: **171**

54. Which of the following are outputs of schedule control?

    ❏   A. Schedule updates, corrective action, and lessons learned
    ❏   B. Project schedule, performance reports, and change requests
    ❏   C. Schedule updates, corrective action, and performance reports
    ❏   D. Lessons learned, performance reports, and change requests

Quick Answer: **163**
Detailed Answer: **172**

55. As a project manager, you understand that correlating risk and mitigation costs is a valuable exercise that can isolate financial implications for the risks. A risk database is an output of risk monitoring and control. What is a risk database?

   ❏ A. A repository used to maintain information about risky projects
   ❏ B. A repository used to maintain information about risky customers
   ❏ C. A repository used for data collected and utilized in the risk management process
   ❏ D. All of the above

Quick Answer: **163**
Detailed Answer: **172**

56. Progressive elaborations are common in projects and can help the project develop higher quality standards with each iteration. Rework is

   ❏ A. Never acceptable
   ❏ B. Action taken to bring a nonconforming item into compliance
   ❏ C. Never necessary
   ❏ D. Always required to meet quality control measures

Quick Answer: **163**
Detailed Answer: **172**

57. It is important to maintain high quality standards for your projects and to utilize inspections to maintain those standards. Inspections completed during a project may also be called

   ❏ A. Walkthroughs
   ❏ B. Control tests
   ❏ C. Checkpoints
   ❏ D. Quality checklists

Quick Answer: **163**
Detailed Answer: **172**

58. Green Leaf LLC is an accounting firm that frequently becomes involved with risk audits and the financial implications that are correlated with those risks. What is the major difference between a risk audit and a risk review?

   ❏ A. There is no difference.
   ❏ B. A risk audit is only conducted on a much larger project.
   ❏ C. The project team conducts a risk audit, whereas an outside party conducts a risk review.
   ❏ D. An outside party conducts a risk audit, whereas the project team conducts a risk review.

Quick Answer: **163**
Detailed Answer: **172**

59. Raj is new to Project Management and is perplexed by scope verification and quality control terminology. You explain to him that scope verification differs from quality control in that

- ❑ A. Scope verification is concerned with the acceptance and not the correctness of the work results.
- ❑ B. Quality control is necessary, whereas scope verification is not.
- ❑ C. A and B.
- ❑ D. None of the above.

Quick Answer: **163**
Detailed Answer: **172**

60. You have just learned that a new governmental regulation will cause a change to your project's product specifications. What should you do?

- ❑ A. Set up a meeting with the government to discuss this regulation.
- ❑ B. Create a new project plan.
- ❑ C. Create a new WBS.
- ❑ D. Prepare a change request.

Quick Answer: **163**
Detailed Answer: **172**

61. The vice president of your company has requested that you attend the upcoming change control board meeting that is scheduled this week. Why is a change control board necessary?

- ❑ A. To approve or reject changes to the project plan
- ❑ B. To approve or reject change requests when required
- ❑ C. To approve or reject changes to the WBS
- ❑ D. To approve or reject the selection of project team resources

Quick Answer: **163**
Detailed Answer: **173**

62. Understanding the concept of a schedule performance index might be useful in identifying projects that should not be included in your project portfolio. What does a schedule performance index of less than 1.0 indicate?

- ❑ A. The project is over budget.
- ❑ B. The project is not as valuable as originally estimated.
- ❑ C. The project is running behind the monetary value of work planned to accomplish.
- ❑ D. None of the above.

Quick Answer: **163**
Detailed Answer: **173**

63. Information technology and telecommunication projects frequently offer opportunities for the project manager to develop different scenarios to reach the end result. Some of these scenarios might involve a workaround. What is a workaround?

- ❑ A. A provision in the project plan to mitigate cost or schedule risk
- ❑ B. Compressing the project schedule by overlapping tasks
- ❑ C. An unplanned response to a determined negative risk
- ❑ D. None of the above

Quick Answer: **163**
Detailed Answer: **173**

64. Cost overruns have plagued the introduction of a new factory assembly line at your company and your project's approved cost baseline has been exceeded. What should you do next?

Quick Answer: **163**
Detailed Answer: **173**

   ❏   A.   Request more funds from the customer.
   ❏   B.   Update the project plan.
   ❏   C.   Update the WBS.
   ❏   D.   Issue a budget update.

65. Construction has begun on the new wing at New Life Hospital and Rick plans to use scheduling software to plan his resource allocations. Project Management software and variance analysis are tools and techniques used in

Quick Answer: **163**
Detailed Answer: **173**

   ❏   A.   Schedule control
   ❏   B.   Risk response planning
   ❏   C.   Administrative closure
   ❏   D.   Quality control

Quick Check Answer Key

1. D	28. B	55. C
2. C	29. A	56. B
3. A	30. A	57. A
4. D	31. B	58. D
5. C	32. D	59. A
6. A	33. B	60. D
7. A	34. D	61. B
8. A	35. A	62. C
9. D	36. B	63. C
10. D	37. A	64. D
11. B	38. D	65. A
12. B	39. C	
13. A	40. C	
14. D	41. C	
15. D	42. A	
16. D	43. B	
17. A	44. A	
18. A	45. B	
19. D	46. D	
20. B	47. A	
21. C	48. C	
22. C	49. A	
23. A	50. D	
24. C	51. D	
25. D	52. B	
26. B	53. C	
27. A	54. A	

Answers and Explanations

1. **Answer D** is correct. Configuration management is a tool used for integrated change control. It is a procedure that is used to identify characteristics of an item and control any changes, record any changes, and audit such items to ensure that requirements are met. A performance report is an input to integrated change control. Answers A, B, and C are incorrect because they are not tools or techniques that are used with integrated change control.

2. **Answer C** is correct. Performance reports include information regarding the performance of the project. They may also include possible project issues. A change control system and a performance measurement are tools and techniques used in integrated change control, whereas lessons learned are an output of integrated change control. Answers A, B, and D are incorrect because they are not inputs to integrated change control.

3. **Answer A** is correct. A work authorization system requires that all work be completed at the right time and in the proper order. Such a system prevents work from being duplicated, neglected, or completed out of sequence. Although a formal sign-off system would aid such a concern, the proper term of a work authorization system is the best answer. Control charts graphically show the results of a given process over time. A change control board is a group of stakeholders responsible for reviewing and approving change requests. Answer B is incorrect because work sign off is generally done after the work is completed and does not proactively control work to be done in the future. Answer C is incorrect because control charts are graphic displays of results and are used to monitor types of output variables. Answer D is incorrect because the change control board is involved with changes to the scope of the project and generally does not micromanage the resources or work to be completed.

4. **Answer D** is correct. Corrective action is an output of integrated change control, not a tool or a technique. A change control system, performance measurement, and additional planning are all tools and techniques of integrated change control. Answers A, B, and C are incorrect because they are tools that are used in integrated change control and therefore are incorrect for this question.

5. **Answer C** is correct. The work breakdown structure is utilized during the scope management process and is an input to scope change control. It is not an input to scope planning, scope definition, or initiation. Answers A, B, and D are incorrect because they are not inputs to the scope management process.

6. **Answer A** is the correct answer. Answer B is incorrect because a positive slack is beneficial to the project manager and negative slack is not. Answer C is incorrect because no slack indicates that the project will be performed within the time constraints that are mandated by the project. Answer D is incorrect because critical success factors are not associated with network diagrams.

7. **Answer A** is correct. Answers B, C, and D are associated with scope change control and are therefore incorrect answers to this question.

8. **Answer A** is correct. Proposed changes must either be rejected or approved and therefore incorporated into a new project baseline. Answer B is incorrect because all changes must be approved; none are automatically approved and performed within the project. Proposed changes must be included in an updated project baseline. Answer C is incorrect because the project plan does not necessarily change if the project is well planned. Answer D is incorrect because, although it is true that the project plan does facilitate communication between stakeholders, this is not the best answer. The project plan is important to change control because it documents the original approved schedule baseline.

9. **Answer D** is correct. Change requests are an input to scope change control, not an output. Scope changes, corrective action, and an adjusted baseline are all outputs of scope change control. Answer A, B, and C are outputs to change control and therefore are incorrect for this question.

10. **Answer D** is correct. Workaround plans and corrective action are outputs of risk monitoring and control, along with project change requests and a risk database. Answer A is incorrect because risk response audits and periodic risk reviews are tools and techniques for risk monitoring and control. Answer B is incorrect because both a risk management plan and a risk response plan are inputs to the risk monitoring and control process. Answer C is incorrect because, although corrective action is an output of risk monitoring and control, a risk management plan is an input to this process.

11. **Answer B** is correct. Both work results and operational definitions are inputs to quality control. Related work results include both process and product results. Operational definitions outline what something is and how the quality control process measures it. Answer A is incorrect because, although work results are an input to quality control, rework is an output that might result from the quality control process. Answer C is incorrect because quality improvement and rework are both outputs of quality control. Rework might be necessary to bring a defective item into conformance. Answer D is incorrect because control charts and Pareto diagrams are tools that can be utilized in quality control. Although control charts graphically display the results of a process over time, Pareto diagrams show how many results were generated in a specified category in order by frequency.

12. **Answer B** is correct. The cost performance index is the earned value divided by the actual cost. Although the earned value can be determined if the cost performance index and actual cost are known, this is not the best answer; earned value involves calculating the key values of planned value (PV, which is also BCWS) and actual cost (AC). Answer A is incorrect because budgeted cost of work scheduled is the same as the planned value, which is the part of the approved cost estimate planned to be spent on a given activity in a given period. It is therefore involved in the earned value calculation. Answer C is incorrect because earned value includes calculating the planned value, which is the part of the approved cost estimate planned to be spent on a given activity in a given period. Answer D is incorrect because the calculation of actual cost is included in earned value. Actual cost is the cost incurred on a given activity in a given period.

13. **Answer A** is correct. Acceptance by the customer involves scope verification (PMBOK section 5.4) which focuses on acceptance of the work results by the customer (the implication is that they were completed satisfactorily) and quality control, which is focused on the correctness of the results. Answer B is incorrect because the resources of the project team are more important than the human resources of the customer. Answer C is incorrect because the success of a project is not generally judged by being under budget. Answer D is incorrect because there is not correlation between fewer lessons learned and the success of a project.

14. **Answer D** is correct. As stated in the PMBOK, work that is not included in the WBS is not in the scope of the project. Answer A is incorrect because it is the definition of a project plan. Answer B is incorrect because it is a contract. Answer C is incorrect because it is a project scope statement.

15. **Answer D** is correct. Before the change is made, the project manager should communicate the impact to the sponsor so that he can determine if he wants to pursue the change. Answer A is incorrect because it might be necessary to change the scope in order for the project to be a success. Answer B is incorrect because a scope change document might not be necessary after the project manager explains the impact to the timeline and resource allocation to the sponsor. Answer D is incorrect because it is not appropriate to utilize a passive-aggressive approach to handle scope change issues.

16. **Answer D** is correct. Change requests can exist in many forms; however, they must be formal requests, as opposed to informal requests, developed within the context of a change control system consisting of documented procedures. Answers A, B, and C are incorrect because they are forms of change requests and therefore incorrect answers to this question.

17. **Answer A** is correct. The PMBOK defines the WBS as a deliverable-oriented grouping of project elements that organizes and defines the total work scope of the project. Answer B is incorrect because the project plan is not initially the source that should be reviewed to determine an impact to the scope of the project. Answer C is incorrect because the contract is not the first document that is reviewed to compare scope changes. Answer D is incorrect because the scope management plan involves the processes and steps necessary for the change and is not used to assess how the scope will change.

18. **Answer A** is correct. Corrective action is anything that brings expected future project performance inline with the project plan. It often requires root-cause analysis to identify the cause of the problem. Schedule delivery can address the activity causing the deviation. It can also be planned and executed for activities delineated later in the schedule. Answer B is incorrect because corrective action does not necessarily require re-baselining the project plan. Answer C is incorrect because change request preparation would occur after the root cause analysis is performed. Answer D is incorrect because resource leveling is involved with planning and not associated with corrective actions.

19. **Answer D** is correct. Some extreme schedule delays require re-baselining to provide realistic data in which to measure performance. Re-baselining should be used as a last resort, however, and should be used with care so that historical data is not lost. Answer A is incorrect because resource leveling may be needed due to the new baseline. Answer B is incorrect because not all stakeholders would necessarily be involved in the approval of re-baselining the project. Answer C is incorrect because not all management personnel would necessarily be involved in the approval of re-baselining the project.

20. **Answer B** is correct. A schedule change control system is beneficial because it defines procedures for changing the project schedule and includes the documentation, tracking systems, and approval levels required for authorizing schedule changes.

21. **Answer C** is correct. A positive (greater than zero) schedule variance indicates that the project is ahead of schedule. A positive cost variance indicates that the project is under budget. Answer A is incorrect because the schedule variance may not be the only reason for the cost variance. Answer B is incorrect because the variance may not be favorable to the project. Answer D is incorrect because the cost variance may not be the only reason for the schedule variance.

22. **Answer C** is correct. The CPI is equal to the value of work remaining divided by the value of funds remaining. It is used to obtain the cost performance factor needed to complete all remaining work according to a financial goal set by management. Answer A is incorrect because CPI is not used to predict whether the project will be over budget. Answer B is incorrect because CPI is not used to predict all probable change requests. Answer D is incorrect because CPI does not determine the value of all projects being performed in an organization.

23. **Answer A** is correct. The bottom line profits that your client is interested in is operating profit. Operating profit is the amount of money earned and is calculated by subtracting direct and indirect costs from revenue. Answers B, C, and D are incorrect because they do not consider direct and indirect costs in their calculations.

24. **Answer C** is correct. Value engineering is a technique used in product analysis. Answer A is incorrect because a Pareto diagram, as stated by the PMBOK, is a histogram, ordered by frequency of occurrence that shows how many results were generated by each identified cause. Answer B is incorrect because Monte Carlo analysis looks at multiple project simulations to calculate a distribution of likely results. Answer D is incorrect because fast-tracking is shortening the project schedule by overlapping tasks.

25. **Answer D** is correct. The undistributed budget is applied to project work that has not yet been tied to WBS items at or below the lowest level of reporting. Therefore, it is part of the performance measurement baseline and will probably be used in the performance of project work. Answers A, B, and C are incorrect because they are not associated with the undistributed budget for this project.

26. **Answer B** is correct. Performance reports are an input to scope change control, as are the work breakdown structure, change requests, and the scope management plan. Answers A, C, and D are incorrect because they are all tools and techniques used in scope change control.

27. **Answer A** is correct. The PMBOK states that changes may require expanding the scope or may allow shrinking it. Answers B, C, and D are incorrect because they do not fully answer the question.

28. **Answer B** is correct. Preventing change from affecting execution is impossible. Change control allows for the effective execution and incorporation of a change into the project plan. The change control board is the body that accepts or rejects a change request. As such, it must be informed and is part of the change control system. Answer A is incorrect because a change control system is not used to prevent all changes to the project. Answer C is incorrect because it is just part of the change control system.

29. **Answer A** is correct. There is a great deal of uncertainty in initiating. As a project progresses through the different phases, the degree of uncertainty decreases. Answers B, C, and D are incorrect because they have a lesser degree of uncertainty than the initiation phase and therefore less risk.

30. **Answer A** is correct. PMIS stands for Project Management Information System, which is the system that is used to provide communication throughout the project, including historical information. Answers B and C are incorrect because they do not describe the Project Management Information System.

31. **Answer B** is correct. A work breakdown structure is not a way to build a project schedule. Answers A, C, and D are factual statements about the WBS.

32. **Answer D** is correct. Re-baselining a project is not a way to reduce the duration of activities. Answer A, B, and C are correct information and therefore incorrect answers to this question.

33. **Answer B** is correct. The PMBOK definition for a change control system says that it must have Answers A, C, and D (paperwork, approval requirements, and tracking mechanisms); therefore, Answer B is not part of a change control system.

34. **Answer D** is correct. Additional planning is a tool and technique used in scope change control. An adjusted baseline, lessons learned, and scope changes are all outputs of scope change control. Answers A, B, and C are incorrect because they are not tools or techniques that are used in scope change control.

35. **Answer A** is correct. Re-baselining is only necessary if a major change to the scope or timeline of the project has occurred. Weekly meetings are not a requirement; task updates can occur through other means. Answer B does not require re-baselining. Answer C is incorrect because weekly meetings are not required for schedule control.

36. **Answer B** is correct. Although Answers A and C might be correct, Answer B is the best answer. Rework will be deemed necessary and required through the quality control process.

37. **Answer A** is correct. Revised cost estimates are an output of cost control. The four inputs are cost baseline, performance reports, change requests, and a cost management plan. Answers B, C, and D are inputs to cost control and therefore incorrect answers for this question.

38. **Answer D** is correct. The PMBOK defines EAC as a forecast of most likely total project costs based on project performance and risk quantification. Answers A, B, and C are incorrect because they do not describe the estimate at completion.

39. **Answer C** is correct. Both positive and negative lessons learned should be documented throughout a project. Answers A and B are incorrect because they do not capture everything that should be incorporated into lessons learned that should be documented.

40. **Answer C** is correct. Risk monitoring and control keeps track of identified risks, monitors residual risks, identifies new risks, and ensures the effectiveness of risk plans at reducing risk to the project. It occurs throughout the project. Answers A and B are incorrect because risk monitoring should occur throughout the project, not just at the start or end of a project.

41. **Answer C** is correct. The PV, or planned value, is the originally scheduled project cost, or baseline. Answers A, B, and D are incorrect because they do not describe the performance measurement baseline.

42. **Answer A** is correct. A trend analysis is forecasting future outcomes (or in this case, errors) based on historical results. The PMBOK strongly supports using historical data. Answers B, C, and D are incorrect because they are not used to monitor the number of errors.

43. **Answer B** is correct. A Pareto diagram, as stated by the PMBOK, is a histogram, ordered by frequency of occurrence that shows how many results are generated by each identified cause. The errors that are causing the largest number of defects should be fixed first. Answers A, C, and D are incorrect because they do not describe the ordering of defects or errors to guide the corrective action in the project.

44. **Answer A** is correct. The project plan should continually be updated to reflect modifications to the project. Answers B, C, and D are incorrect because they are not documents that would be used to reflect project modifications.

45. **Answer B** is correct. If there are pending change requests that might have a positive or negative effect on the budget, these are important documents to review and consider.

46. **Answer D** is the best answer. Special causes are linked to unusual events, whereas random causes are more normal process variations. It is important to understand these terms so that unusual event causes can be identified, controlled, and corrected. Answer A could be correct but is not the best answer. Answer B is incorrect because statistical sampling is just part of the statistical quality control aspect of a project. Answer C is incorrect because attribute sampling is just one aspect of statistical quality control.

47. **Answer A** is correct. The PMBOK states that the cost change control system includes the documentation, tracking systems, and approval levels required for a change. Answers B, C, and D are incorrect because they do not describe the procedures by which the cost baseline can be altered, which is an important aspect of the cost change control system.

48. **Answer C** is correct. This is a PMBOK definition of a project scope change control system. Answer A is incorrect because the system is not part of the project plan, although it may be identified in this document. Answer B is incorrect because the scope control system is not part of the work breakdown structure.

49. **Answer A** is correct. Such a checklist is a tool and technique for risk identification as described in the PMBOK. It can be formulated by using lessons learned from previous projects and other historical information. Answer B is incorrect because the work breakdown structure is more important at the beginning of the project, rather than the end of the project. Answers C and D are incorrect because the original contract and vendor audits are generally not associated with lessons learned.

50. **Answer D** is correct. The PMBOK states that the purpose of risk monitoring is to determine whether risk responses have been implemented as planned, project assumptions are still valid, and a risk trigger has occurred.

51. **Answer D** is correct. Answers A, B, and C are all inputs to risk monitoring and control. The other inputs are scope changes and additional risk identification and analysis.

52. **Answer B** is correct. Periodic project risk reviews are a tool and technique for risk monitoring and control. The others that are defined in the PMBOK are project risk response audits, EVA, technical performance measurement, and additional risk response planning. Answer A is incorrect because project risk reviews are not an output of risk monitoring and control. Answer C is incorrect because project risk reviews are not inputs to risk monitoring and control. Answer D is incorrect because periodic project risk reviews are necessary for the success of a project.

53. **Answer C** is correct. The project schedule is an input to schedule control. The other inputs are performance reports, change requests, and the schedule management plan. Answers A, B, and D are incorrect because the project schedule is not an input to either activity definition, activity sequencing, or activity duration estimating.

54. **Answer A** is correct. The PMBOK states that the three outputs of schedule control are schedule updates, corrective action, and lessons learned. Therefore, Answers B, C, and D are incorrect because they are not completely correct answers.

55. **Answer C** is correct. The PMBOK defines a risk database as a repository that provides for collection, maintenance, and analysis of data gathered and used in the risk management processes. Answers A, B, and D are incorrect because they are not the correct definition according to the Project Management Body of Knowledge (PMBOK).

56. **Answer B** is correct. The PMBOK states that rework is an output of the quality control process. Although rework must be minimized, it is sometimes required to bring a nonconforming item into compliance. Answers A and C are incorrect because rework is sometimes unavoidable and must be accepted. Answer D is incorrect because rework is not always required to meet quality control measures.

57. **Answer A** is correct. Inspections are performed during a project to certify that results are conforming to requirements. They may also be called walkthroughs, audits, or reviews. Answers B, C, and D are incorrect because they are not inspections that are completed during a project.

58. **Answer D** is correct. An outside party conducts a risk audit, whereas the project team conducts a risk review. Risk reviews should be scheduled regularly. Answer A is incorrect because there are significant differences between risk audits and risk reviews. Answer B is incorrect because risk audits can be done on projects regardless of their size. Answer C is incorrect because a project team does not generally conduct a risk audit; however, it frequently performs the risk review.

59. **Answer A** is correct. Scope verification differs from quality control in that scope verification is concerned with the acceptance, and not the correctness, of the work results. Both scope verification and quality control are necessary in a successful project. Answer B is incorrect because scope verification is concerned with the correctness of the work results. Answer C is incorrect because scope verification is required for a project. Answers C and D are incorrect because Answer A is the only correct answer to this question.

60. **Answer D** is correct. Your first step is to document the change, the reasons for the change, and its effect on the project in a change request. Answer A is incorrect because a government regulation will likely not be changed to accommodate your project. Answers B and C are incorrect because you do not necessarily need to prepare a new project plan due to a new government regulation.

61. **Answer B** is correct. The change control board's responsibilities should be agreed upon by the project stakeholders. A change control board is usually necessary to approve or reject change requests. Answers A, C, and D are incorrect because the change control board's main focus is to approve or reject change requests and not changes to the project plan, work breakdown structure, or selection of project team resources.

62. **Answer C** is correct. The schedule performance index (SPI) is an index utilized to show how much of the originally scheduled work has been accomplished at a specific point in time. Answer A is incorrect because SPI is not associated with a project being over budget. Answer B is incorrect because SPI does not gauge if the project is not as valuable as originally estimated.

63. **Answer C** is correct. Workarounds are used when necessary in risk monitoring and control. Answer A is the PMBOK's definition of reserve. Answer B is the PMBOK's definition of fast tracking.

64. **Answer D** is correct. A budget update is necessary when there is a change to an approved cost baseline. Such an update is usually made in response to an approved project scope change. Answer A is incorrect because you can only request more funds if the customer has approved a change control document to approve the additional costs. Answer B is incorrect because you should only change the project plan if it is affected by the budget and has gone through appropriate approval processes. Answer C is incorrect because the budget overrun will not have an impact upon the work breakdown structure (WBS).

65. **Answer A** is correct. Project management software and variance analysis are tools and techniques used in schedule control. Other tools and techniques utilized in schedule control are a schedule change control system, performance measurement, and additional planning. Answers B, C, and D are incorrect because Project Management software and variance analysis are not tools and techniques that are used in risk response planning, administrative closure, or quality control.

Project Closing

Exam Prep Questions

1. Project closing is the last phase of the project life cycle and Howard is excited to be near project completion. In his research on closing processes, he identifies several areas in which he needs to concentrate his efforts. Which of the following two processes is a part of project closing?

   ❑ A. Schedule control and quality control
   ❑ B. Information distribution and contract administration
   ❑ C. Activity definition and activity sequencing
   ❑ D. Contract closeout and administrative closure

2. As you develop your project closeout documents, you begin to review the project deliverables and develop your checklist of project requirements. You can typically find the requirements for formal contract closeout in the

   ❑ A. Project plan
   ❑ B. Contract terms and conditions
   ❑ C. Work breakdown structure
   ❑ D. Charter

3. The solicitation and procurement process can be a challenge if your vendors are not responsive to customer requests for information. Part of this procurement process might include a procurement audit. What is the goal of a procurement audit?

   ❑ A. To determine whether the vendor has been overcharging
   ❑ B. To expose errors of the vendor
   ❑ C. To improve the procurement management process of an organization
   ❑ D. All of the above

4. Administrative closure can sometimes be viewed as an unnecessary "busy work" task; however, it is imperative in the closing phase of the project. Which of the following are inputs to administrative closure?

- ❏ A. Performance measurement documentation
- ❏ B. Product documentation
- ❏ C. Project archives
- ❏ D. All of the above

5. Greg is reviewing the project artifacts for his project and is amazed about the volume of good information the team has developed throughout the project, including the lessons learned. The PMBOK states that lessons learned are

- ❏ A. An input to administrative closure
- ❏ B. An output of administrative closure
- ❏ C. Only necessary on large projects
- ❏ D. None of the above

6. Sometimes Mark feels like a lawyer as he reviews and critiques vendor contracts for ACME Asphalt Company. During the contract closeout, he develops a checklist of topics that he needs to discuss so he is prepared to talk with the vendor about its services. All of the following should be reviewed during contract closeout except

- ❏ A. Invoice and payment records
- ❏ B. Risk log
- ❏ C. Approved change requests
- ❏ D. Inspection documentation

7. What is the difference between contract closeout and administrative closure?

- ❏ A. Contract closeout is only performed once in a project.
- ❏ B. Administrative closure is only performed once in a project.
- ❏ C. Only contract closeout is required in every project.
- ❏ D. There is no difference.

8. While preparing for the PMP exam, Sabrina is relieved to realize that she is finally getting to the last sections of the PMBOK, but she wants to review the tools and techniques for all of the project phases. Which of the following are tools and techniques recommended by the PMBOK in the administrative closure phase?

Quick Answer: **189**
Detailed Answer: **190**

- ❑   A.   Control charts and Pareto diagrams
- ❑   B.   Flowcharting and trend analysis
- ❑   C.   Project reports and presentations
- ❑   D.   Trend analysis and inspection

9. As a vendor, Big Blue Corporation has valued its customer's input during the entire project life cycle, and looks forward to meeting the executives at Small Company for the closeout meeting. Part of this meeting will include the review of the administrative documents for sign-off by the customer. All of the following are outputs of administrative closure except

Quick Answer: **189**
Detailed Answer: **191**

- ❑   A.   Correspondence
- ❑   B.   Contract changes
- ❑   C.   Lessons learned
- ❑   D.   Payment requests

10. After attending the PMI Professional Development Day in Los Angeles, Emelee was encouraged about all the information she acquired on administrative closure of a project. All of the following are outputs of administrative closure except

Quick Answer: **189**
Detailed Answer: **191**

- ❑   A.   Project archives
- ❑   B.   Project closure
- ❑   C.   Lessons learned
- ❑   D.   Rework

11. Differentiating between closeout terms can sometimes be confusing. Contract closeout and administrative closure are similar in that they both include

Quick Answer: **189**
Detailed Answer: **191**

- ❑   A.   Project plan verification
- ❑   B.   Product verification
- ❑   C.   A and B
- ❑   D.   None of the above

Quick Answer: **189**
Detailed Answer: **191**

12. After leading a two-year project at The Project Management Company, David is ready to complete his project and get sign-off from the project sponsor. Which of the following must happen before a project can officially close?

❑　A.　The customer has to formally accept the project's product.

❑　B.　Lessons learned must be documented.

❑　C.　The project team must have a new project.

❑　D.　All of the above.

Quick Answer: **189**
Detailed Answer: **191**

13. Which of the following is defined in the PMBOK to be an output of contract closeout?

❑　A.　Contract documentation

❑　B.　Procurement audits

❑　C.　Contract file

❑　D.　None of the above

Quick Answer: **189**
Detailed Answer: **191**

14. As part of finishing her project notebook, Carmen is compiling the paperwork for the project auditor to review. As she completes her final reports for the administrative closeout, she confirms that she has performed all of the necessary requirements. Which of the following is not a part of administrative closure?

❑　A.　Performance measurement documentation

❑　B.　Return on investment (ROI) reports

❑　C.　Project closure

❑　D.　Lessons learned

Quick Answer: **189**
Detailed Answer: **191**

15. On your current project, you are utilizing the skills of many subcontractors. You look forward to working with some of them again. However, one of them has submitted expensive change orders every week. Now that you are in the closing phase, what should you do?

❑　A.　Utilize earned value analysis (EVA).

❑　B.　Fire the subcontractor for submitting too many change orders.

❑　C.　Conduct a procurement audit.

❑　D.　Conduct a subcontractor trend analysis.

16. Marsha is an engineer who is developing a new line of stereo speakers for Big Bad Boom Company. The project manager of the speaker project is Hans Tweeter, and he is requiring the specifications, technical documentation, and blueprints for these revolutionary speakers for the closeout of the project. These inputs to the administrative closeout are known as

❑ A. Product documentation

❑ B. Deliverables

❑ C. Project archives

❑ D. Project reports

Quick Answer: **189**
Detailed Answer: **191**

17. You are the program manager of an organization and have a project that is nearing completion. Although the project has not been formally closed, the project manager would like to leave early so she can begin her role as the project manager of another project. What should you do?

❑ A. Forbid this, and dictate that she stay through the closing process.

❑ B. Complete the closing duties yourself.

❑ C. Appoint another resource as the closing manager, but dictate that she is available for any required customer meetings.

❑ D. Any of the above.

Quick Answer: **189**
Detailed Answer: **191**

18. Tonya can't wait to be finished with her project in Indiana and move on to new adventures in Project Management in Chicago, but she realizes that she has not performed the administrative closure on the project. Why is it important that administrative closure is not saved until project completion?

❑ A. The customer might not approve the project.

❑ B. The project will not succeed.

❑ C. The project manager might be on a new assignment.

❑ D. Useful information might be lost or forgotten.

Quick Answer: **189**
Detailed Answer: **191**

19. Scott has noticed that due to mergers and acquisitions, the team culture at Worldwide Memorabilia has drastically changed since the beginning of his project. During the closing phase, the team's culture is typically

❑ A. Focused on information gathering

❑ B. Focused on information transfer

❑ C. Competitive

❑ D. Participative

Quick Answer: **189**
Detailed Answer: **191**

20. A new customer at Jack's construction company has just formally accepted a new project. What is the next thing you should do?

Quick Answer: **189**
Detailed Answer: **191**

   ❑ A. Give the formal acceptance documentation to other stakeholders.

   ❑ B. File the formal acceptance documentation in the project archives.

   ❑ C. Dismiss the project team.

   ❑ D. Schedule a final meeting.

21. Getting formal sign-off for a project from a sponsor can almost be impossible at some companies. How is formal acceptance and closure of a contract described in the PMBOK?

Quick Answer: **189**
Detailed Answer: **192**

   ❑ A. Any of the following.

   ❑ B. The signature of the primary stakeholder.

   ❑ C. The person or organization responsible for contract administration should provide the seller with verbal notice that the contract has been completed.

   ❑ D. The person or organization responsible for contract administration should provide the seller with formal written notice that the contract has been completed.

22. Due to hurricane Francis, many construction project contracts in Charlotte, North Carolina had to be canceled or closed out quickly due to the damage caused by the high winds and rain. Which of the following does the PMBOK state is a special case of contract closeout?

Quick Answer: **189**
Detailed Answer: **192**

   ❑ A. Early termination of a contract

   ❑ B. A lost contract

   ❑ C. A and B

   ❑ D. None of the above

23. Which of the following does the PMBOK not contain in its definition of what is included in contract documentation?

Quick Answer: **189**
Detailed Answer: **192**

   ❑ A. The contract itself

   ❑ B. The statement of work

   ❑ C. Requested and approved contract changes

   ❑ D. Supporting schedules

24. Friction Partners is finishing its first government contract and preparing the closing documents. Matt, the project manager for Friction Partners, is in charge of coordinating the necessary documents. Which of the following is an output of contract closeout?
   - ❑ A. Contract file
   - ❑ B. Formal acceptance and closure
   - ❑ C. Contract documentation
   - ❑ D. A and B

Quick Answer: **189**
Detailed Answer: **192**

25. Because it is an ISO-9000 certified supplier, Fillmore Vision Limited is developing its own Project Management style, which is based upon PMI methodology. The lead project manager, Lars, is charged with preparation of project contract closeout artifacts, and he consults the PMBOK for assistance. Which of the following does the PMBOK describe as a useful tool and technique to utilize during contract closeout?
   - ❑ A. Bidder conferences
   - ❑ B. Advertising
   - ❑ C. Project presentations
   - ❑ D. Procurement audits

Quick Answer: **189**
Detailed Answer: **192**

26. While closing out project contracts, which of the following documents do you not need to review?
   - ❑ A. The contract itself
   - ❑ B. Procurement audit
   - ❑ C. Invoice records
   - ❑ D. Payment records

Quick Answer: **189**
Detailed Answer: **192**

27. What is a primary way that a project manager can assess project effectiveness?
   - ❑ A. Use trend analysis.
   - ❑ B. Perform an inspection.
   - ❑ C. Conduct a performance review.
   - ❑ D. Perform a vendor audit.

Quick Answer: **189**
Detailed Answer: **192**

28. Harold is a Six Sigma Black Belt and is savvy at statistical process flows and supply chain management. During a recent lecture, he is questioned by a student about variance analysis and how it relates to Six Sigma. How does the PMBOK explain variance analysis?
   - ❑ A. Comparing actual project results to expected
   - ❑ B. Comparing actual project results over time
   - ❑ C. A and B
   - ❑ D. None of the above

Quick Answer: **189**
Detailed Answer: **192**

. . . .

29. John has a phobia of project risk and how to handle changes within the project. The ambiguity and chaos during certain parts of the project have encouraged him to seek another line of work outside of Project Management. Which phase of the project life cycle gives John the greatest degree of uncertainty?

   ☐ A. Initiating
   ☐ B. Planning
   ☐ C. Executing
   ☐ D. Closing

Quick Answer: **189**
Detailed Answer: **192**

30. As a project manager, you should confirm that the project has met all customer requirements for the project. This output is commonly referred to as

   ☐ A. Project closure
   ☐ B. Sign-off
   ☐ C. Project artifacts
   ☐ D. None of the above

Quick Answer: **189**
Detailed Answer: **192**

31. Earned value (EV) analysis is a performance reporting tool and technique used in administrative closure. What is EV?

   ☐ A. Budgeted cost of work scheduled
   ☐ B. Cost of the work actually completed
   ☐ C. Value of the work actually completed
   ☐ D. None of the above

Quick Answer: **189**
Detailed Answer: **192**

32. EV – AC is equal to what?

   ☐ A. SPI
   ☐ B. CPI
   ☐ C. SV
   ☐ D. CV

Quick Answer: **189**
Detailed Answer: **192**

33. As you prepare for the PMP exam, you might be confused by many of the terms and acronyms. For the contract closeout section of the test, it is important to know that contract closeout is similar to administrative closeout because both

   ☐ A. Are performed at the end of the project
   ☐ B. Involve project sign-off
   ☐ C. Include the sponsor and other key stakeholders
   ☐ D. Involve administrative closeout and product verification

Quick Answer: **189**
Detailed Answer: **193**

Quick Check

34. How does the PMBOK describe product documentation?

    ❏ A. The statement of work

    ❏ B. Documents produced to describe the product of the project

    ❏ C. All project contract documentation

    ❏ D. All of the above

Quick Answer: **189**
Detailed Answer: **193**

35. Project deliverables are provided throughout the entire project and are frequently tied with milestones. Which of the following best describes project archives?

    ❏ A. A list of an organization's prior projects

    ❏ B. Similar to lessons learned

    ❏ C. Indexed project records

    ❏ D. None of the above

Quick Answer: **189**
Detailed Answer: **193**

36. Your company has just completed a project for the county and has received final payment for its services. Who should formally notify you that the contract has been closed?

    ❏ A. The person in charge of contract administration

    ❏ B. The project manager

    ❏ C. The project sponsor

    ❏ D. Any of the project stakeholders

Quick Answer: **189**
Detailed Answer: **193**

37. During a recent company retreat, there was considerable debate about what topics would be discussed. The leader of the group, Alfred, decided that the group would focus on problems it recently encountered during the project closeout with its newest customer, DC Designs. Because the customer was dissatisfied that it did not receive its product on time, it asked for refund of its initial payment. This early termination of the contract is a case of

    ❏ A. Contract cancellation

    ❏ B. Contract closeout

    ❏ C. Customer dissatisfaction

    ❏ D. Contract fraud

Quick Answer: **189**
Detailed Answer: **193**

38. Construction project estimates tend to be more accurate than IT project estimates due to the historical data that is available to builders and designers. Which of the following is the way the PMBOK defines estimate at completion (EAC)?

    ❏ A. It is the same as AC.

    ❏ B. It is the same as EVA.

    ❏ C. It is a forecast of most likely total project costs based on previous projects' performance.

    ❏ D. It is a forecast of most likely total project costs based on project performance and risk quantification.

Quick Answer: **189**
Detailed Answer: **193**

39. Unless customers are satisfied with the project outcomes, they will not likely bring more business to a vendor. Therefore, a post-project evaluation should be provided to solicit feedback from the customer to ensure it is satisfied. What is another potential consequence of a dissatisfied customer?

❑ A. Negative return on investment (ROI)

❑ B. Procurement chain interruptions

❑ C. Lost credibility

❑ D. Corrective actions

40. The benefits that come from a successful project range from knowledge development to financial gains. Sometimes, project managers do not identify problems with a project until it is too late. In the final days of a project, most problems that arise are due to

❑ A. Lack of communication

❑ B. Collocation

❑ C. Schedule problems

❑ D. Technical issues

41. Jessica is a financial whiz and can develop a budget for projects very quickly. When she develops a project budget, she frequently utilizes a performance baseline so she has an understanding of financial implications for the project. The performance measurement baseline is the

❑ A. Actual cost (AC)

❑ B. Earned value (EV)

❑ C. Present value (PV)

❑ D. Budgeted (EVA) cost

42. During which of the following processes should team members update their performed skills in their organization's database?

❑ A. Administrative closure

❑ B. Organization planning

❑ C. Information distribution

❑ D. Team development

43. Project managers tend to dwell upon closure and get excited as they check off their to-do lists. The PMBOK states that a project or phase requires closure

❑ A. After achieving its objectives

❑ B. Being terminated for other reasons

❑ C. If it spans more than 30 days

❑ D. A or B

44. Sieglinde is glad to finally be done with her six-month production-line upgrade project at a local mattress-fabricating company. As she prepares the deliverables for the customer closeout meeting, she reflects upon the activities that will need to occur to properly close out the project. Administrative closure includes all of the following activities except

Quick Answer: **189**
Detailed Answer: **193**

- ❑ A. Collecting project records
- ❑ B. Staffing team members on new projects
- ❑ C. Archiving project information
- ❑ D. Documenting lessons learned

45. Which of the following statements about administrative closure is false?

Quick Answer: **189**
Detailed Answer: **193**

- ❑ A. Each phase of the project should be closed for projects over 30 days.
- ❑ B. Each phase of the project should be closed.
- ❑ C. It includes documenting lessons learned.
- ❑ D. It includes collecting project records.

46. Too frequently, project managers are so glad to be done with a project that they do not go through the necessary final steps in the contract closeout. A written formal statement that the project has been completed should

Quick Answer: **189**
Detailed Answer: **193**

- ❑ A. Be done at the closeout meeting
- ❑ B. Finalize the project
- ❑ C. Be provided by the contact administration representative or organization to the seller
- ❑ D. Resolve any outstanding contract disputes

47. The post-project evaluation frequently identifies areas in which the team and project managers can improve. This evaluation also provides all of the following except

Quick Answer: **189**
Detailed Answer: **194**

- ❑ A. Cost performance reporting
- ❑ B. Formal acceptance
- ❑ C. Cost performance
- ❑ D. Recommendations for future projects

48. Team celebrations are an integral part of a project that encourage future success and camaraderie among stakeholders. When should a team celebration occur?

Quick Answer: **189**
Detailed Answer: **194**

- ❑ A. Upon completion of major milestones
- ❑ B. Project closeout
- ❑ C. Whenever the project manager deems it necessary
- ❑ D. All of the above

49. Lessons learned are important to document because an organization can use them to improve future projects and the Project Management process. Therefore, in project closing procedures, it is important to review the

Quick Answer: **189**
Detailed Answer: **194**

  ❏   A. Checklists for risk identification
  ❏   B. Work breakdown structure (WBS)
  ❏   C. Original contract
  ❏   D. Vendor audits

50. Meredith and Mantel identify several varieties of project termination. These include all of the following except

Quick Answer: **189**
Detailed Answer: **194**

  ❏   A. Termination by extinction
  ❏   B. Termination by integration
  ❏   C. Termination by subtraction
  ❏   D. Termination by starvation

51. The five Project Management process groups include all of the following except

Quick Answer: **189**
Detailed Answer: **194**

  ❏   A. Startup
  ❏   B. Planning
  ❏   C. Executing
  ❏   D. Closing

52. Which of the following is not a Project Management knowledge area?

Quick Answer: **189**
Detailed Answer: **194**

  ❏   A. Integration management
  ❏   B. Scope management
  ❏   C. Risk management
  ❏   D. None of the above

53. Contract closeout falls in which of the following Project Management knowledge areas?

Quick Answer: **189**
Detailed Answer: **194**

  ❏   A. Communications management
  ❏   B. Procurement management
  ❏   C. Contract management
  ❏   D. Vendor management

54. All of the following are included in the contract closeout process except

Quick Answer: **189**
Detailed Answer: **194**

  ❏   A. Contract documentation
  ❏   B. Procurement audits
  ❏   C. Contract changes
  ❏   D. Formal acceptance and closure

55. A procurement audit is used to identify successes and failures in the procurement process. It is conducted during

- ❏ A. Procurement planning
- ❏ B. Solicitation planning
- ❏ C. Vendor review
- ❏ D. Contract closeout

Quick Answer: **189**
Detailed Answer: **194**

56. Tom, a scientific project manager with a large pharmaceutical company, has been assigned a very difficult R & D project that does not appear to be aligned with the goals of his department. Novice project managers frequently do not know how or when to appropriately terminate a project. What is the most important factor to consider when you terminate an R & D project?

- ❏ A. Low probability of achieving technical objectives or commercializing results
- ❏ B. Low profitability
- ❏ C. Patent problems
- ❏ D. Change in market needs or competitive factors

Quick Answer: **189**
Detailed Answer: **194**

57. Project archives are an indexed set of project records that should be maintained for any size or length of project. They should be prepared as a part of which process?

- ❏ A. Organizational planning
- ❏ B. Administrative closure
- ❏ C. Procurement planning
- ❏ D. Communications planning

Quick Answer: **189**
Detailed Answer: **194**

58. Which of the following is not an input to administrative closure?

- ❏ A. Project reports
- ❏ B. Performance measurement documentation
- ❏ C. Product documentation
- ❏ D. Other project records

Quick Answer: **189**
Detailed Answer: **194**

59. The actual cost (AC) is the total costs incurred in accomplishing work on an activity. It is also known as

- ❏ A. Cost variance (CV)
- ❏ B. Actual cost of work completed (ACWP)
- ❏ C. Earned value (EV)
- ❏ D. Present value (PV)

Quick Answer: **189**
Detailed Answer: **195**

. . . .

60. Which of the following is an output of administrative closure?

Quick Answer: **189**
Detailed Answer: **195**

- ❑ A. Project closure
- ❑ B. Project reports
- ❑ C. Project presentations
- ❑ D. Product documentation

61. Earned value (EV) involves the calculation of three key values for an activity. These values can be used to measure whether work is being accomplished as planned. What are these three values?

Quick Answer: **189**
Detailed Answer: **195**

- ❑ A. PV, AC, and SV
- ❑ B. PV, EV, and SV
- ❑ C. AC, SV, and AT
- ❑ D. PV, AC, and EV

62. What does a schedule performance index of less than 1.0 indicate?

Quick Answer: **189**
Detailed Answer: **195**

- ❑ A. The project is over budget.
- ❑ B. The project is not as valuable as originally estimated.
- ❑ C. The project is running behind the monetary value of work planned to accomplish.
- ❑ D. None of the above.

63. Which of the following is not a part of the administrative closure process?

Quick Answer: **189**
Detailed Answer: **195**

- ❑ A. Performance measurement documentation
- ❑ B. Performance reports
- ❑ C. Project reports
- ❑ D. Project archives

64. What formula can you use to determine the cost performance index (CPI)?

Quick Answer: **189**
Detailed Answer: **195**

- ❑ A. AC/EV
- ❑ B. EV – AC
- ❑ C. EV/AC
- ❑ D. AC – EV

65. Administrative closure falls within which of the following Project Management knowledge areas?

Quick Answer: **189**
Detailed Answer: **195**

- ❑ A. Procurement management
- ❑ B. Cost management
- ❑ C. Communications management
- ❑ D. Human resource management

Quick Check Answer Key

1. D	28. A	55. D
2. B	29. A	56. A
3. C	30. A	57. B
4. D	31. C	58. A
5. B	32. D	59. B
6. B	33. D	60. A
7. A	34. B	61. D
8. C	35. C	62. C
9. C	36. A	63. B
10. D	37. B	64. C
11. B	38. D	65. C
12. A	39. C	
13. C	40. C	
14. B	41. C	
15. C	42. A	
16. A	43. D	
17. C	44. B	
18. D	45. A	
19. B	46. C	
20. A	47. B	
21. D	48. D	
22. A	49. A	
23. B	50. C	
24. D	51. A	
25. D	52. D	
26. B	53. B	
27. C	54. C	

Answers and Explanations

1. **Answer D** is correct. Contract closeout and administrative closure are the only two processes in project closing. Answer A is incorrect because schedule control and quality control are controlling processes. Answer B is incorrect because information distribution and contract administration are executing processes. Answer C is incorrect because activity definition and activity sequencing are processes within project planning.

2. **Answer B** is correct. If there are such formal procedures required during contract closeout, they can typically be found in the contract terms and conditions. Answer A is incorrect because the project plan is used to document planning assumptions, decisions, scope, cost, and schedule. Answer C is not correct because the WBS defines and organizes the total work scope. Answer D is incorrect because the charter formally authorizes the existence of a project.

3. **Answer C** is correct. A procurement audit is a review of each process step within the procurement management activity with the key objective of improving this process on future procurement initiatives within the same organization. Answers A and B are incorrect because the goal is not to find or expose errors on the vendor's part. Therefore, Answer D is incorrect as well.

4. **Answer D** is correct. Answers A and B are both correct because performance measurement documentation and product documentation are both inputs to administrative closure. Answer C is an example of other project records and therefore is also correct as an input.

5. **Answer B** is correct. Lessons learned are an output of administrative closure, and are necessary no matter how large or small the project is.

6. **Answer B** is correct. A project risk log is not considered by the PMBOK to be contract documentation. Answers A, C, and D are considered contract documentation and should be reviewed during contract closeout.

7. **Answer A** is correct. A contract is closed when the contract work has been completed or terminated. Answer B is incorrect because administrative closure is performed at the end of every phase of a project. Answer C is incorrect because administrative closure is necessary on all projects. Contract closure only occurs for projects that have contracts.

8. **Answer C** is correct. Project reports and presentations are tools and techniques in administrative closure. Answer A is incorrect because control charts and Pareto diagrams are tools and techniques used in quality control. Answer B is incorrect because flowcharting and trend analysis are also tools and techniques in quality control. Answer D is incorrect because again, trend analysis and inspection are tools and techniques used in quality control.

9. **Answer C** is correct. Lessons learned are not an output of contract administration. The outputs of contract administration are correspondence, contract changes, and payment requests. Therefore Answers A, B, and D are outputs of contract administration and therefore incorrect answers to this question.

10. **Answer D** is correct. Project archives, project closure, and lessons learned are all outputs of administrative closure. Rework is an output of quality control.

11. **Answer B** is correct. It must be verified that the work product meets the specifications. Answer A is incorrect because the project plan is verified during the project plan development phase.

12. **Answer A** is correct. Before a project can officially close, the customer must accept the product of the project. Answer B is a part of the closing process, but even if lessons learned have been documented, the project can remain open. Answer C is incorrect because a team obviously doesn't need a new project, and therefore Answer D is incorrect as well.

13. **Answer C** is correct. The two outputs of contract closeout are the contract file and formal acceptance and closure. Answer A is incorrect because contract documentation is an input to contract closeout. Answer B is incorrect because procurement audits are a tool and technique in contract closeout.

14. **Answer B** is correct. ROI reports are financial reports that are not a part of administrative closure. Answer A is an input to administrative closure. Answer C is an output of administrative closure. Answer D is also an output of administrative closure.

15. **Answer C** is correct. The goal of the procurement audit is to identify successes and failures. Through this audit, your organization can determine which subcontractors to work with again on future projects.

16. **Answer A** is the best answer.

17. **Answer C** is correct. The newly appointed closing manager will be able to contact the previous project manager with any technical questions. The project manager should be available for any customer meetings.

18. **Answer D** is correct. It is quite possible that if administrative closure is saved until project completion, project archives or records could be lost, or useful information could be lost. Each phase of a project should be closed.

19. **Answer B** is correct. During the closing phase, the emphasis is typically on the transfer of information. As team members leave, information is transitioned to the customer or project owner.

20. **Answer A** is correct. After you receive formal acceptance of the project, you should then distribute this formal acceptance documentation to the appropriate stakeholders, as previously determined.

21. **Answer D** is correct. The person or organization responsible for contract administration should provide the seller with formal written notice that the contract has been completed. This is usually defined in the contract.

22. **Answer A** is correct. The PMBOK specifically states that early termination of a contract is a special case of contract closeout.

23. **Answer B** is correct. The statement of work is not included in the PMBOK's definition of contract documentation. The PMBOK defines contract documentation as including, but not limited to, the contract itself along with all supporting schedules, requested and approved contract changes, any seller-developed technical documentation, seller performance reports, financial documents such as invoices and payment records, and the results of any contract-related inspections.

24. **Answer D** is correct. Both the contract file and formal acceptance and closure are outputs of contract closeout. Contract documentation is an input to contract closeout.

25. **Answer D** is correct. Procurement audits are a tool and technique to use during contract closeout. Answers A and B are tools and techniques for solicitation. Answer C is a tool and technique for administrative closure.

26. **Answer B** is correct. Procurement audits are not documents that need to be reviewed while closing out project contracts. However, you should review the contract itself, and invoice and payment records.

27. **Answer C** is correct. A performance review can be utilized to determine the successes and failures of a project.

28. **Answer A** is correct. Variance analysis involves comparing actual project results to planned or expected results. Trend analysis involves examining project results over time to determine if performance is improving.

29. **Answer A** is correct. There is a great deal of uncertainty in initiating. As a project progresses through the different phases, the degree of uncertainty decreases.

30. **Answer A** is correct. A PMIS stands for a project management information system. The PMBOK strongly supports the use of historical project information.

31. **Answer C** is correct. EV, also called the budgeted cost of work performed (BCWP), is the value of the work actually completed.

32. **Answer D** is correct. EV – AC is equal to CV, the cost variance. In Answer A, the SPI is equal to EV/PV. In Answer B, the CPI is equal to EV/AC. And finally, in Answer C, SV is equal to EV – PV.

33. **Answer D** is correct. Performance measurement documentation, product documentation, and other project records are all inputs to administrative closure. Project archives are an output of administrative closure.

34. **Answer B** is correct. The PMBOK states that product documentation is all documents produced to describe the product of the project (plans, specifications, technical documentation, drawings, electronic files, and so forth).

35. **Answer C** is correct. This set of indexed project records should contain all project documents, communications, financial records, and other data.

36. **Answer A** is correct. The person in charge of contract administration should let you know in writing that the contract has been closed.

37. **Answer B** is correct. The PMBOK defines the three inputs to administrative closure to be performance measurement documentation, product documentation, and other project records.

38. **Answer D** is correct. The PMBOK defines EAC as a forecast of most likely total project costs based on project performance and risk quantification.

39. **Answer C** is correct. Both positive and negative lessons learned should be documented throughout a project.

40. **Answer C** is correct. Schedule problems cause most conflicts in the final days of a project. Any slippage in the timeline will become very apparent at this time.

41. **Answer C** is correct. The PV is the originally scheduled project cost, or baseline.

42. **Answer A** is correct. The PMBOK specifically says that employee skills in the staff pool database should be updated to reflect new skills and proficiency increases.

43. **Answer D** is correct. The PMBOK specifically states that a project or phase, after either achieving its objectives or being terminated for other reasons, requires closure.

44. **Answer B** is correct. Administrative closure does not include the activity of staffing the project's team members on new assignments. However, it does include collecting project records, archiving project information, and documenting all lessons learned.

45. **Answer A** is correct. Each phase of a project should be closed in all projects, not only lengthier ones. It's also true that lessons learned are documented and project records are collected in this process.

46. **Answer C** is correct. The PMBOK specifically states that contract closeout is similar to administrative closure in that it involves both product verification and administrative closeout.

47. **Answer B** is correct. Procurement audits are a tool and technique used in contract closeout. Answer A is a tool and technique used in contract administration. Answer C is an input to contract closeout. Answer D is an output to contract closeout.

48. **Answer D** is correct. This is what the PMBOK defines to be formal acceptance and closure, which is an output of contract closeout.

49. **Answer A** is correct. Such a checklist is a tool and technique for risk identification as described in the PMBOK. It can be formulated by using lessons learned from previous projects and other historical information.

50. **Answer C** is correct. The two processes in the closing process group are administrative closure (within the project communications management knowledge area) and contract closeout (in the project procurement management knowledge area).

51. **Answer A** is correct. Startup is not one of the process groups. The five Project Management process groups are initiating, planning, executing, controlling, and closing.

52. **Answer D** is correct. All answers listed are Project Management knowledge areas. The nine Project Management knowledge areas are integration management, scope management, time management, cost management, quality management, human resource management, communications management, risk management, and procurement management.

53. **Answer B** is correct. Contract closeout falls within the project procurement management knowledge group.

54. **Answer C** is correct. Contract changes are an output of contract administration. Answer A is an input to contract closeout. Answer B is a tool and technique utilized in contract closeout. Answer D is an output of contract closeout.

55. **Answer D** is correct. A procurement audit is a tool and technique used during contract closeout. The PMBOK defines it as a review of the procurement process from procurement planning through contract administration.

56. **Answer A** is correct. Contract closeout and administrative closure are closing processes.

57. **Answer B** is correct. Project archives should be kept for all projects, and are an output of the administrative closure process.

58. **Answer A** is correct. Project reports are a tool and technique used in administrative closure. The three inputs to administrative closure are performance measurement documentation, product documentation, and other project records.

59. **Answer B** is correct. AC was previously called ACWP, the actual cost of work performed. CV is cost variance, EV is earned value, and PV is planned value.

60. **Answer A** is correct. Project closure is an output of administrative closure, as are project archives and lessons learned. Answers B and C are tools and techniques used during administrative closure. Answer D is an input to administrative closure.

61. **Answer D** is correct. Earned value involves the calculation of PV (planned value), AC (actual cost), and EV (previously called the budgeted cost of work performed, or BCWP).

62. **Answer C** is correct. The SPI is an index utilized to show how much of the originally scheduled work has been accomplished at a specific point in time.

63. **Answer B** is correct. Performance reports are an output of performance reporting. Performance measurement documentation is an input to administrative closure. Project reports are a tool and technique used during administrative closure. Project archives are an output of administrative closure.

64. **Answer C** is correct. The CPI (cost performance index) is earned value divided by actual cost.

65. **Answer C** is correct. Administrative closure falls within the communications management–Project Management knowledge area.

Professional Responsibility

Exam Prep Questions

1. PMI's ethical standards document describes the professional obligations to which a member must adhere. These fall into which of the following categories?

   ❑ A. Responsibilities to the profession, to customers, and to the public
   ❑ B. Professional practices
   ❑ C. Advancement of the profession
   ❑ D. Truthful advertising

2. You and your friend Jim are both PMPs. Jim is advertising himself locally as an expert in human resources. He is listing projects you know he never worked on. What should you do?

   ❑ A. Nothing. Unless Jim actually gets a job in the field, no violation has occurred.
   ❑ B. Confront Jim and tell him you feel he is engaging in false advertising. Ask him to pull the ad, or you will have to report him to PMI.
   ❑ C. Gather the data you need, including copies of the ad, and report Jim to PMI.
   ❑ D. The doctrine of caveat emptor applies here. Let the buyer beware. You do not have any obligation to do anything.

3. As a PMP, you need approximately 20 hours of professional development units (PDUs) per year to maintain your certification on a three-year cycle. You are now in your third year, and realize you are desperately short of PDUs. A friend recommends submitting early for classes you are scheduled to take. What do you do?

   ❑ A. Go ahead and submit the forms for credit. You are planning to take the classes.
   ❑ B. Do not submit for credit in advance. You might be suspended for not meeting your PDU requirements, but may be able to make them up.
   ❑ C. If you have already paid for the classes, you can submit for the credit.
   ❑ D. Do not submit for credit in advance. You will be permanently barred from PMI for false reporting.

4. The PMI Member Code of Ethics pledges all but which of the following?

   ❑ A. Professional conduct
   ❑ B. Taking responsibility for your actions
   ❑ C. Enhancing professional capabilities
   ❑ D. Accepting reasonable and customary profits

5. Renee orders printer ink cartridges for her project from a new supplier who appears to have the lowest cost. After delivery of the cartridges, the sales rep calls Renee to thank her for the order, and tells her he will be sending her a portable grill as a thank-you gift for her order. What should Renee do?

   ❑ A. Accept the gift. It did not influence her decision to purchase the cartridges.
   ❑ B. Refuse the gift to avoid the appearance of impropriety.
   ❑ C. Report the cartridge company to the Better Business Bureau.
   ❑ D. Ensure the gift becomes a company asset and not a personal asset.

6. Bob works at a manufacturing firm as a contract project manager. He is responsible for choosing a circuit component supplier for his project. Bob is also a silent investor in CIRQ, a circuit component startup that is on the vendor selection list for his project. What should Bob do?

Quick Answer: **217**
Detailed Answer: **218**

❑ A. Select CIRQ. His project benefits and he reaps side benefits for his investment.

❑ B. Immediately disclose to the manufacturing company that he is a silent investor in one of the vendors on the list.

❑ C. Recuse himself from the vendor selection process.

❑ D. Disqualify CIRQ from the vendor selection list.

7. Ralph is a PMP creating an in-house Project Management website. He has used a number of PMBOK and RUP diagrams and materials, but you notice he has not attributed them to the source. What should you do?

Quick Answer: **217**
Detailed Answer: **218**

❑ A. Report Ralph to the in-house legal group.

❑ B. Document the website and send it to PMI so that Ralph is properly sanctioned.

❑ C. No action by you is necessary. Because it is an in-house website, there is no issue with intellectual property.

❑ D. Approach Ralph and indicate that he might be violating copyright laws. Suggest that he obtain permission for use and provide proper attribution on the website.

8. Your co-worker has written a report, which is really your job. You want to take it and re-form it slightly, and then submit it to your boss yourself. Your co-worker is fine with this approach. Should you?

Quick Answer: **217**
Detailed Answer: **218**

❑ A. No. It is a failure to disclose conflicts.

❑ B. Yes. It is simply an example of a co-worker helping you out.

❑ C. No. It is an example of failure to recognize and respect intellectual property.

❑ D. No. This is an example of improper research.

Quick Answer: **217**
Detailed Answer: **218**

9. Jerry, a PMP, needs a job badly, and has tweaked his resume to imply he has experience in customer relationship management (CRM) in order to land a job with a local CRM marketing company. How would you characterize his behavior?

- ❑ A. Jerry is within normal limits of exaggeration. It is the hiring company's responsibility to check Jerry's credentials.
- ❑ B. Jerry's behavior is a violation of PMI's ethical standards regarding relationship to the public.
- ❑ C. Jerry's behavior is a violation of PMI's ethical standards regarding professional practices.
- ❑ D. B and C.

Quick Answer: **217**
Detailed Answer: **218**

10. Rob is an old hippie turned project manager and is very successful in the warehousing industry. At work, Rob is impeccable, truthful, and well qualified. At home, he likes to indulge in some of his old habits, including smoking marijuana occasionally on weekends. How does this affect his status with PMI?

- ❑ A. It doesn't. What is done in the privacy of your own home is not of concern to PMI.
- ❑ B. PMI is only concerned with professional behavior. Rob is clearly an exemplary PMP.
- ❑ C. Rob is actually violating one of the PMI responsibilities of membership, which is to abide by the laws of the community and not knowingly engage in criminal conduct.
- ❑ D. Rob is violating responsibilities to customers and to the public.

Quick Answer: **217**
Detailed Answer: **219**

11. Ray is a project manager working on strategic projects for a coat manufacturer. He has developed a business case for a new warehouse, but the return on investment (ROI) is negative. "I need to have a 10% positive ROI for this project," his boss tells him. "Change the forecast so we can get the project approved." What should Ray do?

- ❑ A. Change the forecast to get the positive ROI, because his boss asked him to.
- ❑ B. Refuse to modify the data, and risk losing his job.
- ❑ C. Explain that ROI might not be the only consideration for the approval of a project, and ask his boss to focus on the strategic nature of the project, rather than changing the ROI.
- ❑ D. Modify the data, as his boss requested, and add a disclaimer to the report that he disagrees.

Quick Check

12. Liz is a PMP, and values the process discipline of Project Management. In a conversation with her, she complains about the professional responsibility requirements of PMI. How would you describe the purpose of maintaining an ethical standard as a PMI member?

   ❑   A. That it maintains the integrity of PMI as an organization

   ❑   B. That it is good for profits

   ❑   C. To ensure all PMI members behave in a professional manner

   ❑   D. To earn and maintain the confidence of team members, colleagues, employees, employers, customers and clients, the public, and the global community

Quick Answer: **217**
Detailed Answer: **219**

13. As a contract project manager, you have just finished a major product development project for a bicycle manufacturer, Racebikes. Bike-Tech, a competitor to Racebikes, has approached you to develop a similar product for it. What should you do?

   ❑   A. Take the job. Leverage the knowledge of Racebikes to create an even better product for Bike-Tech.

   ❑   B. Decline the engagement due to confidentiality issues.

   ❑   C. Determine whether the new engagement will cause you to breach any confidentiality issues with Racebikes.

   ❑   D. This situation represents your ability to leverage your industry knowledge. Take the engagement.

Quick Answer: **217**
Detailed Answer: **219**

14. You are a PMP working as a project manager on a new fiberoptic circuit that you know will revolutionize the computer industry. You decide to buy stock in your company one week before the product announcement and have told several friends to do so also, without disclosing why. Would PMI sanction this behavior?

   ❑   A. Yes. You did not disclose why your friends should buy the stock.

   ❑   B. No. You are engaging in insider trading.

   ❑   C. Yes. It is only your opinion that the product will revolutionize the computer industry.

   ❑   D. Yes. PMI would invoke sanctions against you as a PMI member.

Quick Answer: **217**
Detailed Answer: **219**

Quick Check

15. Richard owns 10% of a company that competes with the one he is currently doing a project for. He decides he will bring up his stock ownership only if it becomes necessary in the course of his project. Has Richard made the right decision?

Quick Answer: **217**
Detailed Answer: **219**

- ❏ A. No. Richard is violating the timeliness of the disclosure clause in the PMI Member Standards of Conduct.
- ❏ B. Yes. Richard, as an individual, cannot affect the stock value of either company, so therefore he does not need to disclose anything.
- ❏ C. Yes. Unless Richard is an employee of the competing company, it does not matter.
- ❏ D. Yes. Unless Richard is working on a strategic project, his stock ownership does not matter.

16. Iman is working in a Middle Eastern country and knows that bribes are a legitimate custom in doing business. Iman works for a U.S. company and knows that U.S. law prohibits bribery. He is attempting to win a contract to construct a water treatment facility and is expected to pay a $5,000 "finder's fee" to the local utility official. What should Iman do?

Quick Answer: **217**
Detailed Answer: **219**

- ❏ A. Provide the fee. PMI approves of obeying local customs.
- ❏ B. Provide the finder's fee. Because it is a fee, there is no issue.
- ❏ C. Do not provide the fee and risk losing the business. It is illegal in the U.S., and Iman works for a U.S. firm.
- ❏ D. Provide the fee outside of his business capacity.

17. Ben is working a bridge construction project that is running over budget and he is getting pressure from his customer to cut costs. He has an opportunity to cut costs by using a rebar that is not as high quality as originally planned. There is some risk that the substitute rebar could fail with high winds, but Ben feels the risk is small, even though the area occasionally gets hurricanes. Should Ben use the substitute rebar?

Quick Answer: **217**
Detailed Answer: **219**

- ❏ A. Yes. The cost/benefit shows it is worth it.
- ❏ B. Yes. The sponsor wants the project to come in on budget.
- ❏ C. No. Ben should use the originally specified rebar, and look to cut costs elsewhere.
- ❏ D. Yes. Ben should tell the customer and use the cheaper rebar.

18. Joe, a PMP, is providing research into customer purchasing behavior of electronics. To sell the research to a pool manufacturer, he changes the white paper and results to be more generic, but does not actually research consumer behavior on pool purchases. How would you characterize Joe's behavior?

Quick Answer: **217**
Detailed Answer: **220**

- ❑ A. It is typical for the consulting world. Joe is just trying to develop another market for his research. Consumer behavior is generally the same, regardless of product.
- ❑ B. Joe is providing a legitimate product to the customer.
- ❑ C. Although Joe can make some generic assumptions about his research, he should really do some additional work before he sells it to groups outside of the electronics industry.
- ❑ D. Joe is violating the PMI Member Standards of Conduct with regard to research.

19. You are on a time and materials contract. You have finished your work product an hour earlier than expected and want to go home. However, you were expecting a full eight hours of billable time to make your personal income goals. What should you do?

Quick Answer: **217**
Detailed Answer: **220**

- ❑ A. Bill eight hours. Just because you were especially efficient does not mean you shouldn't get a full day's pay.
- ❑ B. Stay an extra hour and surf the Web or chat with other co-workers to make up the time.
- ❑ C. Find an additional one-hour task that you can do and legitimately bill the client, even though they did not ask for it.
- ❑ D. Bill the seven hours you worked and go home.

20. Randy is writing a book about Project Management and is using case studies that reflect his experience in working for several local companies who are named in the case studies. You are a PMP editing his manuscript. What would you do?

Quick Answer: **217**
Detailed Answer: **220**

- ❑ A. Remove specific names due to confidentiality issues, unless Randy gets written permission.
- ❑ B. Get contact information and verify that the case studies are accurate.
- ❑ C. Remove the case studies from the book.
- ❑ D. Approve the case studies if they are accurate.

21. You are a new project manager for a telephone company. One of your suppliers invites you to an all-expenses-paid golf weekend. He states that your predecessor always went. It is just for customers of the supplier. Should you accept?

    ❏   A.   Yes. Other customers are going; therefore, there is no conflict of interest.

    ❏   B.   Yes. An event is not considered a gift.

    ❏   C.   No. This is considered a gift that could provide unfair advantage for the supplier.

    ❏   D.   Yes. Your predecessor used to go.

Quick Answer: **217**
Detailed Answer: **220**

22. At a CRM convention, you are given tickets to a free dinner by one of the software vendors. The ticket states that the dinner is a courtesy, and that during it you will see a demo of the latest version of their software. Should you go?

    ❏   A.   No. This violates the appearance of impropriety.

    ❏   B.   No. The dinner is a gift, and therefore should not be accepted.

    ❏   C.   No. You do not want to see the demo.

    ❏   D.   Yes. This is a typical custom at conventions, and there is no impropriety in attending the event.

Quick Answer: **217**
Detailed Answer: **220**

23. As a PMP, Ed is taking several classes on Project Management topics each year. His boss questions, "If you are already certified, why are you taking additional classes?" How should Ed answer?

    ❏   A.   To get PDUs.

    ❏   B.   I like to learn.

    ❏   C.   The classes are covered by the training budget.

    ❏   D.   As a PMI member, part of my professional behavior responsibilities is to strive to enhance my professional capabilities.

Quick Answer: **217**
Detailed Answer: **220**

24. Ron is asked to provide an estimate of cost for a project. After getting scope carefully defined, he provides an estimate that is 300% higher than he really expects the project to cost, just in case. What technique is Ron using?

    ❏   A.   Ron is not using good Project Management techniques. He should provide the real estimate and then negotiate and discuss risk and contingency.

    ❏   B.   Ron is using contingency in his estimate.

    ❏   C.   Ron is not using a bottom-up approach, but he should at least provide an order of magnitude estimate.

    ❏   D.   All of the above.

Quick Answer: **217**
Detailed Answer: **220**

. . . .

25. Ellen wants to get a contract badly. When she hears that
    Havert Consulting is her competition, she says to the hiring
    manager, "I heard that Havert is having financial difficulties,"
    even though she really does not know their financial status.
    Has Ellen crossed the line?

Quick Answer: **217**
Detailed Answer: **220**

   ❑ A. Yes. Ellen has violated the member standard of not knowingly
           engaging in an activity intended to cause harm.
   ❑ B. No. Ellen is merely suggesting there is a problem, and she is
           trying to get the business for herself. The company has a
           responsibility to look into the financials anyway.
   ❑ C. Yes. Ellen has violated the confidentiality of Havert
           Consulting.
   ❑ D. Both A and C.

26. Gregg, a PMP, is developing a radio for an automotive supplier.
    He knows if he uses a certain type of circuit, the radio could
    catch fire in a low probability of cases in very rare circum-
    stances. He reviews his findings with several other team
    members and management, as well as the risk management
    department. Based on these reviews and for cost purposes, he
    chooses that circuit. Has Gregg violated PMI ethics?

Quick Answer: **217**
Detailed Answer: **221**

   ❑ A. There is insufficient information to answer the question.
   ❑ B. Yes. Gregg has violated the member responsibility to protect
           the public from harm.
   ❑ C. No. Gregg has done due diligence and is conforming to pro-
           fessional standards; therefore, he is not in violation of PMI
           ethics.
   ❑ D. Yes. Even with the advice of others, Gregg is not absolved of
           his responsibility to prevent the public from harm.

27. During a PMI ethics dispute, who has the only authority to
    resolve and end an ethics matter?

Quick Answer: **217**
Detailed Answer: **221**

   ❑ A. The individuals involved
   ❑ B. PMI
   ❑ C. The appropriate local legal system
   ❑ D. The attorneys involved in litigation

28. Jeff is a PMI member who is the subject of an ethics com-
    plaint. Does he need an attorney?

Quick Answer: **217**
Detailed Answer: **221**

   ❑ A. Yes
   ❑ B. No

29. Jane is involved in a PMI ethics dispute, but decides to resign from PMI prior to resolution. Does that resolve the issue?

Quick Answer: **217**
Detailed Answer: **221**

   ❏ A. Yes
   ❏ B. No

30. Mike is submitting an ethics complaint to PMI. Mike must do which of the following?

Quick Answer: **217**
Detailed Answer: **221**

   ❏ A. Provide a detailed factual description of the allegations and note the specific provisions of the Code of Ethics that were violated.
   ❏ B. Sign a confidentiality agreement in order to protect the privacy of the parties involved in the case.
   ❏ C. Notify the respondent within the time requirements specified in the ethics procedures.
   ❏ D. Engage an attorney and communicate with the institute through the PMI legal counsel.

31. Ellen receives notice of an ethics complaint against her. As a PMP, she knows that the consequences of an ethics violation include

Quick Answer: **217**
Detailed Answer: **221**

   ❏ A. Private or public reprimand
   ❏ B. Suspension of membership
   ❏ C. Loss of PMI membership
   ❏ D. All of the above

32. Jan is studying for the PMI exam and quizzing a friend: "The definition of confidential information according to PMI is _____."

Quick Answer: **217**
Detailed Answer: **221**

   ❏ A. Any sensitive information considered proprietary
   ❏ B. Any material marked "Confidential" by an organization
   ❏ C. Any material not explicitly in the public realm
   ❏ D. Any material considered confidential, sensitive, or proprietary, either implicitly or explicitly that is not in the public realm

33. Ricky happens on a file of potential new product releases left at a copier at a convention. He works for the competitor. Can Ricky divulge the information?

Quick Answer: **217**
Detailed Answer: **221**

   ❏ A. We do not know whether Ricky is a PMI member or applicant. Therefore, it is impossible to determine the answer.
   ❏ B. Yes. Ricky has no responsibility to the company that left out the information where anyone could find it.
   ❏ C. No. Ricky should return the folder to the owner if he can find him.
   ❏ D. Yes. However, Ricky should return the folder to the owner.

34. Gregg is not sure whether he has a conflict of interest. He looks up the definition on the PMI website. A conflict of interest is defined as

Quick Answer: **217**
Detailed Answer: **221**

  - ❑ A. A transaction in which an individual is directly or indirectly a beneficiary or party to the transaction
  - ❑ B. A transaction in which an individual's family members are party to the transaction
  - ❑ C. A transaction in which a company and an individual engage a third party
  - ❑ D. A transaction in which an individual and his family engage a company for a particular service

35. B.J. is a project manager working on a project for his company's annual meeting. B.J.'s sister owns the local conference center, which is one of the locations on B.J.'s list for a company event. Should B.J. consider his sister's location?

Quick Answer: **217**
Detailed Answer: **221**

  - ❑ A. No. Conflict of interest includes family members.
  - ❑ B. Yes. As long as B.J. has no financial interest in his sister's business, he can consider her location.
  - ❑ C. Yes. B.J. can still consider his sister's business as long as he fully discloses his relationship, and the evaluation is done fairly.
  - ❑ D. Yes. A company's annual meeting is not a strategic project; therefore, this is not a conflict of interest.

36. Robert, a project manager on a human resources project, has access to the employment records of Dave, who is applying for a loan from Robert's friend Jeff. Robert knows Dave is on probation. Should Robert tell Jeff not to issue the loan?

Quick Answer: **217**
Detailed Answer: **221**

  - ❑ A. Yes. Robert has a responsibility to report accurate information to Jeff.
  - ❑ B. No. Robert is violating the confidentiality of private information.
  - ❑ C. Yes. Because Jeff and Robert are friends, there is no issue.
  - ❑ D. No. Robert should refer Jeff to the human resources individual responsible for employment inquiries.

37. You work for BigTV, a privately held TV company that is planning to purchase a privately held TV parts supplier. You know Ed, who works at the supplier, and tell him a purchase is being considered. Your boss finds out you've told Ed. Are you in trouble?

Quick Answer: **217**
Detailed Answer: **222**

   ❑ A. Of course! You have violated the confidentiality of the company you work for.
   ❑ B. No. The purchase plans are public.
   ❑ C. No. Neither company is publicly held, so this is not insider trading.
   ❑ D. It depends on how seriously your boss feels you have violated the company's confidentiality.

38. Joan makes a decision to put off buying certain computer hardware for her project until the second quarter, based on feedback from her team. She has submitted her budget and is now locked into the schedule. Joan now finds out that she does indeed need the hardware in the first quarter. What should she do?

Quick Answer: **217**
Detailed Answer: **222**

   ❑ A. Blame her team and try to get the funding back.
   ❑ B. Do nothing and let her schedule be late.
   ❑ C. Admit the error and attempt to get the financing moved back.
   ❑ D. Juggle the project funding to get the hardware now.

39. Aaron is a tough manager and expects his staff to obey the strictest interpretation of company policy, especially with regard to time off. Aaron, however, comes in late and leaves early. What type of behavior is Aaron displaying?

Quick Answer: **217**
Detailed Answer: **222**

   ❑ A. Lack of integrity by not conforming to the same standards he expects of others.
   ❑ B. Management prerogative.
   ❑ C. Flextime.
   ❑ D. Aaron is actually going to management meetings, but his staff does not know.

. . . .

40. Jane is a PMP who is running a project at a rug manufacturer. Jane works as an employee of a contracting company, but is also able to send her expenses through the rug company. You find out that Jane is expensing both her contracting company and the rug company for the same expenses because the policies do not prevent her from doing so. What should you do?

- ❑ A. Inform Jane that although she is expensing according to the procedures, she is "double dipping," which is illegal and unethical.
- ❑ B. Document the transactions and report her to the management of both companies.
- ❑ C. Do not get involved. If the policies enable her to do so, she is doing nothing wrong.
- ❑ D. Start using the process yourself because it has been successful for Jane.

41. Ralph works hard on his project. He works late hours and often takes work home. His three children are about to start school tomorrow, and he realizes he has forgotten to buy them some school supplies. Ralph raids the company supply cabinet for three notebooks and six pens, and when he sees you on the way out, he murmurs something about needing supplies for work at home. Has Ralph violated the ethics code?

- ❑ A. No. Everyone on occasion walks off with a work pen. Ralph works overtime and at home. It is legitimate for him to take the supplies.
- ❑ B. Yes. Even for small things we might take for granted, taking supplies for nonbusiness purposes is stealing.
- ❑ C. Yes. You should report him to the corporate authorities as well as PMI.
- ❑ D. No. Ralph stated clearly that he was taking the supplies for work. Whether he actually does or not, you will never know.

42. In an abusive, autocratic corporate environment, workers will often get even in passive but destructive ways, even though in general they are persons of high ethics. This phenomenon is known as

- ❑ A. The Boomerang effect
- ❑ B. A retaliatory response
- ❑ C. Theory X
- ❑ D. Theory Y

43. John, a PMP, is studying ethics. He comes across the term *ethical congruence* and finds that it is defined as

Quick Answer: **217**
Detailed Answer: **222**

❑   A.   When two ethical behaviors collide

❑   B.   An organization's capability to effectively develop a code of ethics

❑   C.   The alignment of an organization's stated values, the decisions of its leaders, the behaviors that are encouraged by its systems, and the values of its employees

❑   D.   The prioritization of ethics

44. Brenda uses the Internet frequently for her job researching different aspects of Project Management and for publishing a newsletter for her organization. As she surfs the Web, she happens upon other sites that interest her personally and notes them for use at home. Her corporate Internet usage policy states that the Internet is to be used for business purposes only. Has Brenda acted accordingly?

Quick Answer: **217**
Detailed Answer: **222**

❑   A.   Yes. Brenda may come across the sites during legitimate searches. She is not spending her time reviewing them, but noting the sites for later use.

❑   B.   The PMI Code of Ethics is not intended to address details such as this.

❑   C.   No. If she is searching properly, she would not come across sites of interest to her personally.

❑   D.   No. By even looking at the other sites, she is in violation of corporate policy, and therefore not acting according to PMI ethics standards.

45. Carol is a project manager for a construction project, and is sending a couple of workers to get supplies for a part of the construction. She also needs to have the mulch for her home picked up and delivered, and instructs them to do that on the way to getting the supplies. Is this a violation of the PMI Code of Ethics?

Quick Answer: **217**
Detailed Answer: **222**

❑   A.   No. Carol is simply making use of the synergies available to her.

❑   B.   No. Carol's house is on the way, so there is no conflict of interest.

❑   C.   Yes. Carol is engaging in the wrongful use of resources, and is behaving in a dishonest manner.

❑   D.   No. The workers work for Carol, so there is no conflict.

46. Dwayne is currently working on a major software development project involving a new technology and has been asked by a software development convention to speak. He will be provided with expenses and an honorarium. Dwayne eagerly accepts. You are a PMP working on his project. How would you advise him?

Quick Answer: **217**
Detailed Answer: **223**

   ❑ A. Indicate that you think accepting an honorarium is a conflict of interest, and that he should not accept the request.
   ❑ B. Congratulate him. It is an honor to be asked to speak at a convention.
   ❑ C. Tell him he may speak at the convention as long as he takes no fee or expense reimbursement.
   ❑ D. Gather the information you need to report him as a violator of the PMI Code of Ethics.

47. Lawrence is a PMP and researcher in the marketing field. He is working on a project and keeping meticulous records of the questions asked, responses, and individual respondent information, and is compiling the information to sell in aggregate about consumer behavior in grocery stores with respect to "cherry picking." You are reviewing his research and are concerned that he is keeping individual respondent information. What should you do?

Quick Answer: **217**
Detailed Answer: **223**

   ❑ A. Nothing. Lawrence is keeping the records appropriately, preparing honest research, and protecting the privacy of the individuals involved by aggregating the data.
   ❑ B. Approach Lawrence and indicate you feel he is violating the privacy of the individuals in question.
   ❑ C. Gather the evidence of the privacy violations and prepare to report them to PMI.
   ❑ D. Do nothing. A privacy violation, although not preferred, is not a violation of the PMI Member Code of Ethics.

48. Al is attempting to perform a risk assessment on his project. As a seasoned project manager, he knows assessing risk probability is difficult because

Quick Answer: **217**
Detailed Answer: **223**

   ❑ A. Probability assessment is a mathematical process that requires a mathematician.
   ❑ B. Data precision is unknown.
   ❑ C. At the beginning of a project, the risk is higher.
   ❑ D. It often requires expert judgment, and is often done without the benefit of historical information.

49. Mike has a friend from church, Jack, who owns a paper supply company. Jack's company is on the vendor supply list for one of Mike's projects. Does Mike have a conflict of interest?

   ❑ A. Yes. Depending on the extent of the relationship between Mike and Jack, there could be a conflict of interest.

   ❑ B. Yes. Because Mike and Jack are friends, Mike has a conflict of interest he needs to disclose.

   ❑ C. No. Mike has no financial interest in Jack's company, nor does any member of Mike's family.

   ❑ D. No. As long as Mike does not choose Jack's company, there is no issue.

50. Gordon is using part of a presentation from Jeff in a speech he is doing for a local PMI chapter. Jeff has given permission. During his speech, Gordon does not attribute the information other than to mention that others had contributed and are listed at the end. At the end of the presentation, he recognizes Jeff's contribution in small print. Has Gordon violated Jeff's intellectual property rights?

   ❑ A. No. However, Gordon should have gotten written permission from Jeff, as well as made the attribution more prominent.

   ❑ B. Yes. Attribution should be bold and clear. Gordon should be sanctioned.

   ❑ C. No. Gordon attributed the information to Jeff. Even if it was in small print, it still counts.

   ❑ D. Yes. Gordon did not adequately obtain permission because it should be in writing.

51. Peter has worked as a project manager on a large and complex systems security project for two years, and is now advertising himself as an expert in security projects. Is he being truthful?

   ❑ A. No. Without the CISSP certification, Peter cannot claim expert status and is in violation of the PMI Code of Ethics in truthful advertising.

   ❑ B. Maybe. We do not have enough information about Peter's qualifications to determine.

   ❑ C. Yes. Two years of experience on a complex project can qualify an individual as an expert. Peter is advertising truthfully.

   ❑ D. Yes. In Peter's mind, he is being truthful; therefore, there is no violation.

52. Nick is a PMP, and in his first year of certification, he has written several books and attended three 40-hour classes. He has ample PDUs to requalify in three years. Therefore, Nick is not planning on any training for the next two years, and is focusing on his practice. Is Nick failing to strive to enhance his professional capabilities?

Quick Answer: **217**
Detailed Answer: **223**

    ❑ A. Yes. By not taking classes or improving himself for two years, Nick is actually violating the Member Standards of Conduct.

    ❑ B. No. Working on his practice is still a form of learning.

    ❑ C. Yes. Nick should be sanctioned for failure to take classes.

    ❑ D. No. Nick has met the requirements of PMI for professional development for his certification cycle.

53. AAA Lock Company is hiring Charlie's company, PMP Consultants, and specifically Charlie, as a contract project manager to run a project to improve its lock manufacturing process. The project is expected to be in the middle of execution during August. Charlie takes the contract, knowing that in August he will be in Hawaii on a long-planned family vacation, but he does not tell this to AAA Lock Company in the negotiation. Because Charlie owns PMP Consultants, he plans to have another person fill in for him during that time. In August, AAA Lock Company files a complaint with PMI. What do you think will happen?

Quick Answer: **217**
Detailed Answer: **224**

    ❑ A. Charlie will most likely be disciplined by PMI because he violated section B1 of Member Standards of Conduct by not fully disclosing how he planned to execute his services.

    ❑ B. If Charlie's contract does not stipulate that he must be the project manager, there will be no finding.

    ❑ C. Charlie's company agreed to provide services, not Charlie himself, so no disciplinary action will be taken.

    ❑ D. No disciplinary action will take place because at project initiation, there is no way to guarantee that project execution will really take place in August.

54. Kyle wants the inside track on Xtreme Software. Steve, a PMP who works for Xtreme, has easy access to the public financial statements. Kyle asks Steve for financial information, and Steve forwards him parts of the financial statements from the Web. Has Steve provided insider information?

Quick Answer: **217**
Detailed Answer: **224**

❑ A. Yes. Steve has provided Kyle financial statements; therefore, he has violated section B3 of the Member Standards of Conduct.

❑ B. No. Steve has forwarded information from the website; therefore, it is not insider information.

❑ C. No. The financial statements are public information, and Steve has forwarded publicly available data.

❑ D. Yes. Steve has clearly violated the confidentiality of information for his company.

55. Jennifer, a new PMP, overhears her co-worker, Isaac, talking to Ellen, another co-worker. Isaac brags about a consulting fee he has earned from one of the company's suppliers, just for recommending the supplier as a source for their department. Isaac is going to buy a new TV with the money. Isaac is not a PMP, so Jennifer knows PMI can't do anything in this situation. What should Jennifer do?

Quick Answer: **217**
Detailed Answer: **224**

❑ A. Determine whether there is a company ethics policy and, if so, have a conversation with Isaac about how the consulting fee is really a kick-back.

❑ B. Talk to Isaac's supervisor and advise her of the overheard conversation.

❑ C. Contact PMI anyway because they have ethics advisors.

❑ D. Report Isaac to the company ethics board.

56. Don and Frank are both PMPs working for the same company. Don is reviewing Frank's work and does not feel he has done an adequate job. Should Don report Frank to PMI for failure to conform to professional standards?

Quick Answer: **217**
Detailed Answer: **224**

❑ A. Yes. Frank is violating section C2 of the Member Standards of Conduct.

❑ B. Yes. Frank is violating section B1 of the Complete and Accurate Information section of the Member Standards of Conduct.

❑ C. No. Don should mind his own business.

❑ D. No. The conformance to professional standards is applied to preventing the public from harm, as in a construction project or medical environment.

57. Henry has reported a fellow PMI member for an ethics violation. He has provided the necessary information, and wants to
be done with it. PMI has asked him for more information and
to participate in the hearing. Henry refuses. Can Henry be
disciplined by PMI?

- ❏ A. No. Henry is the complainant; therefore, after he has completed the complaint, his responsibilities are finished.
- ❏ B. Yes. Henry is violating the Member Standards of Conduct C3
to cooperate with the institute concerning review of ethics
violations.
- ❏ C. No. However, the ethics complaint will be dropped.
- ❏ D. Yes. Henry is violating his fellow PMI member's privacy, and
therefore can be disciplined under section B2.

Quick Answer: **217**
Detailed Answer: **224**

58. Carl is filling out a professional development units (PDU)
form online, and cannot remember the event code. He completes the form, providing all the information he has, except
for the event code. Is Carl violating the Member Ethics Code
to provide accurate and complete information?

- ❏ A. No. Carl gave as complete a set of information as he had.
- ❏ B. No. Carl is not misrepresenting the information in any way.
- ❏ C. No. Intent needs to be considered when looking at an ethics
violation.
- ❏ D. All of the above.

Quick Answer: **217**
Detailed Answer: **224**

59. Larry likes to have a martini at lunch. Because he is self-
employed, he does so at his leisure. As a PMP, Larry is working as a contractor for a company that prohibits drinking
during working hours. Larry still has his martini at lunch.
How would you characterize Larry's behavior?

- ❏ A. Larry has a drinking problem.
- ❏ B. As a self-employed individual, Larry may drink at lunch.
- ❏ C. Larry is violating the Member Standards of Conduct C1
because he is not abiding by the rules of the community in
which he is working.
- ❏ D. Larry is violating the Member Standards of Conduct C2, protecting the public from harm.

Quick Answer: **217**
Detailed Answer: **224**

Quick Answer: **217**
Detailed Answer: **224**

60. Nathan, a PMP, is working on a project with Trevor without a written agreement. Trevor has put in a lot of hours since his last payment, and suddenly and unexpectedly dies of a heart attack. Trevor's wife comes to Nathan to get the last check. Nathan refuses, citing he has no legal obligation, because there was no contract. How would you characterize Nathan's behavior?

❏ A. Unethical and subject to discipline by PMI via C1, stating that Nathan must meet all legal and ethical obligations.

❏ B. Although not nice, Nathan is perfectly within his rights to refuse payment to Trevor's wife.

❏ C. Nathan is a bad, bad person and will get what is coming to him eventually.

❏ D. Nathan is a smart business person. Why pay, when he doesn't have to?

Quick Check Answer Key

1. A	**28.** B	**55.** A
2. B	**29.** B	**56.** D
3. B	**30.** A	**57.** B
4. D	**31.** D	**58.** D
5. B	**32.** D	**59.** C
6. B	**33.** A	**60.** A
7. D	**34.** A	
8. C	**35.** C	
9. D	**36.** B	
10. C	**37.** A	
11. C	**38.** C	
12. D	**39.** A	
13. B	**40.** A	
14. B	**41.** A	
15. A	**42.** B	
16. C	**43.** C	
17. C	**44.** A	
18. D	**45.** C	
19. D	**46.** B	
20. A	**47.** B	
21. C	**48.** A	
22. D	**49.** C	
23. D	**50.** C	
24. D	**51.** C	
25. A	**52.** D	
26. C	**53.** A	
27. B	**54.** C	

Answers and Explanations

1. **Answer A** is correct. Answers B, C, and D are subcategories of the professional obligations category.

2. **Answer B** is correct. Although it is tempting to believe Answers A and D, as a PMI member or candidate, you have a responsibility to report possible violations of the code of professional conduct. Answer C is incorrect because you need to first discuss the situation with Jim, exercising the "reasonable and clear factual basis" rule.

3. **Answer B** is correct. Answer A is tempting, but would be submitting a false report. Answer C is incorrect; you must attend and attain the learning objectives to count PDUs. Answer D is tempting but incorrect because a false report is a violation of the Code of Ethics, but it might not necessarily result in permanent barring from PMI.

4. **Answer D** is correct. Answers A, B, and C are all parts of the Code of Ethics. There is no provision for the evaluation of profits.

5. **Answer B** is correct. Although Answers A and D might be tempting, the appearance of impropriety (A4) is important, and should be disclosed or avoided. Answer C is not necessary unless the cartridge company has done something illegal.

6. **Answer B** is the best answer. Answer A is incorrect because Bob definitely has a conflict of interest. Answers C and D are tempting, and could be options, if the manufacturer feels the conflict is too big. Bob's first step, however, should be to disclose the conflict, and then decisions on actions can be made.

7. **Answer D** is correct. Approaching Ralph is the first step. Answers A and B might be necessary if Ralph refuses to correct the error. Answer C is incorrect because intellectual property needs to be protected in-house as well as in public realms.

8. **Answer C** is correct. Answer A is incorrect because this situation is not a conflict of interest. Answer B might be true, but you are taking credit for someone else's work. Answer D is incorrect because you don't know whether the research was done properly.

9. **Answer D** is correct. Jerry needs to represent his qualifications to the public accurately. This is stated in both the Professional Practices section and Responsibilities to the Public section of the Code of Ethics. Answer A is incorrect; lying is not exaggeration, regardless of how badly Jerry needs a job.

10. **Answer C** is correct. Although Answers A and B might seem to be true, they are not. Answer D is incorrect because applicable laws are not part of the section on responsibilities to the public or customers.

11. **Answer C** is correct. This type of problem occurs often in business and is tricky because it can end with a confrontation and possible job loss. No job, however, is more important than your integrity. Answer A is incorrect unless his boss has new data that would change the ROI significantly. Answer B is incorrect because it is not the best approach to a situation. Answer D is also incorrect because it is unlikely that any disclaimer will be allowed into a project proposal.

12. **Answer D** is correct. This is in the preamble to the Member Code of Ethics. Answers A, B, and C are byproducts of ethical behavior.

13. **Answer B** is correct. Although opportunities arise often in which we have industry information without causing confidentiality problems, this is a case in which a competitor wants a similar product. The likelihood that confidentiality will be breached is very high. Answers A and D are tempting because we are often asked as PMs to do projects within the same industry. Answer C is possible, but not likely.

14. **Answer B** is correct. Answers A and C are incorrect because you are taking financial advantage of confidential information, which is considered an ethics violation. Answer D is incorrect and tricky because it is an alternative use of the word *sanction*. The question asks whether PMI would *sanction* the behavior, using the verb, meaning approve. Answer D talks about *sanctions*, (nouns) or punishments.

15. **Answer A** is correct. Under professional behavior, A1 timely and full disclosure is a requirement of members. Answer B is incorrect because a 10% ownership is significant and can affect stock values. This is also a conflict of interest for Richard to be working for a competing company. Answers C and D are not correct in any way. Neither employment nor the strategic nature of a project are factors in disclosure decisions.

16. **Answer C** is correct. Answer A is incorrect because, although PMI approves of obeying local customs, it does not approve of breaking the law. Because Iman works for a U.S. company, he is subject to U.S. laws. Answers B and D are incorrect because they are trying to use other ways to justify the bribe.

17. **Answer C** is correct. To use rebar that has a risk of failure could put the public in danger. This is a violation of Member Standards of Conduct C2: relationship to the public and global community for PMI members to perform their work in conformance to professional standards to ensure the public is protected from harm. Answer A is incorrect because the cost benefit is not detailed in the question. Answer B is incorrect because it is improper to do the wrong thing, even when the sponsor wants it. Answer D is incorrect because it does not absolve Ben of his responsibilities.

18. **Answer D** is correct. Although Answers A and C might be true, Joe is still misrepresenting his research, and is violating A3 of the member standards. Answer B is incorrect because it is not true. The research should not be considered valid for the pool industry.

19. **Answer D** is correct. Although this can happen, meeting your financial goals should be considered in your rate and contract type negotiations. Answers A and B are incorrect because they are not accurately reporting the time worked. Answer C is incorrect because you were not contracted to provide additional work—you should not do it, nor should you bill for it. Answers A, B, and C are violations of Member Standards of Conduct B1.

20. **Answer A** is correct. Due to confidentiality of assignments undertaken and identities (B2), Randy would have to get permission to mention or use them. Answers B and C are probably things an editor would do after permission is granted. Answer D is incorrect because it would be the last resort.

21. **Answer C** is correct. This type of gift could provide an unfair advantage to the supplier. Answer A is incorrect because, even if other customers go, you still have a responsibility not to. Answer B is incorrect because an event can be a gift. Answer D is incorrect because your predecessor should not have gone either.

22. **Answer D** is correct and the best answer. Conventions are venues for sharing information. Because the dinner is not specific to you individually, and you will be seeing a demo, there is no ethics violation. Answer C might be true, but it is not the best answer. Answers A and B are incorrect because there is no impropriety in attending events such as this when attending a convention.

23. **Answer D** is correct. See A5 of the Member Standards of Conduct. Answers A, B, and C might be true, but they are not the best answers.

24. **Answer D** is correct. Ron is actually violating B1 of the Member Standards of Conduct. He is not accurately providing complete information in his estimates. Ron is factoring in contingency by ballparking an additional 300%. Ron might have used a bottom-up approach, but we don't know. In any case, he should provide a plus or minus % in his estimate.

25. **Answer A** is correct. By implying Havert is having financial difficulties, Ellen has crossed the line and violated PMI member ethics. Answer B is not true. Answers C and D are incorrect because Havert's confidentiality has not been violated.

26. **Answer C** is correct. Gregg has performed his work consistently with Professional Standards C2, and therefore is not in violation of the ethics code. This is a fine line because there was the potential to cause harm. However, because he had the findings reviewed and the risk was considered negligble, he is in compliance. Answer A is incorrect because there is adequate information. Answer B is not possible because due diligence was done and the circuit was approved. Answer D is incorrect because Gregg conformed to professional standards.

27. **Answer B** is correct. According to the PMI member ethics case procedures general provisions, only PMI has the authority to resolve and end an ethics matter.

28. **Answer B** is correct. The ethics policy is designed to operate without the assistance of attorneys (general provisions 1, second paragraph).

29. **Answer B** is correct. PMI reserves the right to continue a matter to a final binding resolution (general provisions A9).

30. **Answer A** is correct. Answers B, C, and D are not requirements of submitting an ethics complaint.

31. **Answer D** is correct. PMI can use these and several other disciplinary actions for violations of the ethics code (D8 of the Member Code of Ethics).

32. **Answer D** is correct. Answers A, B, and C all have elements of the definition, but not the complete definition. See the PMI Confidentiality Operations policy.

33. **Answer A** is the best answer. This is a difficult question. PMI only governs PMI members and applicants. Answer B could possibly be construed as correct too, but because the question was not clear about his PMI membership status, Answer A is the best choice. Answers C and D pose possible actions but, again, his PMI status is in question, thus making Answer A the better answer here, as well.

34. **Answer A** is correct. See the PMI Conflict of Interest policy. Answers B, C, and D are all legitimate transactions.

35. **Answer C** is correct. Although Answer A is correct, B.J. can still consider her company as long as full disclosure and fair assessment is done. Answer B is incorrect because B.J.'s financial position in his sister's company is irrelevant. Answer D is incorrect.

36. **Answer B** is correct. Answers A and C are incorrect because Robert has no responsibility to Jeff, even though they are friends. Answer D is tempting because that is what Robert should do if he receives an inquiry, but it is not the best answer because the question does state that Jeff asked for the information.

37. **Answer A** is correct from a PMI perspective. Answer B is incorrect because the question does not state whether the information is public. Answer C is incorrect because confidentiality does not depend upon the public or private status of a company. Answer D is not the best answer.

38. **Answer C** is correct and the best answer. Answer A is incorrect because even though her team gave her input, Joan made the decision. Answers B and D are not the best answers. Joan needs to accept responsibility for her decisions and actions.

39. **Answer A** is the best answer. Answers B and C are incorrect and bad practices, although they are often used as justification. Answer D might be true, but it is not part of the question information.

40. **Answer A** is the correct answer. Even though Jane is complying to the letter of the policy, the intent is clearly not to allow for double reimbursement of expenses. This is a violation of B1 of the ethics code.

41. **Answer A** is correct. Answer B is incorrect because, although this behavior is often typical, and considered no big deal, it costs corporations millions. Answer C is tempting, but not realistic. To report him to PMI, you would have to have factual documentation. Answer D is tempting because you don't know whether he really took them for himself, but the question states otherwise.

42. **Answer B** is correct. When workers feel undervalued or their perception of the organization's requirements is out of sync with their personal values, they can engage in retaliatory behavior such as stealing, lying, and cheating. Answer A is incorrect and is a term associated with grown children returning to live with their parents. Answers C and D are incorrect because Theories X and Y are about types of organizational behaviors.

43. **Answer C** is correct. Answer A is incorrect because when two sets of ethics collide, you have incongruence. Answer B is incorrect because developing a code of ethics is simply a starting point for developing organizational ethics. Answer D is incorrect for the same reason.

44. **Answer A** is correct. Answer B is incorrect because behaving honestly and following organizational policies is part of the PMI Code of Ethics. Answer C cannot be determined because we do not know what sites interest her personally. Answer D is not correct because we know she is simply noting them, and not using them during work hours.

45. **Answer C** is correct. Answers A, B, and D are all incorrect because Carol is using a project resource (worker time) for her personal gain.

46. **Answer B** is correct. Dwayne has no conflict of interest as long as he is not speaking for a specific supplier. Honorariums and expenses are a common incentive for speakers. Answer A is incorrect because there is no conflict of interest. Answer C is also incorrect because accepting an honorarium and expenses is neither illegal nor unethical. Answer D is incorrect for the same reasons.

47. **Answer B** is correct. An ordinal scale is rank-ordered values. Answer A is incorrect because a probability scale is between 0 and 1. Answer C is incorrect because a cardinal scale assigns values to impacts. Answer D is incorrect because linear and nonlinear values are used in cardinal scales.

48. **Answer A** is correct. By aggregating the data, Lawrence is not disclosing personal information. Further, keeping the source data records of the research is good practice and encouraged. Answer B is incorrect. You might do it and find out you are wrong. Answer C is incorrect because Lawrence is not violating the privacy concerns of the individuals. Answer D is incorrect because privacy is of concern to PMI (Standards of Ethics B2).

49. **Answer C** is correct. Answer A is incorrect because the friendship does not create a conflict of interest. There might be an appearance of impropriety depending on the depth of the relationship between Mike and Jack, but not a conflict of interest. This could be a gray area if the relationship was very strong. Answer B is incorrect because friendship does not pose a conflict of interest. Answer D is incorrect for the same reason.

50. **Answer C** is correct. Gordon has properly given Jeff credit for his work. Answer A is incorrect because verbal permission is sufficient. Answer B is incorrect because the font size of the attribution is not defined by PMI. Answer D is incorrect because permissions do not have to be in writing.

51. **Answer C** is correct. Peter clearly has experience in systems security, or he would not have been running a project for two years in the field. The amount of information learned in that two years could indeed have made him an expert. Therefore, Peter is fully within his rights to advertise as an expert. Answer A is incorrect because the CISSP certification is an indication of expertise, but not necessarily the only qualification for it. Answer B is incorrect because we do have adequate information. Answer D is incorrect because what Peter thinks is immaterial to the issue.

52. **Answer D** is correct. Just because Nick doesn't take classes for two years doesn't mean he hasn't put the effort into enhancing his professional capabilities. Therefore, Answer A is incorrect. Answer B is true, but not the best answer. Answer C is incorrect because Nick is meeting PMI requirements.

53. **Answer A** is correct. Charlie did not fully disclose the nature of how his services would be performed. This is truly the difference between legally correct and ethically correct. Answer B is incorrect because, although Charlie has done nothing wrong legally, he has ethically. Answer C is incorrect because Charlie clearly implied he would be the project manager. Answer D is incorrect because the timing of the project is not at issue, just the fact that Charlie substituted someone else without telling AAA Lock Company.

54. **Answer C** is correct. Answers A and D are incorrect because the information was public; therefore, Kyle could have accessed it himself. Answer B is tricky because we do not know whether Steve got the information from an intranet or extranet website. Therefore, it is not the best answer.

55. **Answer A** is correct. If there is no ethics policy, Jennifer could still confront Isaac and try to educate him on conflicts of interest and kickbacks. Answer B is incorrect because Jennifer should confirm the facts with Isaac first. Answer C is incorrect because PMI has no advisory personnel for this type of issue. Answer D is incorrect for the same reason as Answer B.

56. **Answer D** is correct. Answers A and B are incorrect because they are citing the wrong section of the Member Standards of Conduct. Answer C is incorrect because if Don did see inadequacies in Frank's work, he should work with Frank to help Frank to improve.

57. **Answer B** is correct. A complainant must cooperate with PMI requests during an ethics review. Answer A is incorrect for the same reason. Answer C is incorrect because PMI can pursue an ethics violation review to completion. Answer D is incorrect because Henry is not violating anyone's privacy.

58. **Answer D** is correct. The member standard of conduct is not meant to be misused. A test of reasonableness and a review of intent with any ethics matter is crucial.

59. **Answer C** is correct and hinges on the definition of a community. A business organization can be considered a community. Answer A may or may not be true—we do not know, so therefore it is incorrect. Answer B is incorrect because the organization prohibits it. Answer D is incorrect because we do not know the nature of Larry's job or whether he is putting the public in jeopardy.

60. **Answer A** is correct. PMI requires that members honor all legal and ethical obligations. Answer B is correct legally, but not ethically. Answer C might be true, but does not answer the ethical question. Answer D is not true because a truly savvy business person knows that ethical behavior pays off far better in the long run.

CD Contents and Installation Instructions

The CD features an innovative practice test engine powered by MeasureUp™, giving you yet another effective tool to assess your readiness for the exam.

Multiple Test Modes

MeasureUp practice tests are available in Study, Certification, Custom, Missed Question, and Non-Duplicate question modes.

Study Mode

Tests administered in Study Mode enable you to request the correct answer(s) and explanation(s) to each question during the test. These tests are not timed. You can modify the testing environment *during* the test by selecting the Options button.

Certification Mode

Tests administered in Certification Mode closely simulate the actual testing environment you will encounter when taking a certification exam. These tests do not enable you to request the answer(s) and/or explanation(s) to each question until after the exam.

Custom Mode

Custom Mode enables you to specify your preferred testing environment. Use this mode to specify the objectives you want to include in your test, the timer length, and other test properties. You can also modify the testing environment *during* the test by selecting the Options button.

Missed Question Mode

Missed Question Mode enables you to take a test containing only the questions you have missed previously.

Non-Duplicate Mode

Non-Duplicate Mode enables you to take a test containing only questions not displayed previously.

Random Questions and Order of Answers

This feature helps you learn the material without memorizing questions and answers. Each time you take a practice test, the questions and answers appear in a different randomized order.

Detailed Explanations of Correct and Incorrect Answers

You'll receive automatic feedback on all correct and incorrect answers. The detailed answer explanations are a superb learning tool in their own right.

Attention to Exam Objectives

MeasureUp practice tests are designed to appropriately balance the questions over each technical area covered by a specific exam.

Installing the CD

The minimum system requirements for the CD-ROM are

➤ Windows 95, 98, Me, NT4, 2000, or XP

➤ 7MB disk space for testing engine

➤ An average of 1MB disk space for each test

To install the CD-ROM, follow these instructions:

NOTE | If you need technical support, please contact MeasureUp at 678-356-5050 or email support@measureup.com. Additionally, you'll find Frequently Asked Questions (FAQ) at www.measureup.com.

1. Close all applications before beginning this installation.

2. Insert the CD into your CD-ROM drive. If the setup starts automatically, go to step 5. If the setup does not start automatically, continue with step 3.

3. From the Start menu, select Run.

4. In the Browse dialog box, double-click Setup.exe. In the Run dialog box, click OK to begin the installation.

5. On the Welcome screen, click Next.

6. To agree to the Software License Agreement, click Yes.

7. On the Choose Destination Location screen, click Next to install the software to C:\Program Files\Certification Preparation.

8. On the Setup Type screen, select Typical Setup. Click Next to continue.

9. After the installation is complete, verify that Yes, I Want to Restart My Computer Now is selected. If you select No, I Will Restart My Computer Later, you will not be able to use the program until you restart your computer.

10. Click Finish.

11. After restarting your computer, choose Start, Programs, MeasureUp, MeasureUp Practice Tests.

12. Select the practice test and click Start Test.

Creating a Shortcut to the MeasureUp Practice Tests

To create a shortcut to the MeasureUp practice tests, follow these steps:

1. Right-click on your desktop.

2. From the shortcut menu, select New, Shortcut.

3. Browse to C:\Program Files\MeasureUp Practice Tests and select the MeasureUpCertification.exe or Localware.exe file.

4. Click OK.

5. Click Next.

6. Rename the shortcut MeasureUp.

7. Click Finish.

After you have completed step 7, use the MeasureUp shortcut on your desktop to access the MeasureUp practice test.

Technical Support

If you encounter problems with the MeasureUp test engine on the CD-ROM, please contact MeasureUp at 678-356-5050 or email support@measureup.com. Technical support hours are from 8:00 a.m. to 5:00 p.m. EST Monday through Friday. Additionally, you'll find Frequently Asked Questions (FAQ) at www.measureup.com.

If you'd like to purchase additional MeasureUp products, telephone 678-356-5050 or 800-649-1MUP (1687), or visit www.measureup.com.